WOMEN EMPOWERMENT
A FUNCTIONAL MODEL

WOMEN EMPOWERMENT

A Functional Model

Dr K. Manoharan Nair
Dr L. Valsalakumarikunjamma

KALPAZ

Women Empowerment: A Functional Model

ISBN : 978-93-5128-022-4

Published in 2014 in India by
Kalpaz Publications
C-30, Satyawati Nagar,
Delhi - 110052
E-mail: kalpaz@hotmail.com
Ph.: 9212142040

Laser Typesetting: Rajender Vashist, Delhi
Printed at: G. Print Process, Delhi

Contents

Preface

Women Empowerment has become an important topic today discussed at length world over in the wake of globalisation. This is basically because of the fact that women have been the most vulnerable sections of the society which is prone to poverty. Not only that they constitute a sizeable segment of the poverty struck population needs to be empowered on account of lack of opportunities for education, decision-making, control over assets, wealth, fertility and they disproportionately suffer from malnourishment and anaemia.

In Kerala, comparing to other states in India, the status of women is relatively better in the state on account of women awareness, women movement at the grassroots level, greater mobility, education women and child health interventions have led to the overall development of women in Kerala.

Education, employment and entitlement may enhance the material conditions of women which in turn helps in eradicating their poverty at its root.

This text book is the result of a research study and it is useful to the academicians, research scholars and policy makers for understanding the methodological aspects and the factors required for empowerment of women for their development in diverse fields.

Suggestions for improvement of this text book will be highly appreciated. We are thankful to Kalpaz Publications for taking special effort in its publication.

We gratefully acknowledge the support extended by Dr M. Suresh Kumar and Sreelekha L for their help in finalising the work and make it a grant success.

Dr K. Manoharan Nair

Dr L.Valsalakumarikunjamma

List of Tables

1

Introduction

Women empowerment and full participation of women on the basis of equality in all spheres of society including participation in the decision-making process and access to power are fundamental to the achievement of equality, development and peace. Through empowerment, they can generate income by starting micro-enterprises, joining in Neighbour Hood Groups (NHGs), joining in employment, engagement in societal activities and participation in politics.

In India, the trickle-down effects of macro-economic policies have failed to resolve the problems of gender inequality. Women have been the vulnerable section of the society and they constitute a sizeable segment of the poverty-struck population. Women face gender-specific barriers in access to education, health and employment. Compared to men, women in India are disempowered. They are denied the opportunities for education and economic independence. Again, women have little control over assets, wealth and fertility and they disproportionately suffer from malnourishment and anemia. Women are often underpaid for their work. Their contributions to society and the economy are often ignored. Thus, women's contribution to the family and society development cannot be measured economically.

Without women, home, society, nation and even human existence would collapse. There is no work on this earth which women cannot do. What is required is something like tapping potential energy and changing it into kinetic energy so as to make life meaningful for women, in particular, and humanity, in general. Therefore, there is a need to understand women's vast and tremendous potentialities and develop them, which would result in automatic empowerment.

Before the Neolithic period, man and woman seem to have been more or less equal in status. But, by the time humanity emerged into the light of recorded history, man became the master. This distorted concept of superiority of man over woman has always aroused interests of thinkers all over the world. Any serious enquiry that searches for woman's identity, whatever be the approach or ideological underpinnings, brings one fact clearly into focus that no country or region can claim development, in its real sense, without the support, co-operation and involvement of women. This factor slowly attained the status of a fact of life and was handed down through centuries.

The development experience of women is not uniform in India. History, geography and cultural pattern of religion, along with other various socio-economic factors play a significant role in the development of women anywhere in the world. This is very true in the case of the development of women in Kerala also. The status of women is relatively better in the state. Women awareness, women movements at the grassroots level, greater mobility, education, women and child health interventions have led to the overall development of women in Kerala.

Women's development has assumed greater significance in the context of globalisation. The various neoliberal policies introduced at national and state levels, with the intention of the restructuring of the national and state economies, have serious implications on women's development.

Education, employment and entitlements may enhance the material conditions of women, which in turn helps in eradicating their poverty at its root levels. The work participation rates among women are low, rates of unemployment among them are higher than that prevailing among men and gender differentials in the labour market persist across caste, income and educational categories. The socio-economic status of the women in Kerala are not appreciable. The working women and their autonomy and empowerment in organised and unorganised sectors are not up to the mark. Their empowerment and social status, basically, depend on the religious and caste beliefs of women in Kerala. Globalisation has intensified the existing inequalities and heightened the vulnerability of poor women. There exists the problem of status, employment, autonomy, income, assets, entitlements and empowerment among women in Kerala.

Significance of the Study

Kerala had a favourable sex ratio of 1058 in 2001 census, whereas all-India figures stood at 933. The 2001 census reflects that Kerala is the only Indian state where the sex ratio is above one and it is worth mentioning that Kerala has never had a female-male ratio below unity at any time in the country. Similarly, in terms of literacy (88 per cent), life expectancy (72.4 years) and mean age at marriage, women in Kerala score higher than the women in any other state of the country. All these paved the way for outstanding achievements of Kerala in terms of women's development which resulted in overall human developments. Kerala's highest levels of human development and gender development are the results of its achievements in the field of health and education for women. Kerala has the highest mean age at marriage for women. Lowest fertility rate, lowest percentage of women with anemia, maternal mortality rate and female infant mortality—all these, clearly indicate that there exists a better health status for Kerala women. Inclusion of women in the labour force has increased worldwide during the past few decades. Participation of women in economic activities outside *grama* has an important bearing on gender relations within the household. The social influences of women's work are also quite extensive. Women's earnings give them access to and control over an independent income, which makes their economic contribution visible and high.

Background of the Study

The empowerment of women is a process, a continuum of several interrelated and mutually reinforcing components. Women empowerment and their full participation on the basis of equality in all spheres of society which include the participation in the decision-making process and access to power are fundamentals for the achievement of equality, development and peace. Historically, Kerala has been quite different from the rest of the country in terms of the indicators of women's development. It owes its attributed success to the achievements in the areas of health and education where the contribution of women is particularly significant in eradicating poverty through earning income, assets and improving the standard of living through participation in SHGs, NHGs and micro-enterprises. Work participation is low and unemployment among the educated is high in Kerala compared to other states in India. There is political participation of women to act as leaders in the grassroots in which statutory reservation of seats in contesting in the Gram Panchayats, Block Panchayats, District

Panchayats, Municipalities and Corporations are provided through the Act, which calls for further development and growth of women in India, in general and Kerala, in particular.

Scope of the Study

The present study incorporates employment, income and entitlements leading to empowerment of women in selected activities under organised and unorganised sectors of Kerala. For it, socio-economic and historical factors influencing the status of women in Kerala have been analysed. The study aims at providing deeper insights into issues relating to employment, income and entitlement, which are considered to be the essential ingredients of empowerment of women in Kerala. The scope of the study is limited to working women in the selected activities in the organised and unorganised sectors in Thiruvananthapuram district. The study also developed a women empowerment index and a predictor regression model for women empowerment in selected activities.

Relevance of the Study

The study is highly relevant on the following grounds:

The issues relating to the empowerment of working women in Kerala have not so far been subjected to any deeper analysis. There is an increasing incidence of domestic violence, separation and divorce in Kerala. The rate of suicide among women has also increased over the years. In the absence of any scientific study, haphazard and ad hoc policy measures are suggested to address the various problems confronting the women in Kerala. The present study thus, has implications for policy with reference to earning income, protection through legal measures, empowerment, and property rights.

Statement of the Problem

Their strengths rather than their weaknesses. But due to the weaknesses embedded in them, they find it difficult to utilise all opportunities available to them in this digital age and face the threats coming from various corners of the society they live in.

Kerala is an industrially backward state and does not have a thriving unorganised sector in the manufacturing and trading activities. A significant proportion of working women is engaged in agricultural and construction activities. With the spread of education, more and more women have entered into paid employment in the formal sector, i.e., government, public and private sectors.

In the organised sector, though there may not be any gender disparity in salary and service conditions, male domination and sexual harassment are not entirely unheard of. Unfortunately, there is a tendency even among educated and highly placed professional women in Kerala to ignore such experiences as part of everyday life and suffer silently.

In the unorganised sector, significant wage rate disparity exists in respect of unskilled female paddy field workers, when compared to their male counterparts. The problems of gender discrimination and sexual harassment are equally applicable to women in the unorganised sectors. However, only an in-depth study can bring out the extent of their incidence.

Given the patriarchic social structure of Kerala, the environment which the working women confront at home cannot be expected to be very different. There does not exist any study worth the name on the extent of autonomy which working women enjoy with regard to decisions on spending their earned income. It appears that irrespective of caste, religion and educational backgrounds, by and large, the expenditure-related decisions in Kerala families are taken by the husbands. The cultural background and social ethos of Kerala society approve of male dominations in such aforesaid type of decisions. It is also likely that an increasing proportion of working women resist such domination and assert their right to have a role in the expenditure-related decisions. The pertinent issues are, in what proportion the working women enjoy autonomy in taking decisions regarding spending on their income, in what proportion the women assert their rights, is there any significant difference between the response of working women in the organised and unorganised sectors, and what is the extent of differences across women of various religions, caste and educational backgrounds. Though women empowerment is a combination of such complexities, pertinent studies focusing on the issues stated above have not emerged so far. A specific study highlighting their entitlements towards employment, income and status, which leads to empowerment in the selected activities is a matter of great concern, in which no study has yet been made, hence the present study.

Objectives of the Study

The objectives of this study are:

(i) To identify a tentative set of variables influencing the empowerment of women in the selected activities with special reference to employment, income and entitlement.

(ii) To categorise homogeneous empowerment groups for ranking based on women empowerment.

(iii) To fit a predictor regression model of women empowerment with particular reference to factors of employment, income and entitlement.

(iv) To examine whether there exist significant disparities in women empowerment across different religions, localities, job status, educational groups, age groups and occupational groups.

Hypotheses

The following are the hypotheses formulated for the study:

1. **H_1:** There is no significant difference in women empowerment as to income, employment and entitlement among women in different locations viz., urban and rural areas.
2. **H_2:** There is no significant difference in women empowerment as to income, employment and entitlement among women in different organisational set-ups viz., Government, Non-government and Unorganised sectors.
3. **H_3:** There is no significant difference in women empowerment as to income, employment and entitlement among women of different job status, viz., Gazetted and Non-gazetted officials.
4. **H_4:** There is no significant difference in women empowerment as to income, employment and entitlement among women in different levels of educational attainments viz., Below Primary, Primary, SSLC, Degree, and Above Degree.
5. **H_5:** There is no significant difference in women empowerment as to income, employment and entitlement among women in different religions, viz., Hindu, Muslim, Christian and Others.
6. **H_6:** There is no significant difference in women empowerment as to income, employment and entitlement among women in different occupational groups, viz., Farm activities, Hospitality, Micro Enterprises, Solid waste management, Health sector, and Education.
7. **H_7:** There is no significant difference in women empowerment as to income, employment and entitlement among women in different age groups, viz., Below 20 years, Between 20 – 35 years, Between 35 – 50 years, and Above 50 years.

Design of the Study

The way in which the study is designed is described as under:

Method of Study

The present study is a descriptive one which analyses the empirical data relating to employment, income, entitlement and empowerment of women in Kerala in selected activities.

Methodology

Sources of Data

For the present study, data has been collected both from secondary and primary sources.

Secondary Data

It has been collected from research reports, articles, reports of the Government— both Central and State, books, journals and publications brought out by the women organisations. In order to obtain a clear picture of the factors influencing the status of *Malayali* women, the archival and historical source materials have been surveyed besides the available literature.

Primary Data

The primary data has been collected from those who are engaged in selected organised and unorganised sectors by using Purposive Sampling Technique.

Sample Design

A sample of 400 respondents was selected for the study, 200 drawn each from the organised and unorganised sectors. The selection of sample is made based on the Purposive Sampling Technique. The details of sample selection are stated in Chapter III.

Tools for Data Collection

A structured interview schedule is specifically developed for collection of primary data. The interview schedule is finalised after a pilot study.

Tools Used for Analysis

For analysis and interpretation of the data, statistical tools like correlation, regression, mean, median, standard deviation, co-variance,

t – test and analysis of variance – One way classification (ANOVA) are used with the help of computer software package and Statistical Package for Social Sciences (SPSS).

Period of Study

The period of study includes a five-year span from 2006-07 to 2010-11 of the Tenth and Eleventh five year plans.

Definition of Terms

(a) Employment

The term 'Employment' for the purpose of the study refers to the possible opportunities of occupation in different sectors of activities and the field of employment, either government or private.

(b) Income

The term 'income' for the study is the return both in monetary as well as non-monetary terms earned by the women employees out of various activities of employment either in the organised or unorganised sector.

(c) Entitlement

The term 'entitlement' refers to the guarantee of access to benefits based on established rights or legislative protection provided to women, which includes women's accessibility and control over private and public properties, control over employment and income, autonomy on mobility, politics, acquiring knowledge and information and accessibility to legislature.

(d) Empowerment

'Women Empowerment' in a wider sense connotes a process whereby women can overcome most of the deprivations that they face, such as education, work status, employment opportunities, health care, social security and position in decision-making by virtue of their gender. Women empowerment in its narrower sense refers to making them powerful to do away with "subordination" or "discrimination" and "injustices" done to them in the male-dominated society. The present study in this context has targeted the working class women in the organised and unorganised sectors in Thiruvananthapuram district.

Main Variables Used for the Study

The following are the main variables analysed in the present study:

(a) Savings; (b) Family Income; (c) Food; (d) Clothing; (e) Shelter; (f) Accessibility to housing loans; (g) Accessibility to vehicle loans; (h) Accessibility to consumption loans; (i) Status and Property laws; (j) Impact of globalisation in expenditure pattern; and (k) role in decision-making.

Chapterisation Scheme

Chapter 1 : Introduction : This chapter explains the methodological description of the study.

Chapter 2 : Review of literature.

Chapter 3 : Women status and development the world over : This chapter gives detailed information about the status and development of women in the world, India and Kerala.

Chapter 4 : Theoretical framework for analysis: This chapter deals with the theoretical background for analysis and interpretation of the collected data.

Chapter 5 : Analysis on employment, income, entitlements and women empowerment.

This chapter gives details regarding the socio-economic profiles, women empowerment index, variable-wise analysis and regression model of women empowerment in Kerala.

Chapter 6 : Empowerment disparities across different women groups: This chapter contains description about the testing of hypotheses to find out the disparities and their level of significance.

Chapter 7 : Summary of findings.

Chapter 8 : Conclusions.

Chapter 9: Suggestions.

2

Review of Literature

The literature survey on the past studies is made for knowing the gap in research. Through an extensive literature survey on the studies made in the past, the authors identified the area to be conducted. The important studies and articles relating to women empowerment are reviewed and listed below :

Lucy (1995)[1] has pointed out in her study on women empowerment for sustainable development, that the society, both national and international, will miss a lion's share of it if it disregards the contribution of women in sustainable development. For empowerment to become real, she advocates the need to bring in a change in the mindset of men who can aid in establishing gender equality. She further suggests that investing in human capabilities and enabling people to exercise choices is the surest way to contribute to economic growth and overall development.

Mahajan (1996)[2] analyses the conflicts which modern women in India have to encounter, if they decide to pursue a career along with their traditional domestic role. The social and cultural milieu of India has been such that, even today, it assigns to its women, the traditional family roles, and not the career roles. Hence, even the educated women are in a dilemma, when they have to play both the roles simultaneously.

Gopalan Sarala (1997)[3] in her case study on women empowerment in Andhra Pradesh, has pointed out that it is knowledge and awareness rather than mere literacy that count for empowerment. For growing in strength and accessing information, she suggests for organising people in groups.

Gopalan Suseela (1999)[4] notes that empowerment of women with job opportunities and earning capacity is highly essential for alleviating discrimination. She further cites that high literacy rate has not influenced the status of women.

Kulathoor Nair and Premakumaran (1999)[5] commenting on the political empowerment of women, list the factors like unsuitability of political work at the grassroots level, fear of demoralisation, mental harassment and political assault, that force women to refrain from political participation. They categorise the obstacles in this connection under three heads, namely, money, mafia and manipulation.

Subha K and Bhargava (2001)[6] in their article on Panchayati Raj system and political empowerment of women, state that PRIs have provided an important channel for women's involvement in their own development through participation in the representative structures of the local government. Representation aims at involving women in decision-making. Their roles should be recognised and strengthened so that they get full access to resources and services.

Shalu Nigam (2001)[7] in her article on empowering women, discloses that the influence of socio-economic changes, especially consumerism, migration, urbanisation and liberalisation, has led to a rise in single-parents family breaking the traditional joint family structure. This has led to apparent evils of domestic violence, insecurity and increased divorce rates. Further, the dream of empowering society and enriching the family can witness early accomplishment only with empowering the major constituent of the family, that is, women.

Murugaiah K (2002)[8] in his article on women's work and empowerment intervention to enhance women's income, states that the subject of empowerment of women is deeply rooted in the globally determined and accepted goals of equality, development and peace for all. It is multi-dimensional and refers to the expansion of freedom of choice and action in economic, social and political spheres. It also implies control over means and decisions for women; such freedom is often curtailed due to gender inequality in the household as well as in the society.

Anand Jaya (2002)[9] in her case study on the performance of selected SHGs and NHGs in empowering women, acknowledges that NHGs and SHGs were instrumental in effecting an attitudinal change in women. She has also hinted that factors such as distrust in leaders, autocratic leadership style, inability to evolve suitable income-generating activities, and the inability to lend the required skills are hindering the successful functioning of the groups.

Das Srimathi (2002)[10] points out that even after effecting constitutional guarantees and penal enactments, women remain the victims of exploitation, alienation and dehumanisation. They are the objects of discrimination in the womb, at home, and at the work place. She has also hinted on other inequalities–economic, political, social and educational, which women have to deal with.

Paricha (2002)[11] in an attempt to prescribe the strategies for empowering women in Panchayat Raj Institutions, has put forth an array of measures. They include creating awareness among women, winning to effect men's mental transformation in favour of women's emerging equal partners, imparting training to the elected representatives to discharge their duties, organising women from the poorer households especially and granting them a minimum financial assistance to enable them to associate with Panchayat activities.

Srivstava Ramesh (2002)[12] in his article, policies for socio-economic development of women pointed out that the full fledged development of a nation is possible only if it utilises the potentialities and capabilities of women to the fullest extent. He depicts the essential role of empowerment in making women self-reliant and self-confident. He further puts forth the necessity to instill social awareness and motivation among women and men in all women empowerment efforts.

Vasudev Rao (2002)[13] in a conceptual analysis of women empowerment, notes that empowerment cannot be restricted merely to sharing or distribution of power; it also involves changes in social, economic and institutional arrangements, political ideologies and traditional practices. He stresses the significance of participation of marginalised group, especially women in the formulation, implementation and evaluation of policy decisions, reminding further that both uncritical and safe-distance participation would not benefit women.

Nanavathy Reema (2003)[14] advocates from SEWA experience that an effective empowerment strategy should raise the income-deprived status of workers, planners and managers besides assisting them to earn their livelihood. She has appraised the integrated approach of SEWA to attain a state of full employment through unions and co-operatives in building collective and organisational strength, providing social security and capacity to face competitive market.

Nandal Santhosh (2003)[15] in a critical analysis of women's empowerment perspectives, states that only a multi-dimensional approach can assist in achieving women empowerment, economic, social and political. He further holds that mere passing of social legislations and keeping them as dead letter without change in the attitudes of persons responsible for implementing will not accentuate empowerment.

Tucker Veena (2003)[16] in her article, "Perspective analysis of empowerment" has laid down the processes involved for empowerment and calls for community involvement, developing skills, taking decisions and solving problems independently. Accessibility of government media and other community services contribute to empowerment at the community level.

Kamalam (2004)[17] in her article on women empowerment and role of women's commission, points out that the younger generation can take our society to a state where women enjoy greater freedom and equality in the society.

Mridual Eapen (2004)[18] in her article on empowering Kerala women, points out that economic empowerment of women, which places women's economic vulnerability at the centre of their powerlessness and builds its strategies around strengthening women's position as workers and income earners, interprets the question of empowerment narrowly. While there is no doubt that it improves women's economic position and conditions, it is not clear that their change necessarily empowers them in other dimensions of their lives. However, in the context of Kerala, this narrow interpretation of empowerment in economic terms has a critical relevance since women's well known achievements in the social sections like education and health are not matched by economic indicators such as workforce participation, and their share of income from work, reflected in low levels of female workforce participation and high rates of unemployment.

Bala Madhur and Monga (2004)[19] revealed through an impact study on women's employment on decision-making in Himachal Pradesh that employed women enjoy greater role in decision-making in families than unemployed ones. They conclude that employment enhances economic independence leading to elevated status and enhanced ability to influence the decision-making process.

Kishor Sunita and Gupta Kamala (2004)[20] recorded the evidence from National Family Health Survey that the status of women depends on the quality of gender existing in the society. Gender quality, they conceive, on the other hand, revolves around the clearly defined sex differentiated rights. They have identified the role of empowerment in dictating the health and nutritional status of the household, quality and quantity of human resources available for development, and opportunities for realising their potential.

In an analysis of women engaged in grassroot-level welfare services delivery systems in Aligarh District in Uttar Pradesh, Mohammad Noor and Shahid Mohammad (2004)[21] find a direct relationship among women's participation in outdoor socio-economic and political activities, empowerment and greater equality. They note that enhanced outdoor participation can ignite the empowerment process, leading to a state of gender equality.

Ramanathan Malathi (2004)[22] infers from *Lijjat papad* experience that though economic empowerment is much more than an earning capacity, the capacity to earn one's livelihood and the resultant self-confidence can provide a strong foundation to the empowerment initiatives of women.

Connecting education and empowerment from experiences in India, Ram Kumar Usha (2004)[23] reiterates the role of education in making women economically, politically and socially empowered. She adds that education equips women to participate in development programmes and makes them competitive and productive.

Renganathan (2004)[24] in his article on women's empowerment through development programmes, opines that women participation in development programmes, by engaging them in participatory planning, can pave the way for their empowerment. He also suggests measures like strengthening people's institutions and institutional arrangements to cater to their needs and field-based applied research for ensuring effective people participation.

Rosa (2004)[25] who conducted a study on empowerment of women through employment, points out that, though overall empowerment of a person increases with employment, empowerment in the societal matters does not exhibit any sign of hope. She further pinpoints that income is not the sole factor determining the empowerment of a person.

Singh Surat (2004)[26] in his attempt to analyse the empowerment status of women representatives in Panchayati Raj Institutions in Haryana, comments on their minor involvement in the decision-making and other activities of local self-government institutions. He attributes this to their low level of awareness, lack of confidence and low socio-economic status. He also recommended the need to bring about an attitudinal change of men towards women besides advocating the necessity of providing training to women leaders in managing responsibilities and their maintaining contact with the outside world.

Sood Archana (2004)[27] emphasises in his study that empowerment, especially of rural women has a decisive impact on factors governing sustainable development of a country. Women's status in the society can be raised through capacity building, developing leadership traits and social interventions.

In a study on empowerment and poverty reduction, Narayan (2005)[28] gives a wider connotation for eradication of poverty, which includes expansion of freedom of choice and action to shape one's life. It is the expansion of assets and capabilities of poor people to participate in, negotiate with, influence, control and hold accountable, institutions that affect their lives.

A workshop (2005)[29] was organised at the international level to ask the government to use information technology for women empowerment and poverty alleviation. The workshop had three specific objectives:

(a) to share experiences of support and operation of women's information and communication technology- based enterprises among the participants, drawing on their expertise.

(b) to contribute to development of a handbook on women's Information Communication Technology (ICT)-based enterprises; and

(c) to provide workshop participants with direct experience of Kerala's Kudumbasree IT units, which are operated by women from poor communities. The workshop concluded that ICTs can bring direct benefit to the poor (i.e., hardware assembly, data entry, web designs and cyber cafes) and that Kudumbashree is a unique and motivating example of ways in which the government can harness IT to empower women and foster entrepreneurship. The government should see the IT strategies and policies which can be effectively used as a tool for women's empowerment and poverty alleviation.

Emphasising the significance of information technology in the realm of development, Bishoji Deepak (2005)[30] outlines that an effective policy towards initiating socially acceptable, economically and practically viable

IT projects will be a major step towards materialising the dream of empowerment of women: social, economic and political.

Kelkar Govind (2005)[31] has revealed that more than a source of income, access to property rights enhances women's risk-bearing abilities. About the measurement tools of gender development index and gender empowerment measures, he opines that they are unable to grasp the real achievements of women.

Lalithabai (2005)[32] in her article on women empowerment and Panchayati Raj lists the major issues in women empowerment, namely, male-dominated administrative structure, illiteracy, male-based value system, unemployment and lack of gender consciousness among the masses.

Based on a comparative analysis of two micro credit programmes, NGO and State led, Lakshmidevi and Pillai (2005)[33] state that both have a positive impact on poverty alleviation and empowerment of women, though state-led programmes maintain an upper hand. Admitting the improved economic gain and the resultant additional self-esteem, self-confidence and autonomy, they reiterate that the changed income is too small to either raise the economic status or push them out of poverty.

In a critical analysis of micro finance on women empowerment, seeking evidences from the findings of South Asia, Naila Kabeer (2005)[34] opines that though micro-finance is effective in making some economic and social contributions; it does not automatically empower women any more than other interventions like education, political quotas, access to waged work or as any others do.

Omvedi Gail (2005)[35] holds that women can be empowered by engaging them in managing community resources, where the greatest scope for participation of women exists. Though in principle Omvedt Gail agrees that increase in political representation can change women, it cannot be assumed that a quota system alone can lead to it, as women competing only against women may limit their experience.

Pattnaik Sathyanarayana and Trupty Mayee Pradhan (2005)[36] while relating empowerment and violence, deem the empowerment of women to be the urgent need of the hour for ending violence and atrocities committed against them. Strengthening women in leadership roles, involving them in decision-making, and increasing their access to education and control over resources, will pave the way for the empowerment of women assisting in turn to minimise discrimination and violence.

Paul Chithra (2005)[37] noted 'The New Indian Express' report, based on the survey conducted by Sastra Sahitya Parishad that Kudimbasree Mission, had failed as powerful women empowerment machinery. The root cause of failure is attributed to confining the activities within the BPL Group. The report adds several other limiting forces such as lack of management expertise, absence of proper planning, non-availability of raw materials, ineffective marketing strategy, and lack of co-ordination between the Panchayat and the Kudumbasree units besides poor investment in productive sector.

Thambi Binitha and Devika (2006)[38] in their impact study of Kudumbasree programmes, emphasise that Kumdumbasree programme assists only in reaffirming and expanding the prevailing maledomination in the absence of inclusion of any provision for questioning the male dominated power structures. The success of the programme, they underline, to a large extent depends on the prevailing family and social environment. They recommend that Kudumbasree bye-laws should incorporate provisions needed to overcome the restrictions imposed by family, society and institutions on women and steps necessary to achieve women empowerment.

As reported by V Jayanth (2006)[39], the study made by UN General Secretary on tackling violence against women, calls for a cohesive approach which has highlighted that violence against women is yet to receive priority attention among states and other stakeholders. State-sponsored women's enterprises await revival, says a report by 'The Hindu'[40] which pinpoints the Kerala Soap Industries Federation, a State Government-floated enterprise with a view to providing employment to women from the economically backward section, is awaiting revival, in the backdrop of the new impetus being given by the government to uplift the industrial sector in the State.

The Government of Maharastra[41] has decided to hand over ration shops to all women self-help groups in a bid to end the massive diversion of food grains and kerosene towards empowerment of women.

As reported by The Hindu[42], a higher percentage of women hold managerial and executive jobs these days than they used to in the past. True, we have come a long way but it is still not far enough.

An open forum held at *Vibgyor* (a festival of documentaries and short films) organised by the Chetana Media Institute on role of films in women's empowerment (2006)[43], highlighted the role of films in the movement for women's empowerment.

Jyothi S. Nair (2007)[44], who conducted a study on entrepreneurship and empowerment, examines the factors that motivate women to start microenterprises, to measure the group dynamics in microenterprises and entrepreneurial qualities, to measure economic empowerment attained, and to look into the challenges before women while undertaking micro entrepreneurial activities.

Ruby J.A. (2008)[45], who conducted a study on Kudumbasree project in Kerala, examined the role of Kudumbasree in empowering women in Kerala through microfinance. The study concluded that the women in Kerala improved their position in finance and decisionmaking process after joining in the Kudumbasree projects.

Lathika K.K. (2008)[46] conducted a study on women empowerment in Kerala with special reference to Kudumbasree projects. The study concluded that women empowerment improved much after undertaking projects under Kudumbasree projects.

Bushra Beegom (2008)[47], in a study on women executives in Kerala examined the extent of conflict among women executives, role of family in helping them in meeting the challenges, assessing the qualities of leadership and decision-making, job satisfaction, conflicts in their positions and the major challenges that the women executives face in Kerala.

Lalitha K.K. (2008)[48] conducted a study on women empowerment in Kerala with special reference to Kudumbasree project with the objectives of assessing the level of empowerment at the individual level, the spread of empowerment in terms of participation in community activities, measure of empowerment status at group level, and the problems confronted by women. The study concludes that the level of individual empowerment is related to the number of members in the group and empowerment varies within variation in the number of NHGs, leaders of NHGs and that members of the microenterprises.

Ruby J.A. (2008)[49] conducted a study on microfinance and women empowerment – a study of Kudumbasree projects in Kerala – with the main object of understanding the structure, working and progress of Kudumbasree projects in Kerala. The study examines the role of Kudumbasree in women empowerment through micro financing, including identification of the problems in NHGs. The study came to the conclusion that Kudumbasree has been instrumental in achieving empowerment of women through microfinancing.

Beena George (2008)[50], in a study on empowering rural women through microfinancing, attempts to compare the impact of microfinance programmes of governmental and non-governmental organisations on rural women empowerment in central Kerala. The study comes to the conclusion that there is improvement in annual family income, standard of living after joining the SHGs, income-generating activities and women empowerment.

Promila Yadava (2009)[51], in her article on literacy and women's empowerment, states that the consequences of literacy on women has a ripple effect beginning from the individual to the national level. Given the impact of literacy on female well being, empowerment and autonomy, actions aimed at achieving gender parity are urgently needed.

Emmanuel K.A. Kanipilly (2009)[52] conducted a study on empowerment of urban poor through poverty alleviation programmes of Kerala with the main aim of investigating the impact of urban poverty alleviation in Kerala on the empowerment of urban poor women. The study also investigates whether awareness programmes, capacity building and training programmes increased the respondents' human capabilities to face challenging situations, meet people in authority, demand their rights and take up responsibility within organisation, work in team, and provide leadership when required.

Manju Singh (2010)[53], in her article 'Empowerment of Women: Gaps in Technology diffusion' points out that technology empowerment of rural women is identified as a crucial element to ease out their work stress, reduce drudgeries and to improve productivity. In developing countries, technology development and training programmes have not been responsive to household drudgery associated with different production activities undertaken by women. Hence, rural women's need for technology that improves their productivity, while reducing drudgery must be recognised. This article attempts to highlight the need of effective technology transfer for the empowerment of rural women. Considering women's different needs and widening gaps on rural technologies, there is a critical need of technology transfer for enhancing and widening the process of technology diffusion in rural India.

Santhosh Nandal, Kavita, Suman Rani and Gautam N.C. (2010)[54], in their article 'Women's empowerment and national development policies: a critical analysis', opine that women of India are relatively under-empowered and that they have a lower status than men. In spite of so many efforts undertaken by the government, the picture at present is not satisfactory. The tools enabling the empowerment process do not help. However, the march towards this goal depends more on attitude. Unless the attitude towards the acceptance of unequal gender role by the society and even the women themselves are changed, women cannot grab the opportunity provided to them through constitutional provisions, law, etc. Hence, we can say that women are empowered in India in its real sense.

Dijo Augustine and Minu M Kumar (2010)[55] in their article 'Women Empowerment through the SHG Approach – The Kudumbashree Model' state that empowerment is a process where women take control of their lives by expanding their choices. Thus, the women are being empowered by the process of group formation by both governmental and non-governmental organisations, which goes beyond financial intermediation and emphasises social vision. Women empowerment, in its true sense, is the primary focus of Kudumbasree.

Atonu Chatterjee (2011)[56] in his article 'Women in Panchayats: A Review' points out that gradual gendering of local democracy is opening up a new vista in the rural areas. Women are increasingly getting a chances to shape grassroot-level politics which previously was controlled by local power cliques.

Patil B.G. and Nandana G.B. (2011)[57] in their article 'Women Empowerment – A spiritual approach', point out that it is this spiritual connection of the soul with the supreme that really leads to right type of empowerment. Without this, spirituality development is incomplete. Spirituality ends hostility, antagonism, class of interests and divisionism in the society. Thus, spiritual and moral empowerment is the way out for women empowerment.

Paramasivan C (2011)[58] in his article 'Economic Empowerment of Women through SHG in YARCARD' states that empowerment, as a social process, has challenged the fundamental imbalances of power distribution and relations. It was the distribution of power within and between forties, and society's process aiming at social equality, which could be achieved through disempowering some structures, systems and institutions. Social empowerment has promoted sustainable rural structure for dissemination of knowledge about health, nutrition, literacy, education, freedom and opportunities for realising women's potentialities and adoption of new agricultural practices. They highlighted the participation of women in SHG function, awareness towards SHGs and motivation to join in the SHGs.

In an article titled 'Self-Help Groups and Women Empowerment', Rajamani. B (2011)[59] points out that self-help groups have been engaged as a popular method of working with people in the recent years. Power to the people signifies a new social movement, which has probably been borne out of the realisation of society's traditional arrangements for solving their problems. The SHGs are a media for the development of savings habit among womenfolk. It is a window for developing better technology and skill upgradation. The SHGs' collective actions and solidarity are an important women empowerment mechanism and develop savings habit and mobilisation of resources among the womenfolk.

Nripendra Kishore Mishra and Tulika Tripathi (2011)[60] in their article titled 'Conceptualising Women's Agency, Autonomy, and Empowerment' point out that the women's agency, autonomy and empowerment are widely used ideas in development literature. But there is substantial ambiguity in the conception of those ideas. While women's well-being and women's agency are sufficiently distinguished from each other, there seems to be a large overlap between agency and empowerment and between agency and autonomy. The study attempts to examine the degree of empowerment and autonomy across different characteristics like place of residence, religion, caste, education, type of employment and wealth quintiles, at the individual as well as the regional levels. A regional analysis shows that empowerment may not always lead to autonomy.

Staffan Lindbery, Venkitesh. B, Athrey. R, Vidhyasagar, Goran Djurfeldt, and Rajagopalan. A (2011)[61] in their article, 'A Silent Revolution? Women's Empowerment in Rural Tamil Nadu', report that one of the significant changes over the past 25 years in Tamil Nadu is the entry of women into the local political bodies at the village and village union levels through the 33 per cent reservation system. Simultaneously, women are now to a significant extent, organised in self-help groups. Through these, about one-fourth of the households can access loans for small entrepreneurship, or rather more frequently, smaller emergency/ consumption loans. There has also been increasing participation of women in the non-agricultural labour market and the emergency in Tamil Nadu of a rudimentary barefoot welfare state.

Sreekumar S.S. (2011)[62] in his article, 'Education and Empowerment of Women: The case of Andaman and Nicobar Islands', examines the challenges facing empowerment of women. This includes problems related to dropout rates, gender gap in literacy, unemployment of women, to be viewed from a multi-dimensional perspective and specifically studied from a social angle.

Nripendra Kishore Mishra and Tulika Tripathi (2011)[63] in their article 'Conceptualising Women's Agency, Autonomy and Empowerment', state that women's agency, autonomy and empowerment are widely used ideas in development literature. But there is substantial ambiguity in the conception of these ideas. While women's wellbeing and women's agency are sufficiently distinguished from each other, there seems to be a large overlap between agency and empowerment and between agency and autonomy. This paper attempts to examine the degree of empowerment and autonomy across different characteristics like place of residence, religion, caste, education, type of employment and wealth quintiles at the individual as well as the regional levels. A regional analysis shows that empowerment may not always lead to autonomy.

It is seen from the review of literature that studies in respect of analysing the women empowerment through income, employment and entitlement in different activities are profuse, hence the present study.

References

1. Lucy, T.V. : Empowerment of Women for Sustainable Development, Social Action, Volume 45, No. 2, 1995, pp. 224-230.
2. Mahaljan A.: Women's Tow Roles- A Study of Role Conflict in India, Journal of Social Work, Vol. 25, No. 4, 1996, pp. 377-80.
3. Gopalan, Sarala: Empowerment of Women— A Case Study of Andhra Pradesh, Southern Economist, Vol. XXX, No. 15, 1997, pp. 18-23.
4. Gopalan, Suseela: Empowerment of Women Through Education and Employment, Kerala Calling, Vol. 19, No. 5, 1999, pp. 5-6.
5. Kulathoor Nair and Premakumaran, S.V.: Empowering Women, to be or not to be, Kerala Calling, Vol. 19, No. 5, 1999, pp. 7-9.
6. Subha, K. and Bhargava, B.S.: Panchayati Raj System and Political Empowerment of Women, All India Institute of Local Self-Government, Vol. XXI, No.12, January-June, 2001, Mumbai, pp. 11-15.
7. Shalu Nigam: Empower Women, Enrich Family, Social Welfare, Vol. 48, No. 5, 2001, pp. 35-38.
8. Murugaiah, K.: Women's Work and Empowerment, Interventions to Enhance Women's Income, Social Welfare, Vol. 49, No. 7, 2002, pp. 3-8.

9. Anand, Jaya: Self-Help Groups in Empowering Women, A Case Study of Selected SHGs and NHGs, Kerala Research Programme on Local Level Development, Discussion Paper, No. 38, Centre for Development Studies, Thiruvananthapuram, 2002, pp. 1-70.
10. Das, Shrimati: Gender Justice and Empowerment, Social Welfare, Vol. 49, No. 9, pp. 14-19, 2002.
11. Paricha, A.K. : Strategies of Empowerment of Women in Panchayati Raj Institutions, Local Government, Quarterly, Vol. XXII, No. 1. 2, February to March, 2002, pp. 6-7.
12. Srivstava, Ramesh : Policies for Socio-Economic Development of Women, Social Welfare, Vol. 49, No. 7, 2002, pp. 24-27.
13. Vasudev, Rao: Empowerment Concepts and Charity, Social Welfare, Vol. 49, No. 9 2002, pp. 9-13.
14. Nanavathy, Reema : Empowering Women by the Women, for the Women, the SEWA Experience, Women's Link, Vol. 9, No. 3, 2003, pp. 16-19.
15. Nandal, Santhosh : Women's Empowerment Perspectives—A critical Analysis, Women's Link, Vol.9, No. 3, 2003, pp. 28-31.
16. Tucker, Veena : Theoretical Perspectives of Women's Empowerment and the Role of NGOs, Women's Link, Vol. 9, No. 3, 2003, pp. 2-8.
17. Kamalam, M : Women Empowerment Role of Women's Commission, Kerala Calling, Vol. 24, No. 5, March 2004, pp. 5-17.
18. Mridual, Eapen: Empowering Kerala Women, Kerala Calling, March 2004, Vol. 24, No. 5, pp. 9-13.
19. Bala, Madhur and Monga, O.P. : Impact of Women's Employment on Decision-making in Families, Social Welfare, Vol. 5, No. 51, 2004, pp. 14-16.
20. Kishor Sunita and Gupta, Kamala : Women's Empowerment in India and its States Evidence from the National Family Health Survey, Economic and Political Weekly, Vol. XXXIX, No. 7, 2004, pp. 694-703.
21. Mohammad Noor and Shahid Mohammad: Rethinking Women's Participation, Empowerment and Gender Equality: A Micro Analysis, Women's Link, Vol. 10, No. 3, 2004, pp. 7-12.
22. S. Ramanathan, Malathi: Women and Empowerment- Shri Mahila Giriha Udyog, Lijjat Papad, Economic and Political Weekly, Vol. XXXIX, No.17, 2004, pp. 1689-96.
23. Ram Kumar Usha : Education and Empowerment of Women Experience in India, Indian Journal of Adult Education, Vol. 65, No. 1-2, 2004, pp. 22-31.
24. Renganathan, R.: Women's Empowerment Through Development Programmes, Kisan World, Vol. 31, No. 6, June, 2004, pp. 13-14.
25. Rosa, K.D.: Empowerment of Women Through Employment, Ph.D thesis submitted to the University of Calicut, 2004.

26. Singh, Surat : Empowerment of Women Representatives in Panchayati Raj- A Profile from Haryana, Kurukshetra, Vol. 52, No. 10, 2004. p. 18.

27. Sood, Archana : Sustainable Rural Development—Focus on Women, Kurukshetra, Vol. 52, No. 6, 2004, p. 30.

28. Narayan and Deepa : Empowerment and Poverty Reduction—A Source Book, Washington: World Bank, 2005.

29. The Hindu, September 18, 2005, p. 15.

30. Bishoji, Deepak: Information Technology—New Mantra for Women's Empowerment, Social Welfare, Vol. 52, No. 5, 2005, pp. 10-13.

31. Kelkar, Govind: Development Effectiveness Through Gender Mainstreaming, Gender Equality and Poverty Reduction in South Asia, Economic and Political Weekly, Vol. XL, No. 44 and 45, 2005, pp. 4690-98.

32. Lalithabai, K.N.: Women Empowerment and Panchayatl Raj, Journal of Local Governance, April-June 2005, Quarterly Publication, KILA, pp. 38-46.

33. Lakshmidevi, K.R. and Pillai. P.P. : Micro Credit Programmes, Poverty Alleviation and Empowerment of Women—Some Empirical Evidence from Kerala, Institute Francais, Pondicherry, 2005, pp. 322-324.

34. Naila, Kabeer: Is Micro Finance a Magic Bullet for Women's Empowerment? Analysis of Findings from South Asia, Economic and Political Weekly, Vol. XL, No. 44 and 45, 2005, pp. 4709-18.

35. Omvedi Gail: Women in Governance in Asia, EPW, Vol. XL, No. 44 and 45, 2005, pp. 4747-4750.

36. Pattnaik, Sathyanarayana and Trupty Mayee Pradhan : Empowering Women by Ending Gender Violence, Social Welfare, Vol. 52, No. 52, 2005, pp. 21-24.

37. Paul, Cithara: Kudumbasree Mission Failed to Achieve Purpose, The New Indian Express, Kochi, September 2, 2005, p. 5.

38. Thambi Binitha and Devika : Changing Order of Empowerment and Kudumbasree Activities, Shastra Gathi, Vol. 41. No. 7, 2006, pp. 17-21.

39. The Hindu, Oct. 11, 2006, p. 15.

40. The Hindu, November 19, 2006, p. 6.

41. The Hindu, February 6, 2006.

42. The Hindu, March 22, 2006.

43. The Hindu, February 26, 2006.

44. Jyothi S. Nair: Ph.D thesis submitted to the University of Kerala (Dept. of Sociology) in 2007.

45. Ruby J.A.: Micro Finance and Women Empowerment—A Study of Kudumbasree Project in Kerala, Ph.D thesis submitted to the M.G. University (Dept. of Economics,), July, 2008.

46. Lathika, K.K.: A Study of Women Empowerment in Kerala with Special

Reference to Kudumbasree Projects, Ph. D thesis submitted to M.G. University (Dept. of Economics), March, 2008.

47. Bushra, Beegom: Women Executives in Kerala, Ph.D thesis submitted to University of Kerala, (Dept. of Sociology), 2008.
48. Lathika, K.K: Ph.D thesis submitted to the M.G. University, March, 2008.
49. Ruby, J.A. : Ph.D thesis submitted to M.G. University (Dept. of Economics) July, 2008.
50. Beena George : Ph.D thesis submitted to M.G. University (Dept. of Economics), October, 2008.
51. Promila Yadava: Literacy and Women's Empowerment, Yojana, Vol. 83, March, 2009, pp. 47-50.
52. Emmanuel, K.A. Kanipilly: Ph.D thesis submitted to M.G. University (Dept. of Zoology,) January, 2009.
53. Manju Singh : Empowerment of Women: Gaps in Technology Diffusion, Social Change, Vol. 40, No. 4, December, 2010, pp. 564-576.
54. Santhosh Nandal, Kavita, Suman RAni and Gautam.N.C : Women's Empowerment and National Development Policies: A Critical Analysis, Social Action, Vol.60, No.3, July-September, 2010, pp. 302-313.
55. Dijo Augustine and Minu M. Kumar: Women Empowerment through the SHG Approach – The Kudumbashree Model, The Indian Journal of Social Work, Vol. 71, No. 4. October 2010, pp. 601-610.
56. Atonu Chatterjee : Women in Panchayats: A Review, Yojana, Vol. 55, Feb. 2011, Government of India, pp. 24-25.
57. Patil, B.G., and Nandana, G.B.: Women Empowerment – A Spiritual Approach, SELP Journal of Social Science, Vol. 5, January-March, 2011, pp. 14-15.
58. Paramasivan, C.: Economic Empowerment of Women through SHG in YARCARD, SELP Journal of Social Science, Vol. 5, January-March, 2011.
59. Rajamani, B.: Self Help Groups and Women Empowerment, SELP Journal of Social Science, Vol. 5, January-March, 2011, pp. 86-89.
60. Naipendra Kishore Mishra, Tulika Tripathi: Conceptualising Women's Agency, Autonomy, and Empowerment, Economic and Political Weekly, Vol. XLVI, No. 11, March 12, 2011. pp. 58-65.
61. Staffan Lindbery, Venkitesh.B, Athrey.R, Vidhyasagar, Goran Djurfeldt, Rajagopalan: A Silent Revolution ? Women's Empowerment in Rural Tamil Nadu, EPW, Vol. XLVI, No. 13, March 16, 2011, pp. 111-120.
62. Sreekumar, S.S. Education and Empowerment of Women: The Case of Andaman And Nicobar Islands, Social Science in Perspective Achudamen on Study Centre, Thiruvananthapuram, Vol. 3, No. 1, January-March 2011, pp. 39-60.
63. Nripendra Kishore Mishra, Tulika Tripathi: Conceptualising Women's Agency, Autonomy and Empowerment, EPW, Vol. XLVI, No. 11, March 12, 2011, pp. 58-65.

3

Women - Status and Development

Women throughout the world today live longer, healthier lives, are better educated, enjoy more job opportunities and earn salaries than ever before. In many countries around the globe, there are more women than men in colleges and more women than ever in top-level leadership roles, both in business and in public life. The past several decades have witnessed tremendous improvements in women's literacy, longevity, education and employment opportunities, and general standard of living. And as women's lives gotten better, their families have become better educated, better nourished, healthier and more productive where women thrive communities and nations thrive. Now let us see the status of women in the world, India and Kerala.

I. Women in World Scenario

Around the world, millions of women live in societies where centuries old social and religious laws, customs, and traditions have created instrumental barriers to education, jobs and health care as well as depriving women of most of their political and civil rights. And where women have limited access to schooling, health care and economic opportunities, their families tend to be larger, poorer, less educated and debilitated by malnutrition and disease[1].

Since ancient times, women have been considered inferior physically, morally and intellectually. In most of parts of the world, women have traditionally been considered men's property, to be handed over from father to husband. Over the years, laws and customs concerning women's rights have been shaped by a variety of Greek, Roman and other ancient legal systems as well as by Christian, Jewish, Hindu, Islamic and other religious laws and traditions[2].

Women in the Ancient World

In most ancient societies, women were considered legal minors, under the control of either their fathers or husbands. They were seldom allowed to own property or manage their own finance. Yet, the earliest known code of law, the 18th century B.C. Babylonians Code of Hammurabi, afforded women some measure of economic independence. They were entitled to dowries, could pass land and other possessions down to their children and shared equal authority with their husbands over their children. In ancient Egypt, women were considered equal to their husbands in law and business and they could dispose of their own property.

Throughout most of ancient Greece and Rome, women enjoyed very few rights. A wife had no control over her property or children and if the family produced no male heirs, an adult male might be adopted to marry one of the daughters. The Greek colony Sparta was an exception: women enjoyed great freedom and girls were entitled to the same education as boys.

In ancient China, the Yin and Yang philosophy of nature reinforced the notion of women's inferiority; the Yang (male) principle always dominated the Yin (females)

Under the ancient Hebrew law, a women could inherit property. But her contracts could be invalidated by her father or husband. In both Hebrew and Islamic law, polygamy was allowed and divorce was legal; but according to Islam, divorce was the sole prerogative of the husband.

In Jewish law, a woman could not be divorced against her will, but neither could she obtain a divorce decree without her husband's consent. In Islamic law, women were expected to remain secluded in the home and when going out, had to cover themselves from head to toe.

Among some North American Indian tribes too, a girl was kept secluded in the company of other females, rarely seeing even her brothers, and it was not unusual for a man to have more than one wife. Among the Aztecs of ancient Mexico, daughters could inherit their parent's property, and women gained honour and respect by bearing children. A women who died during birth of a child was revered as a goddess.

Although Christian doctrine preached equality of all souls before God, it held that women were inferior to men and taught women to be obedient to their husbands. According to the Hindu laws of Manu, women were subservient to all male relatives. Only a husband could initiate a divorce and disobedience was just cause. In addition, a widow could not remarry and the law sanctioned *sati* system, the burning alive of a widow on her husband's funeral pyre[3].

Women in the Middle Ages

During the Middle ages, most women were still denied an education and their lives generally revolved around managing their homes and caring for their families. Women in rural areas often worked alongside their husbands in the fields, while those in town and cities, sometimes assisted their husbands in a trade or craft practiced.

In the beginning of the 15th century, women in Europe slowly started gaining some rights and freedoms. The inventions of the printing press in Germany in the mid 15th century, made books and other printed materials readily available and the burgeoning Protestants sects encouraged women to read the Bible and conduct religious services at home. In 1533[4], the Protestant Reformation leader Martin Luther explained, "Girls begin to talk and to stand on their feet sooner than boys because weeds always grow up more quickly than good people".

Emergence of Modern Feminism

By the 17th century, a few women had started speaking out for women's rights especially for educational opportunities, but it was not until the 18th century that the seeds of modern feminism were sown. With the intellectual movement known as the Enlightenment, came many democratic ideas and values, including the rights of the individual. Yet, most women were untouched by the social, political and economic rights that the Enlightenment conferred on men.

The first major feminist work was Mary Wollstonecraft's 'a vindication of the rights of women', published in Britain in 1792. It argued for increased educational opportunities for women as well as political equality with men, and gradually women in many countries started to organise themselves to advance their own concerns, such as, educational issues, the right to work and laws pertaining to divorce and child custody.

The Struggle to Vote

Over the next two centuries (19th and 20th), women made tremendous strides towards equality with men. The single most important and most arduous struggle during this period was the fight for women's suffrage, which originated in Western Europe and spread ironically, largely through colonisation around the globe.

In many countries, women attained the right to vote only after years of difficult struggle. In most Western countries, the women's suffrage movement grew out of decades of women's increasing public involvement in social issues, such as, abolition of slavery and the temperance movement. In Britain and the United States, as the movement for suffrage gained momentum, it sometimes grew militant and even violent.

Despite these efforts, by the dawn of the 20th century, only one country had granted its female citizens the right to vote. In 1893, New Zealand granted women equal voting rights with men. In 1902, Australia granted women the right to vote in federal elections, even though some states still barred them from voting in local elections. Finland (1906), Norway (1913), Denmark (1915) and a host of other European countries followed in quick succession[5].

In 1918, Canada became the first North American country to extend the franchise to women followed by the United States in 1920. Ecuador, in 1928, was the first South American country to grant women's suffrage, and in 1931, Sri Lanka became the first Asian country to do so, followed by Thailand in 1932. The first African country to grant women the right to vote was Senegal in 1945. Cameroon and Liberia followed in 1946.

Following World War II, the process greatly accelerated and today, practically every women in the world has the right to vote. In only a small handful of countries – Bahrain, Brunei, Kuwait, Oman, Qatar, Saudi Arabia and United Arab Emirates – women are still denied access to the ballot box. Although a separate law granting women the right to vote was under consideration, at the same time, it was never adopted.

In a few countries including Russia and China, women's suffrage was adopted practically overnight as part of a national revolution that granted equal political rights to women and men. In certain countries, voting right was given based on fulfilling conditions like completion of secondary or higher education (Portugal); in 1930, South Africa granted such right to white women, to widows or mothers of servicemen and civilians killed during world war I (Belgium).

New Wave of Feminism

In 1960s, a new wave of feminism emerged and by this time

several factors – lower infant mortality rates, rising life expectancy, and the introduction of modern contraceptives – had given women more control over their lives and greater freedom from child bearing responsibilities.

At the same time, rising inflation was propping more women into the labour force, and by 1970, women constituted 40 per cent more of the work force in more than a dozen developed countries, among them Canada, Denmark, France, the United Kingdom and the United States. In the United States and parts of Europe, this resurgence became known as the women's liberation movement, and much attention was given to consciousness raising, that is, making women more aware of their common problems.

Todays Issues

Today almost every country has a wide array of women's organisation, some dealing with the broad issues of women's right, others focusing on specific concerns such as abortion, sexual harassment, violence against women, or the problems of immigrant or minority women. While fundamentalist movement within Catholicism, evangelical Protestantism, Judaism and Hinduism have had serious repercussions in some parts of the world, none has had such a far reaching effect on women as the worldwide resurgence of the various forms of Islamic fundamentalism[6]. Afghani women, who once enjoyed a number of rights and freedoms are now being forced to observe purda, the practice of keeping women in seclusion and prohibiting them from seeing any men other than their relatives. In public, they must be accompanied by a male relative and must always be swathed in the traditional burgoo, a headto-toe covering with only a netted opening for the wearer's eyes.

In Poland in 1993, the church lobbied successfully to greatly restrict the country's liberal abortion law and keep sex education out of the classroom. Other setback for women, especially in the area of employment are evident in those parts of the world currently suffering domestic downturns. Women are bearing the brunt of these crisis, suffering high levels of unemployment coupled with cutbacks in child care and other government services whether a conflict is worth another country or an internal ethnic, religion or civil war, women and girls are often prime targets and those who survive suffer the many devastating effects of armed conflict: torture, mass rape, broken families and the loss of homes and property.

International Organisations

At the international level, a number of non-governmental women's group support research on women's issues and co-ordinate and disseminate information among women of different countries.These groups include:

- Women's Studies International
- Human Rights Watch
- The International Centre for Research on Women; and
- The International Women's Health Coalition.

In recent years, the Asian Foundation founded the Asia-Pacific Women in Politics Network, which conducts workshops, study group and training programmes aimed at encouraging women to vote, speak out on issues and become political leaders. Similar efforts are in the planning stages for Latin America, Africa and the Middle East.

Undoubtedly, the single most important international organisation concerned with women's issues and committed to promoting equal rights for women throughout the world is the United Nations, which in 1975, launched its Decade for Women Programme, and since then, has sponsored four major international women's conferences: Mexico city (1975), Copenhagen (1980), Nairobi (1985), and Beijing (1995).

In addition, several UN agencies and affiliated organisations are concerned primarily with women's issues such as International Research and Training Institute for the Advancement of Women (INSTRAAW), the United National Development Fund for Women (UNIFEM), and the United Nations Division for the Advancement of Women, which services the commission on the status of women, the main UN body responsible for all policies concerning gender issues.

One of the most important ways in which the United Nations has had an impact on the status of women has been through its sponsorship of several major international agreements or conventions. The most recent of these is the convention on the Elimination of All Forms of Discriminations Against Women (CEDAW), an international bill of rights for women that also includes guidelines for implementing the policies and laws required to guarantee those rights.

Women in Politics and Leaders of Politics

There is not a single country where women enjoy the same political status, access, or influence as men do. The first women ever elected to lead a country was Srimavo Bandaranaike, who became Prime Minister of Sri Lanka (then called Ceylon) in 1960. By 1970, two other countries, India and Israel, were led by women and in 1988, Benazir Bhutto became the first women to head a Muslim country when she was elected Pakistan's Prime Minister. By 1997, five countries were headed by women.

Women in Indian Scenario

Ancient Period

With the coming of Manu Code in post-Vedic age, the Vedic custom of husband and wife jointly taking part in religious functions slowly rejected women's rights and made them depend entirely on her husband and declared that she was not man's equal in her own right. A husband must be worshiped; by a faithful wife just as a God is done. A married women was not allowed to do anything according to her own pleasure even in her dwelling place. When young she depends on her father, after marriage on her husband, and in old age on her son. The famous dictum of Manu, the law giver which equates drums, rustics, shudras, animals with that of the then prevailing status of women in India[7]. Historians have eulogised the position of women during the Vedic age, when they were considered a moral force in the society and held in pivotal position in the family. The fall in the status of women has been attributed to the Muslim invaders. But history bears witness to the fact that even in the Vedic times, Sita the consort of Rama, was turned out of the royal place in Ayodhya in deference to public opinion. Women have, over centuries, been used, abused and exploited and the scenario has not changed much as we move into the twenty first century[8].

The inferior status of women is established right at the birth. The birth of a girl child is unwelcome as she is considered to be an economic burden. Female infanticide was very common in states like Rajasthan.[9]

Economic development is the progress towards an increasingly intricate patterns of labour specialisation. In communities at earliest stages of development, practically all goods and services are produced and consumed within the family group but with economic development, more people become specialised in particular tasks and the economic autonomy of the family group is superseded by the exchange of goods and services. The position of women differs in many basic features in the community groups[10]. If the nation is to develop, it is essential that the basic standard of living of the people is alleviated. This cannot be achieved unless women who constitute half of the population are mobilised towards contribution to the national development and growth. This has to be a two way process as women cannot contribute meaningfully in the process of development until their own development is taken care of.

Women have not belied the faith which has been reposed in them. They participated in a big way during the national freedom struggle. There have been agitations against atrocities on women. Women have launched anti-dowry campaigns. The Chipko movement has become a possibility because of the efforts and foresightedness of women in fighting for better environment[11]. However, there are a host of inhibiting factors namely, social, economic and political factors which prevent women from being active participants in the development process.

There appears to be nothing final about the rules that women assumes in our society. But we have to a lot for women because they have been suppressed. They have not been allowed to develop or to contribute in various spheres in a world where they comprise half of the population. If that half is neglected and not allowed to play its full part, nation's development can not be achieved. In our country, women's roles have undergone change in the direction of narrowing of options and towards an expansion in opportunites[12]. Women do have to put in hard labour. Many roles are expected of the responsibility for running domestic activities in addition to whatever they do professionally.

The period between 1500-1000 B.C. is identified as the early Vedic period or the Rig Vedic period. According to various sources, women enjoyed equal status and rights during the early Vedic period. It is evident from available data that many liberal attitudes and practices pertaining to women existed during this period. Women took part of religious and social activities and they had some freedom to choose their partner in marriage. Marriage was not compulsory for women. The daughters were not considered a liability or an unwelcome guest in her parental household. Girls were also initiated into Vedic studies. However, later, the status of women began to decline with the Islamic invasion of Bihar and rise of Mughal empire, and later that of Christianity curtailing women's freedom and rights.[13]

The period of epic Mahabharata is believed to be dated to fifth century B.C. The two great Epics, Ramayana and Mahabharata have played key roles in moulding the ideology of Hindus as well as their attitudes towards women. It thus becomes important to discuss the portrayal of women in these two epics when we are discussing the status of women. As stated earlier, these two epics have a strong influence on Indian society. Even today, girls are being brought up to follow in the footsteps of Sita, the wife of Rama. Sita is considered ideal Hindu woman because she surrendered all her personal desires and followed Rama to the forest. On the other hand, Draupadi—the central female character of Mahabharata—is a woman who exhibits a greater sense of independence and courage. Sita of Ramayana and Draupadi of Mahabharata are well known today. In spite of their subjugated status vis-à-vis their husbands, they are universally respected and have become role models. The self-imposed blindness of Gandhari as a mark of respect for her blind husband did not lower her status as a queen. In fact, she sends the message that a respectable wife is one who humbles herself vis-à-vis her husband. Ancient India's march to civilisation was accompanied by the growth of social discriminations.[14]

Jainism and Buddhism took roots around the sixth century B.C. Both the religions emerged as potent religious reform movements. The post-Vedic varna divided society and the ritualistic domination of the priestly class of the Brahmanas led to the emergence of Jainism and Buddhism as protest movements. Jainism emerged as a religion distinct from Hinduism. Though it recognised the existence of the gods, it placed them lower than the Mahavira (Jina). Jainism made the first serious attempt to mitigate the evils of the varna order and advocated giving up family life to become ascetics. During the time of Mahavira, a large number of women drawn from different background joined the monastic order. In Jaina literature, there are references to women who had achieved remarkable success as ascetics. Buddhism did not recognise the existence of god and soul (atman). This was a kind of revolution in the history of Indian religions. It appealed to the common people. It particularly won the support of the lower orders as it attached the Varna system. Buddhism permitted women to participate in religious discourses and seek membership in Sangha. Many women monks composed verses, which came to be known as Therigatha.

The high status, women enjoyed during the early Rig Vedic period, gradually started deteriorating in the Later Vedic period between 1000 and 500 B.C. Women began to be confined to the household. Because of the importance given to values such as purity (ritual cleanliness) and pollution (ritual impurity or contamination), women began to be considered impure during certain periods of their life. They were kept away from many religious and social occasions. Lineage began to be traced in the male line and sons were the sole heirs to family property. As the economic and social status of sons began to rise, the position of women saw a steep decline. The strong belief of the day was that only a male heir could save his parents from the cycle of rebirth. Since a daughter left her parental home after marriage, it was the son who was left with the responsibility of caring for parents in their old age. This further added value to the sons.

A women's place was the home and her primary responsibility was to bear sons and ensure the continuity of the family lineage. A husband's rights over his wife were total and he had the freedom to go for another marriage if his wife failed to beget sons. A woman was kept constantly under male control and she lost her right to seek knowledge. Over a period of time, marriageable age was also lowered.

There was a general decline in the status of women in the post-Vedic period. But there were still instances of women intellectuals who showed great scholarship and the most well known woman scholar of this period was Gargi Maithreyi. There are also references to women studying Vedas and going through initiation rituals. But by and large, the position of women went on witnessing a steady decline and reached an all time low during the age of Dharmashastras[15].

During the age of Dharmashastras, code of conduct which served as the basis for prescribing behaviour norms for women also were evolved. These belong to a large body of secular literature, compiled in 500-200 B.C. This period saw the exclusion (leaving out) of women both from economic and religious sphere. Since education was virtually denied to women, they had to be dependent on men for their survival and maintenance. The concept that women were inferior to men gained ground and women were pushed to a state of utter despair and ignorance. This period was also characterised by consolidation of religious customs and caste systems assuming rigid proportions.

The Dharmashastras prescribed codes of conduct, which regulated not only family life but also life in society at large. They also prescribed punishments for violation of these codes of conduct. The two most important authoritative law codes of this period were Manusmriti and Yagnavalkyasmriti. Manusmriti upheld the view that a women did not deserve freedom at any point of life (Na stree Swathantriamarhati). Manu's view was that a women, in her childhood is dependent on her father, in her youth on her husband, and in her old age on her son. This view of Manu was not a theoretical idea but also a practice followed *in toto* by the society at that period. The same Manu also told that 'where women are respected there the God's delight'. This is a statement, which is in clear contradiction of his pronouncements about women not deserving any freedom.

Yagnavalkya laid down that parents who did not get their daughter married before they attained the age of puberty would be committing an unpardonable sin. The Dharmashastras planted the impression that an unmarried woman could never attain salvation from these worldly obligations if she remained single. As a result, marriage came to be considered as an unavoidable ritual for a woman. While girls had to be married at a very tender age, no such restrictions were imposed on men. The husband was even given right to enforce the obedience by resorting to physical punishment.

During the period of Dharmashastras, childhood marriage was encouraged and widow marriage was looked down upon. The birth of a girl came to be considered as an ill omen and many parents went to the extreme extent of killing their female infants. The practice of Sati became quite widespread because of the ill treatment meted out to the widows. It was during the period of Dharmashastras that the status of women completely deteriorated. Women lead a life of total subjugation (subordination) and had virtually lost all hopes of emancipation (freedom). This situation, more or less, continued until the nineteenth century when the social reforms movement launched a struggle to improve the conditions of women[16].

Medieval Period

The 11th century saw the emergence of Islam which created hopes of promoting the interests of the oppressed groups, also introduced certain values and practices, which did not help to enhance the status of women or emancipate them from their bondage. The system of Purdah (using a veil to cover the head/face/entire body/mostly remaining indoors), which was generally prevalent among the royal families, nobles and merchant prince classes prior to the advent of Muslims spread to the other classes also. These customary practices of the upper castes, particularly the twice born castes were considered as the practices of all Hindus. The lower castes generally adopted upper caste customs. The strict observance of *purdah* resulted in the seclusion of women from men who did not belong to their family and also the world outside.

Marriage was a contract among the Muslims and it was a man's prerogative to divorce his wife. In a system, where there was no provision for payment of alimony (maintenance after divorce), the wife was left to fend for herself. Among the Muslims, marriage, divorce or inheritance questions are decided as per the provision contained in the Muslim Personal Law (Shariat). Even today, in the absence of a uniform civil code, Shariat governs Muslim family life. The fact that a large number of Muslim women have still not been able to access opportunities for education leaves them at the mercy of rigid patriarchal values and practices.

During the medieval periods, practices such as polygamy (the marriage in which a man has more than one wife), *Sati*, child marriage, ill-treatment of widows already prevalent during the Dharmashastra age gained further momentum. The priestly class misinterpreted the sacred texts to their advantage and created an impression that all these evil practices had religious sanction. Since women are denied the right to education and are kept away from participation in life outside the home, they could neither know the reality nor question the existing practices[17].

Modern Period

The modern period began with the onset of the nineteenth century. The Britishers came to India in 1600 A.D. For nearly 200 years, in their East India Company incarnation, they addressed questions of social inequality or social oppression. Social evils such as *Sati*, suppression of widows, denial of right to education to women, and child marriage flourished. With the dawn of nineteenth century, an era of change began and it was during this period that many efforts were made both by the British rulers and progressive sections of Indian society to put an end to social evils. The modern period may be classified into (i) The period before Independence (The British period) from 1800 to 1947, and (ii) The period after Independence (after 1947).

The British set in motion the era of social reforms when they imposed a ban on the inhuman practice of *Sati* (the practice of self or forced immolation of a widow on the funeral pyre of her husband) in the year 1829[18].

The famous social reformer Raja Ram Mohan Roy's fight against Sati received a positive response from the then Governor General Lord William Bentick and he also took a lead in enacting the Sati Prohibition Act.

Because of the ban on widow marriage and lack of opportunities for education, women who were rescued from the practice of *Sati* had to undergo a great deal of suffering. Many widows preferred to die, because life held no meaning for them.

It was this plight of the young and tortured widows that moved West Bengal's great reformer Iswar Chandra Vidyasagar, who led the movement for lifting the ban on widow marriage. Due to his efforts, the Widow Remarriage Act of 1856 was passed. The role of Vidyasagar in promoting the cause of women's education also deserves special mention.

Many of the woes of women were rooted in child marriage. The Child Marriage Restraint Act of 1929 fixed the minimum age for marriage for girls as 14 years and for boys as 18 years. Today the minimum age at marriage for woman is 18 years and for a man 21 years. These changes were brought about by the Child Marriage Restraint (Amendment) Act, which was passed in 1976.

Gandhiji, under whose leadership women participated in the nationalist movement, opposed such practices as child marriage and dowry. The large scale participation of women in the freedom movement both as known and unknown freedom fighters was a standing testimony not only to their courage but also their capacities.

The British period saw the rise of social reform movement which took up the issues of gender inequality, primarily by passing laws that removed barriers to women's emancipation.

Independence brought new hopes and led to the creation of departments and launching of schemes, meant exclusively for improvement in the status of women.

After India got independence, the Constitution of India laid the foundation for creating a social order where men and women are treated as equals while Article 14 of the Constitution conferred equal rights and opportunities on men and women. Article 15 (1) prohibited discrimination of citizens on grounds of sex. The Constitution, through Article 15 (3) also laid down that the State can make special provisions for women. According to Article 16 (2), no citizen shall be discriminated against in respect of any employment in office under the State.[19] The Directive Principles of the State Policy prescribed that:

(i) Men and women equally have the right to adequate means of livelihood.

(ii) There is equal pay for equal work for both men and women.

(iii) The health and strength of women workers cannot be abused.

(iv) Provision should be made for securing just and humane conditions of work and for maternity.

The Hindu Marriage Act, 1955; The Hindu Succession Act, 1956; The Equal Remuneration Act, 1976; The Indecent Representation of Women (Prohibition) Act, 1986; Hindu Adoption and Maintenance Act, 1956; The Immoral Traffic Prevention Act, 1956 (further amended in 1986); The Family Courts Act, 1984; and The National Commission for Women Act, 1990 have been passed after the nation became independent and were implemented for liberating women from oppressive social customs and protecting their rights.

Women's Relative Status

The female anthropologists in their studies on human societies; who have given more of their attention to this issue, agree that the relative status of women has varied over time and across societies. There is less consensus on the factors determining their relative positions. One anthropologist, Ernestine Fried[20] has emphasised the importance of environmental constraints in shaping human organisation. She argues that the technology employed by a society to produce the necessities of life has tended, in the past, to determine the division of labour on the basis of sex. In turn, she believes that the more important women's role is in production and in controlling distribution outside the family, the higher is their status compared to men. The status of men and women was very unequal in societies where men provided all the needed resources and women devoted themselves to turn these resources into usable form and create a viable atmosphere in which they could be used.

Others tends to disagree, at least with the emphasis on the importance of production roles in determining status. There is little dispute about the fact that property gives owners power over distribution and that this helps to determine status.

There is a common view that the structure of social relationships and participation in productive work both play a role. Specifically, in the case of women, it appears that sharing in the provision for the family's needs is a necessary, though not a sufficient ingredient in achieving a greater degree of equality[21]. Clearly, as Michelle Rosaldo[22] points out, the extent to which women's activities are confined to the home while men monopolise the public sphere, also plays an important role.

Based on the texts of the period 400 B.C. to 1200 A.D., several reasons have been put forward to account for the deterioration of women's position in the society, such as, the imposition of Brahmanical austerities on the entire society (except where Buddhism and Jainism were more prevalent), foreign invasions of India affecting the status of women adversely, discontinuance of Upanayana of girls, lack of educational facilities for women and the role of the caste system, joint family system, feudalism and other such social institutions. Religious idea or philosophy of people influenced to a certain degree man's outlook on society. On the other hand, economic and social changes also react powerfully on the religious ideas or philosophy of a society[23]. If the position of women during this period deteriorated as compared to earlier centuries, its causes are sought as also the variations within social groups and regions, where the change was felt to different degrees. This may provide a complete and systematic view of the status of women during the period of 200 years, i.e., the 11th and 12th centuries A.D. in Northern India.

Family Relationship and the Status of Women

Professor Rivers[24] had distinguished four types of institutions which have been designated by the term family viz., the clan, the matrilocal joint family, the patrilocal joint family, and the individual family comprising only parents and minor children.

Irawati Karve is of the opinion that the stories in the Mahabharata and Ramayana show how stable the joint family system has been through the ages "The Mahabharata family is found today in most joint families. The ideas of status, duties and rights of joint family are those inherited from and deeply rooted in the tradition of these epics[25]. The position of a girl[26] born in the family was such that she was valued as an object for marriage or exchange and occasionally for lending. Women should always be protected with care, never to be killed, the more so as the sages have assigned greater sin to the killing of women. The man who kills women consciously or unconsciously, is certainly boiled in the Maha Raurava hell[27]. Some of the Smritikaras (Manu, Likhita, etc.)[28] giving importance to the son, say that one should not marry a girl who does not have a brother. It is apparent that it was not only women of the lower social groups who had a low status in society but even women of royal families did not enjoy a noticeable higher status in their own families. The parents[29] worshipped the gods so that they could have a son where as the birth of a daughter increased the anxiety of the parents and this increased further when the girl attained the age of marriage.

It is seen that, in general, in Northern India, where patrilineal society prevailed, sons were preferred to daughters. But as a wife, she had a higher status in the family and in society in Rig Vedic times as compared to later centuries as without her presence, no sacrifice or Yajna could be fruitful (Ramayana).

When a women goes to her husband's house, she has to face some unfavourable situations and certain rivalries with her husband's sister, or what comes to the same thing as relationship between a woman and her brother's wife. A woman resents (sometimes) a female stranger coming and occupying her father's house and holding a position of respect. She is active in spying over the young bride and reporting every misbehaviour to her mother. This behaviour accentuated if the husband's sister were widowed or had been driven away from her husband's house and had come to live at her father's house[30]. A man had absolute right over his wife and the prescribed behaviour for a married woman was to be a *pativrata* (following the will of the husband). A man could have more than one wife but there were very strict rules for a woman. The practice of polygamy further deteriorated the position of woman. Aged members, especially old women, face a serious situation in today's family structure.

Status of Women in Social Institutions

According to Ashraf[31], the term *purdah* means a curtain or something to screen off an object or person. In common parlance, it means a veil when applied to women; the term signifies seclusion in a separate building otherwise call *antahpurah*, or otherwise covering the face when appearing before men or going out in public. We do not find any reference to the seclusion of women in the Vedic period. The Arthashastra of Kautilya[32] refers to some women as *aniskasini*, i.e., not going out of their homes. In the works of poet Kalidasa, we find the practice of seclusion of women among the royal families. In eleventh and twelfth centuries, we do find many instances of the recognition of this institution and support for it from the kings. This tended to further lower the position of women as evident from the reference to women rulers and a few to women warriors. But, most of such inscriptional evidence we get from the Deccan and South India. Though reference to women rulers shows the higher status a women enjoyed, nevertheless it was limited to royalty and aristocracy, there too in a very limited sense.

Legal Status of Women

It is essential to study the evolution of property rights of women (inheritance) and the wealth acquired by other means (viz. stridhana). It is seen that the general position of women went on deteriorating some time after sixth and seventh centuries A.D. as evident from work of Baudhayana[33].

Quoting the text of the Vedas, he says that females are generally incompetent to inherit "devoid of prowess and incompetent to inherit", women are useless. Most of the commentators agreed that the wife is entitled to get a share at the time of partition between her husband and her sons. But there is great divergence of opinion amongst them as to the manner of allotting such a share.

In the Agni Purana,[34] a text of tenth-eleventh century A.D., it is said that women and an animal can be kept as a pledge and interest on them is the 17th part of their original value. Another law ordains that the person who places his own children, wife, animals and paddy as deposits is entitled to get twice the value of the original. Thus, it is seen that if a woman was considered a kind of property of her father or her husband, there were very little chances of her owning property. There was a time when a woman was financially independent, in the sense that she could own a share out of her husband's property and had authority over her *stridhana*.

According to Jaimini[35], one effect of marriage is to give each of the parties there to control over the others wealth. Gautama (post-Vedic), who favours niyoga, recommends a widow's right to inheritance only in the absence of her sons. If she submits to niyoga, and that too with her brother-in-law, then only she could inherit the property. It must have been so because people did not like the family property going out of the house. If she has a son through her brother-in-law, he could be closer to her husband and his family and thus, the property would also remain in the same house.

Vasistha Smrti[36] gives a widow only the right of maintenance out of her husband's property. Probably this is so because he thinks that if she is given too much property, more than what she requires to keep herself alive, she would go astray. Since Manu[37] does not recommend niyoga and sati for a widow, he favours the property rights of widow. But, if she was to live in this world, she needed some money to live on and for which Manu prescribes a portion out of her husband's property.

In the Dayabaga[38], it is said that the eldest wife alone, who is ranked as *patni* and who can associate with her husband in the performance of religious rites, is entitled to inherit.

Educational Status

Modern education has a fundamentally different orientation and organisation. Its content is liberal and exoteric and it is steeped in a modern scientific world view. Freedom, equality, humanism and denial of faith in dogmas are the themes which a modern education should contain. It has a professional structure which is not ascribed to any specific group or class but can be achieved by merit by any one in a society. The foundation of modern education in India was established by the British. Its historical landmarks are: Macaulay's policy of 1835 to promote European learning through English, Sir Charles Wood's Dispatch of 1854 which for the first time recognised the need for mass education with private and missionary help and gave up the policy of selective education known as the filtration theory, and finally the first Indian Education Commission of 1882 which recommended the initiative of private India agencies in the expansion of education[39].

Yogendra Singh has analysed the significance of education in the process of modernisation. Singh writes: "from the very beginning, a contradiction between the primary and the college university level of education emerged in India on account of the medium and content of education. At the primary level, the medium of instruction (with the exception of missionary and public schools) was the regional languages, and at the college level, it was English. Teaching of science and European literature was done at the colleges and universities to which a select few had access; but the mass education at the primary level remained isolated from this main current. This lag in the structure of education which started from the time of Macaulay has still not been fully bridged. Modernisation through education thus, right from the beginning in India, has been confined to a sub culture of college and university educated youth and elite never did become a mass phenomenon[40]. In the nineteenth century, the rush for higher education specially among the urban middle class and the growth in higher education was also considerable[41].

Progress has also been made in other spheres of educational planning and modernisation of its organisation. Percentage of girls going to schools and colleges has increased. In many states, schooling of children has been made free and compulsory. New vocational and polytechnical institutions have been started for better utilisation of educated manpower for the economic and social growth of the country[42].

The National Committee on Women's Education had suggested establishing separate educational institutions for girls in order to end the prejudice regarding girls' education because most parents do not want to educate them with boys in the same institution. Therefore, during the period after 1960-61, the number of girls' institutions increased every fast. It has also been always accepted that for development of women's education, increasing the number of female teachers is a compulsory condition.[43]

Women and Economic Development

Economic development is the progress towards an increasingly intricate patterns of labour specialisation. In communities at earliest stages of development, practically all goods and services are produced and consumed within the family group, but with economic development more people become specialised in particular tasks and the economic autonomy of the family group is superseded by the exchange of gods and services. The position of women differs in many basic features in the community groups[44]. If the nation is to develop, it is essential that the basic standard of living of the people is elevated. This cannot be achieved unless women, who constitute half of the population, are mobilised towards contribution to the national development and growth. This has to be a two-way process; women cannot contribute meaningfully in the process of development, until their own development is taken care of.

Women have not belied the faith which has been reposed in them. They participated in a big way during the national freedom struggle. There have been agitations against atrocities on women. Women have launched anti-dowry campaigns. The Chipko Movement has become a possibility because of the efforts and foresightedness of women in fighting for a better environment[45]. However, there are a host of inhibiting factors namely, social, economic, and political which prevent women from being active participants in the development process.

There appears to be nothing final about the roles that women assume in our society. But we have to do a lot for women because they have been suppressed. They have not been allowed to develop, or to contribute in various spheres, in a world where they comprise half of the population. If that half is neglected and is not allowed to play its full part, nation's development cannot be achieved. In our country, women's roles have undergone change in the direction of narrowing of options and towards an expansion in opportunities[46]. Women do have to put in hard labour. Many roles are expected of the responsibility for running domestic activities in addition to whatever they do professionally.

The Shramshakti report by the National Commission on Self-Employed Women and Women Informal Sector in the (1988:93) convincingly argues that: While the work put in by the women and their earnings meet the survival needs of the family, their contribution in the fields of agriculture, food production, forestry, animal husbandry, industry processing occupations, contribute to the growth of GNP, thereby making a direct contribution to the national economy....There is no doubt that women's contribution to the family and national economy is much more than their actual earnings.

Entitlement of Women

The movement for the improvement of the legal status of women was an integral part of the general movement for the emancipation of women and was inspired by the equalitarian idea. The marriage laws, the property laws and the personal laws are some of the legal methods by which woman can be made subordinate to man. The social reformers, and in the later phases, women themselves realised the obstacles in the way of full freedom and free development of women and therefore they advanced demands for improving their legal status also. The rights sought include:

1. Women and Social Rights : Marriage laws.
2. Women and Economic Rights: Diverse property rights for different communities.
3. Laws for Occupation and Employment of Woman.

Amartya Sen[47] makes a compelling case for the notion that societies need to see women less as passive recipients of help, and more as dynamic promoters of social transformation, a view strongly buttressed by a body of evidence suggesting that the education, employment and ownership rights of women have a powerful influence on their ability to control their environment and contribute to economic development.

Economic participation concerns not only the actual numbers of women participating in the labour force, but also their remuneration on an equal basis. Worldwide, outside of the agricultural sector, in both developed and developing countries, women are still averaging slightly less than 78 per cent of the wages given to men for the same work, a gap which refuses to close in even the most developed countries.

For comparing the status of women in various states of India, different variables such as female literacy, sex ratio, maternal mortality rate, percentage of anemic women, married women who participated in household decisions, women who have ever experienced spousal violence and gender disparity index for various states have been taken into account. The attainment of the said variables is high in Kerala compared other states in India.

Women in Kerala Scenario

Kerala has become an interesting case in the development debate of economic growth versus human development, showing that it is possible to put the wellbeing of the people in the state on top of policy agenda, despite low economic performance. Kerala has the Highest Human Development Index (HDI) in India. In fact, the general position of women in Kerala has improved considerably during twentieth century. The land reforms also helped in improving the position of the women there. The replacement of the joint family system with nuclear family also helped the changes in this direction. Again, women also played a prominent role in the freedom struggle. Political consciousness and general awareness of the Kerala women can be considered as high. They are educated and highly politically conscious. However, most of the women in Kerala aspire for jobs that bring them status, financial independence and courage in daily life situations. In general, women are considered to be capable of leading a successful family life. Today, we can find women in middle and high level salaried jobs as senior civil servants, as teachers in universities, colleges, schools and in professions such as nursing. These was made possible because of the efforts taken by the women social reformers.

The development experience of women is not uniform in India. History, Geography and cultural pattern of the region, along with various other socio-economic factors play a significant role in the development of women anywhere in the world. The status of women is relatively better in the state. Women awareness, women movements at the grassroots level, greater mobility, education, women and child health intervention have led to the overall development of women in Kerala. Women development has assumed greater significance in the context of globalisation. The various neo-liberal policies introduced at national and state levels with the intention of the restructuring of the national and state economies have serious implications for women's development.[48]

Relations in the family, class status, and the ideology of the social group to which they belong affect women's status. All these are part of inheritance. Among the ideologies underlying inheritance is patriarchy. In its narrow sense, patriarchy is the rule by the father within the family and the consequent subordination of his wife and children. In a broader concept, patriarchy is used as a term for characterising the society that comprises male dominance in all areas: education, work, and socio-political institutions. Safa[49] mentions three crucial sites of women's subordination, family, workplace and the politics, and maintains that patriarchy is manifested in all the three sites.

Women and Politics

In Kerala, the year 1996 was a landmark in decentralised planning. Local bodies in the state started functioning as institutions of self-government and agents of local development. Women empowerment is an integral part of any development administration. This is more so in a local level development under the Panchayati Raj and devolution of new powers to it.

Participation of Women in Gram Sabhas

The participation in decentralised planning reveal that more than two million persons attended Gram sabhas and ward assemblies in the first phase (1996-2000) of PPC in which women constituted 26.22 per cent. Women's participation ranged from the low of 20.26 per cent in Ernakulam to a high of 35.02 per cent in Thiruvananthapuram according to Jagajeevan and Ramakanthan.[50] As pointed out by Bava Khan, Pareethu P.M., Oomman, John, Kumari, Leela[51], the percentage rate of participation of women had increased from 35.56 per cent in first year to 78.44 per cent in third year. There was a remarkable decrease during the fourth and fifth year. The number of women in Gram Sabha was higher than that of men over the three years—1997-98, 1998-99, 1999-2000, and there was steady decline in the participation of women in the Gram sabhas. While in 1997-98, more than one thousand women attended the meetings in one of Panchayat, while in 1999-2000, their number declined to half. In the other Panchayat too, a steady decline was registered[52].

Elected women representatives opined that the low level participation of women is due to lack of awareness about the relevance of Gram sabhas among women. The women's participation in the Gram sabhas had increased in number compared with that of earlier stages but this does not imply that their participation in the discussions also increased. In many cases, they came on the insistence of families rather than on their own volition. Women mainly constitute the beneficiary groups and normally focussed on the subjects like women welfare, sanitation, or drinking water. But the increased presence of women in the Gram sabhas influenced the discussions over there and women also have a feeling that they are also a part of public action.[53]

Participation of Women in Development Seminars

Development seminars were meant for the assessment of the resources, problems and formulation of local development perspectives and plans, and women's participation in them is indispensable. There was a conscious effort to enhance the participation of women in development seminars. However, women's participation in discussions was mainly confined to the areas of women development, social welfare, drinking water, and education.

There has been paucity of a gender-based perspective in identifying problems and constraints. Symptoms have been identified as problems and simplistic solutions or explanations have been offered[54]. Women's contribution in preparing the development reports was very low and the women elected members were reasonably active but their involvement was mainly confined to writing the chapter on women development[55].

Participation of Women in Task Forces

The objective of task force constituted at the LSGIs was project preparation. There were attempts to include women in the implementing mechanism at the time of formulation of projects. However, there was a considerable decline in the involvement of women in the task forces. Panchayat plan that was formulated was through trial and error method and built up into a system constituted by sectoral task forces to discuss problems and come up with projects of programme-based solutions, like the agricultural and allied task force, the health task force, industry task force, SC/ST task force etc. There were task forces for women's issues as well. Panchayat members headed the task forces. The head of the women's task force was necessarily a woman member. The convener was the VEO/LVEO, and other subject experts if available were co-opted. Over and above this, there was also a well-intentioned but poorly executed attempt to discuss the gender dimensions of all general projects[56]. The elected women representatives opined that the proportion of women in task force was less than 10 per cent.

Participation of Women in the Training Process

In the training programmes organised by the planning board during 1996-1997, altogether 660 Key Resource Persons (KRP) at the state level and 12,000 District Resource Persons (DRP) at the district level participated. One-lakh local resource persons were trained. A suggestion was made at the beginning that one-third of this group may be women but it was not mandatory. In the first phase at state level, out of a total number 373, only 64 were women. In the third phase, the women's participation was increased to 15 per cent, i.e., 219 women. In the fourth phase, in which Panchayat presidents and secretaries were also included as resource persons, the women's participation was 17.4 per cent. But even at that time, women's representation at the KRP level was only one-tenth of the total. But the representation of women as DRP was relatively higher than that of KRPs[57]. Most of the facilitators trained as KRP and DRP were men. It is because, not only local governments were reluctant to take women who they felt would not be able to give the kind of time, commitment and advice needed, there were not too many women volunteers either. At the campaign, this was recognised as a shortfall that needed to be made up and in subsequent years; the training programmes started to focus on training the elected women themselves. Only 34 per cent of women task force members participated in Women Component Plan preparations. In the case of resource persons, only 38 per cent women had been involved in this process; 58 per cent of government officials, LVEO, ICDS Supervisors and some of teachers participated in project formulation. Causes of low participation were identified as lack of knowledge and expertise in project formulation and proper understanding of WCP and lack of skills in transforming gender needs into projects.[58]

Participation of Women in Decision-making

Participation of women in decision-making level is a major factor in WCP. Elected women representatives have power to intervene in the WCP at all levels. In general, women representatives are not empowered fully to intervene effectively in the process from a gender perspective.

More than 90 per cent of Elected Women Representatives (EWRs) were active in Grama sabha. Only 10 per cent reported as having not participated in Gram sabha. However, the level of involvement of EWRs tended to decline in subsequent phases. The average participation of women varies from 33 per cent to 51 per cent in various districts[59].

Women members, in general, were influenced by opinion of male members. Many women members felt that political parties were exploiting them. Male members and husbands of certain members did not allow them to attend trainings, as they did not want them to learn their rights and exercise power. The most important thing was that the Elected Women Representatives felt neglected in not receiving communication from Panchayat to attend meetings[60].

Women Empowerment

In most development strategies, participation and empowerment of women have emerged as an important goal. The primary objective of empowerment of women is to create more equitable and participatory structures in which women can gain control over their lives. Generally, women's empowerment has been based on grassroot initiatives that are designed to meet the special needs and interest of local women themselves[61]. The various aspects of empowerment include empowerment framework, elements of empowerment, empowerment approaches, concept of empowerment and finally about organising women for development. After reviewing the processes of the Panchayat, she concludes by saying that the WCP provision was useful to attain a certain level of economic empowerment and substantial social and political empowerment is still a dream to be achieved in future[62]. While the macro-economic policy changes aimed at opening the national economies have facilitated the emergence of new forms of employment of women, the terms with which women participate in these supposedly gender-neutral labour markets carry and reproduce familial and gender norms that are distinctively biased against women[63].

The Indira Mahila Yojana (IMY) has been functioning through the ICDS programme, and in 2001, it was recast into an integrated programme for women's empowerment, namely, Integrated Women's Empowerment Programme or Swayamsidhha. The long-term objective is the all-round empowerment of women, especially socially and economically, by ensuring their direct access to and control over resources through a sustained process of mobilisation and convergence of all the ongoing sectoral programmes. The immediate objectives were establishment of SHGs, creation of confidence and awareness among members of SHGs regarding women's status, health, nutrition, education, sanitation and hygiene, legal rights, economic upliftment and other social, economic and political issues, strengthening saving habits, improving access of women to micro-credit, involvement of women in local-level planning and convergence of services of DWCD and other departments. It is functioning in 18 blocks of the state. The other programmes are Balika Samridhi Yojana; Education Work for Prevention of Atrocities on Women; Swadhar (a scheme for women in difficult circumstances); Anganwadi Workers Welfare Fund; Women's Welfare Services; Supporting Training and Employment Programme for Women (STEP); Kishori Sakthy Yojana (for adolescent girls in 13 blocks).[64]

Kudumbasree is a mission formed for the total eradication of absolute poverty in 10 years through concerted community action under the leadership of Local-Self Government by facilitating organisation of the poor women for combining self-help with demand-led convergence of available services and resources to tackle the multiple dimensions and manifestations of poverty holistically. It is a woman-based participatory poverty eradication project launched by the State Government with the financial support of NABARD and Central Government. The mission attempts to empower the Gram Panchayats and Municipalities to form neighbourhood groups of women, enable the neighbourhood groups to undertake micro saving and credit activities, converge the poverty eradication programmes of the Local Self-Governments at the neighbourhood level and integrate the neighborhood groups with the local government structure.

Reservation of Seats for Women in Local Bodies of Kerala

The Kerala Assembly on 16th September, 2009, unanimously passed two bills—the Kerala Panchayati Raj (Second Amendment) Bill 2009 that will reserve 50 per cent seats in local bodies for women and was implemented in September, 2010 polls to the local governments in Kerala.[65]

Women's Employment in Kerala

'Kerala, which ranks first among Indian states in terms of Human Development Index (HDI) and Gender Development Index (GDI), presents a very poor picture of female work participation. This is paradoxical since the development experience of the state is universally acclaimed as a model for poor states to follow for transforming the living conditions of their people, through 'enlightened' policies of promotion of health care and education. However, the most tragic failure of development in the state is the acute unemployment and low labour force participation rates of both men and women[66].

Participation of women in the labour force has increased worldwide during the past few decades. Since, most women are actually employed in some kind of productive or other similar work, the issues relating to female employment are different from those of male employment. Participation of women in economic activities outside home has an important bearing on gender relations within the household. Women's economic power relative to that of men is considered as the most important dependent variable affecting gender relations at the household level.

The social influences of women's work are also quite extensive. Work opportunities outside home reduce the economic dependence of women on men and in turn, increase her economic command within the family. Women's work outside the household would alter the concept of male bread-winner and would reduce considerably the societal biases regarding roles of women that are primarily responsible for underestimation of women's work. Women's earning give them access to and control over an independent income, which would make their economic contribution visible and high.

In the context of female labour force participation, it has been generally hypothesised that economic growth and education increases female labour force participation. Kerala, where economic growth has been higher than all India and where women are relatively more educated, experiences one of the lowest female work participation and highest unemployment among the major states in India, especially among the educated. This is contradictory for a state which ranks first in Human Development Index and Gender Empowerment Index among all the states of India[67].

Work participation among women in Kerala is 22.9 per cent, which is one of the lowest in India. This low labour force is accompanied by high rates of unemployment. Kerala has the highest incidence of employment both for males and females and in rural areas as well as in urban areas. The overall unemployment rate in Kerala is 12 per cent showing a wide gender gap with 24.3 per cent for women and 6.5 per cent for men[68].

Women and Economic Crisis

The economic crisis is detrimental for both women and men, whether they are at work, looking for work or outside the labour force. Women are often in a disadvantaged position in comparison to men in labour markets around the world. Increased access to labour markets for women has great potential as a contribution to economic development, but only if the work in which women are engaged is decent and productive. Women are too often trapped in insecure employment situations with low productivity and low earnings. This is particularly true for women in the agricultural sector, which is still the predominant source of employment and livelihoods.

The economic crisis makes the achievement of a path toward sustainable and socially equitable growth and decent work increasingly more difficult and underlines the concerns over the social impacts of globalisation for women. Gender equality should be a key principle in any policy response, as the effects of the crisis go beyond the scope of women in the world of work. Therefore, policy responses should help offset the unequal social and economic burden on women. The crisis is an opportunity to drive new ways of thinking on economic and social policies since women are much more integrated into the world of work than ever before. When governments design and implement fiscal stimulus packages, it is important to recognise the labour market disadvantage that women face and to consider explicit employment growth targets for women.

Since women are overrepresented in the unorganised sector where the conditions of work are insecure and wages are low with hardly any non-wage benefits, it is necessary to understand the type and nature of vulnerabilities women face in this sector, in particular as domestic workers.

In Kerala, the problem of the economic crisis was aggravated for women workers since large numbers are engaged in traditional industries which have historically been dependent on exports. Hence, in the context of declining exports of coir, cashew, handlooms and fish, it is necessary to examine the impact of global economic crisis on women workers in these industries.

Women and Income Generation Process

Kudumbasree introduced several innovative programmes for the financial, economic and social upliftment of poor women by organising them into community-based structures like neighborhood groups.

Micro-finance is being used as a major tool for poverty eradication. Kudumbasree Mission follows a simple model of micro-finance to facilitate easier availability and better utilisation of loans for poor people. Currently about 1.97 lakh NHGs are involved in thrift and credit activities and about 37.14[69] lakh families stand covered. Thrift and credit societies, linkage banking, lease land farming, rural micro-enterprises, etc. are some of the initiatives introduced by Kudumbasree to improve the livelihood of the poor women in the neighbourhood groups.

Rural micro enterprises assistance to women belonging to rural areas started during the financial years 2001-02. A subsidy of Rs 7500, or 30 per cent of the project cost, whichever is less, in the case of individual enterprise and Rs. one lakh, or 50 per cent of the cost of project, whichever is less, in the case of group enterprises having a minimum of five members.[70]

Women and Recent Development

India has been ranked 128th out of 177 nations in terms of UNDP's Human Development Index and is classified in the group Middle Human Development Index which measures the overall achievement of a country in three basic dimensions—longevity and health, education and knowledge and a decent standard of living with Kerala is in forefront in all the above said variable in respect of both genders—males and females.

Kerala, a state of thirty-odd million people in the southern tip of India, has been hailed as the epitome of women's development in a country that does not fare too well in terms of UNDP's gender development indicator[71]. Unlike many other states in this country of billion plus people, literacy levels are high among women as well as men in Kerala, and the differences between the two are relatively low, thereby contributing to a high level of recorded GDI in the state. Health indicators are equally impressive with high levels of life expectancy for women and men, and indeed a fairly strong positive tilt towards women, which is similar to the case prevailing in all developed countries and—given the gender biological vulnerability of the male of the species as compared to the female—is what it should be in all relatively gender-neutral societies. Even those health indicators that do not enter directly into the GDI calculations, such as maternal mortality rates, for instance, are pretty good in Kerala, the estimates being significantly lower than those in many other Indian states. It is little wonder that experts have cited the instance of Kerala as one that can and should be emulated as a case that ensures high levels of gender development and consequently a high status for women[72].

In Kerala, the approach adopted by the government in fifties was to give priority to social sectors like health and education. The state has achieved near universal primary education and total literacy. High expenditure on health and family welfare has resulted in the relatively better health indicators. The universal public distribution system ensured freedom from hunger at low cost. The state has several nutrition schemes and has been successful in providing social security provisions to workers from unorganised sectors and vulnerable groups like widows.

Kerala has been considered relatively free from the conventional inhibitions against women's education and employment and women owning property. The matrilineal forms of family which placed fewer restraints against women's inheritance rights on the one hand, and the early twentieth century social reforms which widened access to education across genders on the other hand, can be associated with this. The missionaries showed particular interest in the development of education of women irrespective of caste or creed. As many historians point out, the result of spread of education was the rise in age of marriage. The birth and death rates also decreased. Freedom to remarry, to dress as per choice, to go for higher studies and for employment, were the result of this early spread of education among women in Kerala. It was mainly women's education, which reshaped and modernised the life of women and society in Kerala.

Yet, gradually one can see a change in women's position as is indicated by the decline in property rights of women, declining work participation rates, rise in dowry and other crimes against women and growing domesticity of women. Subsequent social and legal reforms were instrumental in sanctioning new forms of marriage grounded in modern patriarchal relations.

In spite of high female literacy, as per the data provided by the quinquennial surveys carried out by the National Sample Survey Organisation (NSSO), the state also ranks among the lowest female labour force participation rates. Detailed interviews with women from varied socio-economic backgrounds under different contexts revealed that contrary to popular belief, women do not enjoy the kind of 'freedom' that one would expect to go with high levels of human or gender development. The Gender Network research agenda slowly acquired a new agenda item, namely, unraveling the puzzle of the Kerala woman. We needed to understand why, and how, such high levels of standard (or 'conventional') gender development indicators could co-exist with these other signals of women's powerlessness.

The story begins with the 'discovery' that although bits and pieces of information were already available for some time or the other from different sources that questioned the dominant understanding that women enjoy a non-discriminatory and high social standing in Kerala, this information did not find any place in shaping popular knowledge and understanding of the issue. Such popular understanding has after all been supported by a range of sociological and historical explanations. Kerala has had a long history of social reforms, touching just about every community in the state, and just about every reformer has put an emphasis on the vital role that women can, and should play in the reforms process. The high status traditionally enjoyed by women in matrilineal systems, of which Kerala could boast a few; the history of early spread of female education in the state through the agency of benevolent rulers as well as Christian missionaries; the seemingly pro-active role played by the state government in the post-independence years in terms of early inception of family planning; the long history of left movement which had pushed the interests of the economically disadvantaged sections of the population, were some of the elements of the set of explanations that have been invoked to cement the popular understanding. The major indicators of women's development, such as literacy levels and health indicators, were far ahead of the rest of the states in India, and the dominant understanding about the status of women far too well entrenched for the dissonant bits of information, such as falling infant sex ratios or soaring dowry rates in the state in recent times, to make any dent in the popular perception. High rates of crimes against women could be ignored by ascribing it to reporting bias due to high literacy levels. Low levels of female labour force participation could be explained away by invoking self-selection. Evidence contrary to this dominant understanding coming out of detailed case studies could be ignored as aberrations, and so on. Curiosity drove us to Kerala to understand the nature of the ground reality. A number of studies were conducted under three phases of the Gender Network during the period 1999 to 2006 to find out what, if anything was wrong with the 'status of women' in Kerala. The first of these was designed to review the history of social and legal reforms in the state with a focus on women's position in society.[73]

The claims about the high levels of gender development in Kerala have been based, primarily, on high levels of recorded gender development indicators such as female literacy and life expectancy levels, and women's earnings in the labour market relative to that of men as expounded by UNDP. One has to take cognizance of the fact that a note of caution was indeed sounded in the original UNDP document, with a plea to take these figures with a degree of caution and to desist from reading too much into them.

Subsequent years however, witnessed a virtual flood of research in gender studies with the collection and analysis of data on conventional 'gender development' indicators in a range of social, economic, demographic and political arenas, over time and across space.[74]

Extensive interviews with Kerala women from varied backgrounds using a range of qualitative methods such as case studies, focus group discussions and detailed life histories over the course of the research convinced us that not everything is right for women in 'God's Own Country'[75].

The female literacy is high in Kerala and also the gender gap in literacy is low in Kerala (males 94.2 and females 87.9 whereas in India it was 75.9 in the case of males and 54.2 in the case of females).[76]

In Kerala, the female-male ratio is well above unity; in fact, it is as high as 1,058–a figure comparable to that of Europe and North America. Kerala has a distinguished history of a more liberated position of women in society[77].

The percentage of anemic women in each state depicts the low health status of women. Health has both intrinsic and instrumental importance influence over development and welfare of women. All other states except four states (Kerala, Punjab, Himachal Pradesh and Maharashtra) have more than 50 per cent of their women anemic[78].

Social opportunities, which include provision of basic public services such as, healthcare, child immunisation, primary education, social security, environmental protection and rural infrastructure, are essential aspects of development. The extent of female involvement in decision-making at household level is another indicator of female autonomy. The linkage between investment in education, health and skills; more equitable distribution of income, government social spending; and empowerment of people, especially women have been proved many a times through empirical evidences. Per capita spending on education and health has relatively stronger impact on human development than growth in per capital income per se[79]. Social movements like caste-based reform movements, missionary activities and left movements have helped in rising human development and social security for the poor and the women have also played an active role in raising the levels of social development in the state. Thus, provision of social opportunities have direct link with the overall development of the place, which is further enhanced by improvement in the status of women. Property has traditionally been inherited through the female line for a powerful community in Kerala – the Nairs.

Recently, in most development strategies, participation and empowerment of women have emerged as an important goal. It is true that meaning of the term empowerment is subject to different interpretations. First, it is translated as participation in labour force. But, there is an observation that mere participation in labour force is not a sufficient condition for empowerment if the structure remains unchanged as exploitative and oppressive. The widely accepted view looks at it as development of strategies that empower women by challenging existing social, economic and political structures. The primary objective of empowerment of women is to create more equitable and participatory structures in which women can gain control over their lives. The empowerment should enable them to increase their self-reliance, to assert their right to make choices, and to challenge and eliminate their own subordinates. They were given a chance to express their views on the immediate problems they face and suggest solutions from their own traditional wisdom and acquired knowledge.

Through empowerment, the women can participate in work force and gain employment; and by engaging in the challenging jobs, start micro-enterprises, joining in SHGs, NHGs and micro-finance activities for income generation and asset creation. Not only that, they are now powerful in obtaining their rights legally through empowerment.

The theoretical framework analysis is explained in Chapter 4 and the analysis on the main variables like income, entitlement and empowerment of women for better women development are discussed in Chapter 5.

References

1. Naomi Neft and Ann.D. Levine: Where women stand—An international report on the status of women in 140 countries - 1997-98, Random House, New York, 1998, pp. 1-2.
2. *Ibid.,* p. 8.
3. *Ibid.,* pp. 9-10.
4. *Ibid.,* p. 12.
5. Naomi Neft and Ann.D. Levine: Women's Right, Random House, New York, 1998, p. 13.
6. Naomi Neft and Ann.D. Levine: Women's Right, Random House, New York, 1998, pp. 13-14.
7. YWCA of India : The Educated Women in Indian Society Today, Tata Mac Graw Hill Publishing Company, Bombay-1971, p. 240.
8. *Ibid.,* p. 249.
9. *Ibid.,* p. 248.
10. Ralph E. Smith: Projecting the Size of the Female Labour Force: What makes a difference in Book of Llyod, Andrew and Gilroy, Women in the Labour Market Columbia University Press, New York.
11. *Ibid.,* p. 65.
12. *Ibid.,* p. 59.
13. Sharan R.R.: Status of Women: A Historical Perspective, Uppal Publishing House, New Delhi, 1992.
14. Kane P.V.: History of Dharmashastra, Vol. II, Part I, Hindu Social Organisation, Bombay, 1961.
15. Srinivas M.N.: Social Change in India, Orient Publications, Bombay, 1972.
16. Altekar A.S.: The Position of Women in Hindu Civilisation, The Cultural Publication House, Calcutta, 1938.
17. Tripathi S.N.: Unorganised Women Labour in India, Discovery Publishing House, New Delhi, 1994.
18. Sharma R.R.: Status of Indian Women—A Historical Perspective, Uppal Publishing House, New Delhi, 1992.
19. Article 14th, 15th and 16th of the Constitution of India.
20. Fried: Women and Men, Academic Press, New York, 1983, p. 20.
21. Joyce M. Nielson: Sex in Society: Perspective on Stratification (Belmont C.A., Wordsworth), 1978.
22. Michelle Z. Rosaldo: Women, Culture and Society: A Theoretical Overview, Schocken Books. New York, 1982.

23. Tawney R.H.: Religion and the Rise of Capitalisation, Preface, (Quoted by Neogi H.C. Origin of Feudalism in Ancient India – Land System and Feudalism in Ancient India, ed, D.C. Sircar p. 96.
24. Quoted in A.R. Desai: Rural Sociology in India, p. 33.
25. Karve. I.: Kinship Organisation in India, p. 10.
26. Karve: Kinship Organisation in India, p. 48.
27. Srimad Devi Bhagavatham: Part III, BVII, Chapter XXV, p. 679.
28. Likhita Smriti: p. 153, cited by Vinayaka Ganesha Apte.
29. Dhanapala, Tilakamanjari: pp. 17-18, Upaniti, p. 698.
30. Iravati Karve: Kinship Organisation in India, p. 72.
31. Ashraf K.M. : Life and Conditions of People of Hindustan, p. 135.
32. The Arthasashtra, 2, 23.
33. Baudhayana – II 2, 3. p. 135 ed. by A. Chinnaswami Shastri.
34. Agni Purana, 253, pp. 63-64.
35. Jaimini. Vol. 1–14 p. 983.
36. Vashishta. S., Chapter 17, M.N. Dutt – The Dharmashastra, p. 804.
37. Manu Smriti, Chapter – IX, p. 185.
38. Daya Baga, Chapter XI, Section I, 15 and 47 c.f. D.N. Mitter: Position of Women.
39. Yogendra Singh: 1988, Modernising Indian Tradition, Rawat Publications, Jaipur, p. 101.
40. Yogendra Singh: 1988, Modernising Indian Tradition, Rawat Publications, Jaipur, p. 102.
41. Mishra B.B.: 1960, Supra, pp. 302-305.
42. Yogendra Singh: 1988, Modernising Indian Tradition, Rawat Publications, Jaipur, p. 105.
43. Yogendra Singh: 1988, Modernising Indian Tradition, Rawat Publications, Jaipur, p. 102.
44. Ralph E. Smith: Projecting the Size of the Female Labour Force: What makes a difference, Book of Lloyds, Andrew and Gilroy, Women in the Labour Market, Columbia University Press, New York.
45. *Ibid.*, p. 65.
46. *Ibid.*, p. 59.
47. Amartya Sen: Development as Freedom, Oxford University Press, 1999.
48. Meera Bai, M.: Women's Development in Kerala—Some Current Issues, Women and Economic Reforms Kerala Experience, Serial Publications, 2006, New Delhi. p. 1.

49. Safa, H.T.: Gender Equality and Women's Wage Labour: In Valentine M. (ed), A Theoretical and Empirical Analysis in Patriarchy and Development, 1986.

50. Jagajeevan, N. and Ramakanthan, N. (2000): *Gramasabhas—A democratic structure for development planning*. Paper presented in International Conference on Democratic Decentralisation. State Planning Board.

51. Bava Khan, Pareethu P.M., Oomman, John, Kumari, Leela (2001): *Report of Study of Women Component Plan in Kerala,* State Institute of Rural Development, Kottarakkara.

52. Ramanathan, Mala, Vijayan, Aleyamma, Varatharajan, D. and Sukanya, R. (2002): *A Study Report on Political Decentralisation and Primary Health Care System* Achutha Menon Centre for Health Science Studies.

53. Sukumar, Mini (2003): *Experience of Kerala in Local Governance,* Paper presented in the open forum on 24th October, 2003 at Chinese Academy of Social Sciences Hall, Beijing, organised by ARENA as part of ARENA Regional School in Local Governance.

54. Muraleedharan, Sarada (2005): *Decentralisation and Gender – the Kerala experience of the WCP,* Paper presented in a workshop on 'Gender Based Planning in Local Governance: Issues and Concerns, on 8th February, 2005 organised by Sakhi Women's Resource Centre, Trivandrum.

55. Ramanathan, Mala. Vijayan, Aleyamma. Varatharajan, D. and Sukanya, R. (2002): *A Study Report on Political Decentralisation and Primary Health Care System.* Achutha Menon Centre for Health Science Studies.

56. Muraleedharan, Sarada (2005): *Decentralisation and Gender–the Kerala experience of the WCP,* Paper presented in a workshop on 'Gender Based Planning In Local Governance: Issues and Concerns, on 8th February, 2005 organised by Sakhi Women's Resource Centre, Trivandrum.

56. Muraleedharan, Sarada (2005): *Decentralisation and Gender – the Kerala Experience of the WCP,* Paper presented in a workshop on 'Gender Based Planning in Local Governance: Issues and Concerns, on 8th February, 2005 organised by Sakhi Women's Resource Centre, Trivandrum.

57. Sukumar, Mini (2003): *Experience of Kerala in Local Governance,* Paper presented in the open forum on 24th October, 2003 at Chinese Academy of Social Sciences Hall, Beijing, organised by ARENA as part of ARENA Regional School in Local Governance.

58. Bava Khan, Pareethu P.M., Oomman, John, Kumari, Leela (2001): *Report of Study of Women Component.*

59. Issac, Thomas. Seema, T.N. and Guptha, Smitha (2003): *Women elected representatives in Kerala (1995-2000), From symbolism to empowerment.* Paper presented in a seminar on A Decade of women's empowerment through local government in India.

60. Radha, S. and Choudhary, Roy Bulu (2002): *Women in local bodies,* KRPLLD, Centre for Development Studies, Trivandrum.

61. Muraleedharan, K. (2000): *Women's Participation in Development - the Kerala experience.* Paper presented in International Conference on Democratic Decentralisation.
62. Sanitha, Baby (2003): *Women's empowerment in Ninth Plan–Case Study of Ezhupunna panchayath.* M.A. Dissertation, Mahatma Gandhi University.
63. UNRISD: Working towards a more gender equitable macro-economic agenda, 1997, Report of Unrisd/cpd workshop, 1996.
64. Lalitha Bai: Women's Empowerment, Kerala Institute of Local Administration, 2003.
65. Economic Review, 2009, State Planning Board, Thiruvananthapuram, p. 440.
66. Devi Lakshmy: Determinants of Labour Force Participation among Women in Kerala–Some Evidence from a Micro level study, The Asian Economic Review, 38, April, 1996.
67. Economic Review 2008, State Planning Board, Thiruvananthapuram, p. 432.
68. Economic Review 2009, State Planning Board, Thiruvananthapuram, p. 432.
69. Economic Review 2009, State Planning Board, Thiruvananthapuram, p. 444.
70. Economic Review 2009, State Planning Board, Thiruvananthapuram, p. 322.
71. Human Development Report of UNDP, 2005.
72. Dreze, Jean and Sen, A.K.: India: Economic Development and Social Opportunity, Delhi: Oxford University Press, 1995.
73. Eapen and Kadoth, Praveen: Demystifying the High Status of Women in Kerala: An Attempt to Understand the Contradiction in Social Development, Report submitted to New Delhi, Institute of Social Studies Trust, 2001.
74. Gender, Special Issue, Economic and Political Weekly, Vol. 31, No. 43, 1996.
75. The expression used by the State Government of Kerala to promote tourism in the State.
76. Government of India, Census of India, 2001, URL, www. Censusindia.net
77. Dreze, Jean and Sen, A.K.: India: Economic Development and Social Opportunity, Delhi: Oxford University Press, 1995.
78. Government of India: Women and Men in India 2002, New Delhi, CSO, 2002, p. 20.
79. Chakraborty, Lekh S.: Public Expenditure and Human Development: An Empirical Investigation, 2003 (Http://www.wider.unu.edu/conference-2002-/conference%202003-2 papers/papers pdf/Chakraborty%20120403.pdf).

4

Theoretical Framework for Analysis

The women empowerment today has become an increasingly important variable in the level of economic development of a country than ever before by virtue of its innate intrinsic value and acquired standing worldwide. Recognising its importance, governments in neo-developed countries have formulated policy measures targeting the empowerment of women. In India, the 73rd and 74th Constitutional Amendment made provision for Constitutionalising the elected grassroot level local governing bodies, i.e., Panchayats, Municipalities and Corporations as the third strata of the governance structure gave further impetus to this factor. They witnessed an emergence of new leadership of women leaders at the grassroot governance institutions with distinguishable intrinsic values, contributing to a silent revolution in the realm of women empowerment and governance practices.

In Kerala, the Kudumbashree Mission—an endeavour to mitigate absolute poverty among women by empowering them by means of micro credit and micro entrepreneurship with proper linkages with the local governments, has resulted in good amount of replicable best practices of citizens engagement in civic governance as also asset creation of poor in a massive participation of people especially the women.

The generation of income, employment, entitlement and empowerment of women in selected activities, like farm activities, hospitality activities, micro enterprise activities, management of solid waste, health and education activities in the Government, non-government and unorganised sectors in the urban and rural areas with different status of level of education, religion, age and job status is looked into in depth in the analysis.

Definition of Terms

The definitions of various terms used in the present study are:

Autonomy

The terms empowerment and autonomy in context of gender are complementary. Feminists, economists and thinkers have redefined the concept of autonomy and they state that though education and employment may enhance the material conditions of women, they need not necessarily lead to their autonomy. Thus the term *Autonomy* in its simplest sense refers to the access to and control on deciding upon knowledge, decision-making, interaction and socio-economic matters.

Organised Sector

The term 'Organised Sector' in the context of present study denotes all formally organised common work places consisting of both government and non-government organisations. As far as women are concerned, significant proportion of working women is engaged in organised sector.

Unorganised Sector

The term 'Unorganised Sector' in the context of present study denotes all informally thinly organised scattered work places. As far as women are concerned, significant proportion of working women is engaged in agricultural and construction activities.

Non-gazetted Officers

The term Non-gazetted officer refers to all staff and officers in the scale of pay of Rs. 6500 (pre-revised) working in the government sector and that of staff members in the same status in non-governmental organisations.

Workers

The term workers in this context of study refer to those labourers working in the unorganised sectors with permanent income at regular periodical intervals.

Selected Activities

The activities selected to study the income, employment, entitlement and empowerment include farm activities, hospitality activities, micro enterprises, solid waste management, health sector, and education sector.

Identification of Tentative Variables and their Constituent Sub Variables

There are no set methods and clear-cut prescription to establish women empowerment. After a close review of various theories, models, approaches, research studies on women empowerment and the characteristic features of gender equalities in Kerala, the fact conceived by the researcher is to identify the variables and their constituent items which influence and condition the women empowerment.

The women empowerment is a determinant of the autonomy (in knowledge, decision-making, interaction and socio-economic affairs) which is influenced and shaped through deliberate interventions (economic strategies, legislative measures, political changes and ideological shift) of the governmental and non-governmental agencies. It is quite impossible to identify whether the autonomy or the influence of deliberate interventions that is actually attributable to the women empowerment. It is determined both by the autonomy and deliberate interventions. Thus, the broad constituent items of women empowerment are autonomy and environment for deliberate intervention. The autonomy can be autonomy in knowledge, autonomy in decision-making, autonomy in interaction and autonomy in socio-economic affairs. The environment can be governmental or non-governmental. Economic strategies and legislative strategies are the sub-constituents of governmental intervention. Political changes and ideological shifts are the non-governmental interventions.

The various factors influencing and empowering the women may thus be classified into eight variables viz., (i) Accessibility and Control over Private Properties [V_2], (ii) Accessibility and Control over Public Properties [V_3], (iii) Control over Income and Employment [V_4], (iv) Control over Decision on Own Body [V_5], (v) Independence on Mobility [V_6], (vi) Accessibility and Control over Politics [V_7], (vii) Accessibility and Control over Knowledge, Information and Proficiency [V_8], and (viii) Legal Status and Accessibility to Legislature [V_9]. In order to have an analytical insight and statistical accuracy, each of these eight variables is further sub-divided into a number of sub-variables or 'items'.

Accessibility and Control Over Private Properties

The women empowerment is largely dependent on her accessibility and control over private properties. The various sub-variables (or items) of this main variable are: (i) Savings; (ii) Family Income; (iii) Food; (iv) Clothing; (v) Shelter; (vi) Accessibility to Housing loans; (vii) Accessibility to Vehicle loans; (viii) Accessibility to Consumption loans; (ix) Status and Property Laws; (x) Impact of Globalisation in Expenditure Pattern; and (xi) Role in Decision-making. There is empirical evidence that improvement in these sub-variables (items) has contributed to an increased accessibility and control over private properties which, in turn, leads to empowerment of women.

Accessibility and Control over Public Properties

The empirical evidences show that there is a direct positive relationship between women empowerment and her accessibility and control over public properties. The sub-variables identified under this variable are: (i) Labour issues in bringing water; (ii) Problems related to availability of water; (iii) Problems related to availability of Fuel; (iv) Problems related to availability of sanitation; (v) Problems related to kinds of health issues; (vi) Availability of security; (vii) Expenditure on security; (viii) Food security; (ix) Calorie expense; (x)Nutritional status; (xi) Non-acquisition of primary education nutritional status; (xii) Child welfare services; (xiii) Accessibility to housing; (xiv) Accessibility to banking; (xv) Facilities to basic needs; (xvi) Accessibility to loans; (xvii) Accessibility to electricity; and (xviii) Accessibility to technical education.

Control Over Income and Employment

It is evident that the empowerment of women is directly related to her employment and income earning capacity. The major sub-variables are: (i) Work done which carry wages; (ii) Work done which carry no wages; (iii) Self-reliance in the decision-making process; (iv) Time spent on different jobs and rest; (v) Utilisation of wages earned/spent; (vi) Utilisation of wages earned handed over; (vii) The degree of decision-making power in family expenditure; (viii) Share of woman's income in family expenditure; (ix) Expenditure on personal needs; (x) Accessibility to income generating jobs; (xi) Level of independence for selection of stream of study; (xii) Level of independence for selection of jobs; (xiii) Wage difference; (xiv) Relationship of woman's job with education; (xv) Relationship of woman's job with land holding; (xvi) Relationship of woman's job with men's job status; (xvii) Access and control over trade and commerce; (xviii) Intervention in new products' market; and (xix) Participation (role) of women in trade unions.

Control on the Decisions of Own Body

Women empowerment very largely depends upon the control over the decisions on her own body. The sub-variables are: (i) Freedom for taking decision on marriage; (ii) Control over the decisions on child birth; (iii) Freedom on decision on sexual intercourse with the partner; (iv) Physical and mental torture like rape; (v) Physical and mental torture like caste-religion based atrocities; (vi) Physical and mental torture like sexual harassment at work place; (vii) Physical and mental torture by spouse; (viii) Physical and mental torture by close relatives; and (ix) Societal attitude on women sexuality.

Autonomy on Mobility

Women empowerment is also dependent upon the access and control over the decisions on her own mobility. The sub-variables are: (i) Freedom for mobility as single; (ii) Freedom for mobility with women companion; (iii) Freedom for mobility with men companion; (iv) Freedom for mobility in day time; (v) Freedom for mobility at night; (vi) Lack of freedom for mobility due to caste and religion; (vii) Lack of freedom for mobility due to special conditions; (viii) Lack of freedom for mobility due to special personal issues; (ix) Lack of freedom for mobility due to local customs; (x) Lack of freedom for mobility due to women status; and (xi) Lack of freedom for mobility due to places of worship.

Autonomy Over Politics

Access on and control over politics is another factor determining women empowerment. The important sub-variables (or items) are: (i) Participation in the capacity as voter in general elections; (ii) Participation in the capacity as candidate in general elections; (iii) Freedom to cast vote as per own decision; (iv) Membership in political parties; (v) Membership in community organisations; and (vi) Approach by political parties towards women; (vii) Reservation of seats for women in election to parliament; (viii) Reservation of seats for women in election to legislative assembly; (ix) Reservation of seats for women in election to local government; (x) Method of participation of women; and (xi) Nominations of women to Corporations or Boards.

Professional Autonomy in Knowledge and Information

Professional autonomy in knowledge and information is a leading factor of women empowerment as is evident from the literature. The important sub-variables (or items) are: (i) Women's participation in

Gram sabha; (ii) Women's participation in community organisations; (iii) Ability to bring up own interests; (iv) Ability to bring up consensus building; (v) Ability of bargaining; (vi) Power of women's associations; and (vii) Women's participation in biggest organisation; (viii) Women's participation in biggest networks; (ix) Women's membership in women's associations; and (x) Women's membership in information centres like library.

Legal Status and Accessibility to Legislature

The women empowerment is determinant on their legal status and their accessibility to legislature procedures. The important sub-variables (or items) under this variables are: (i) The attitude of legislative forums towards women; (ii) Women's awareness on laws concerned with women's and their rights; (iii) Women's awareness on their rights; (iv) The decisions on the violation of women's rights; (v) The decisions on the violation of atrocities against women; (vi) Accessibility and experience with the police set-up; (vii) Accessibility and experience with the court of law; and (viii) Accessibility and experience with Women's Commission.

Variables on Interview Schedule

For collecting the opinion of respondents, structured interview schedules were formed. The interview schedule consists of the Variable V_1 – Personal Profile of respondents and Eight variables with sub-components (or items) of independent variables (V_2 to V_9).

Collection of Opinion through Interview Schedule

The opinions of the respondents of female non-gazetted officers of organised sectors and female workers of unorganised sectors in Thiruvananthapuram district, selected on the basis of Stratified Random Sampling Technique are collected by conducting interviews with them. The interview schedule covers eight variables and a number of sub-variables (items). Apart from the above variables, the interview schedule is inclusive of nine questions (items) grouped under the heading 'Personal Details' of the women respondents. For scaling the opinions in the interview schedules, the researcher developed a seven-point rating scale indicating the response mood of the functionaries (Fig. 4.1).

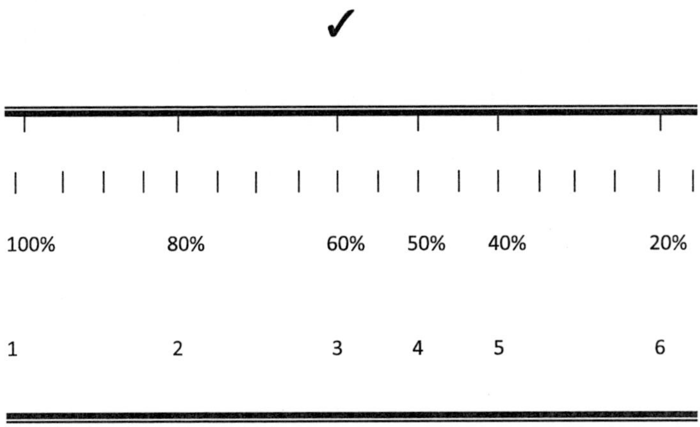

Fig. 4.1: Seven-point Rating Scale

A seven-point Rating Scale (Figure 4.1) was drawn in a card board and presented to each respondent. Each question is asked by the interviewer to the respondent. Care has been taken to give sufficient time to the respondent to think over and answer. They are requested to look at the Rating Scale Board and say to which 'percentage' each of their answers belong and state whether her opinion stands in 1 or 2 or 3 or 4 or 5 or 6 or 7. The interviewer ticked the answer accordingly and proceeded to the next item.

An example of the rating scale is explained below:

Question: What is the extent of your satisfaction on your control over household decisions?

The respondents are asked to state whether she 'is flexible' by 100 per cent or 80 per cent or 60 per cent or 50 per cent or 40 per cent or 20 per cent or 0 per cent by indicating 1 or 2 or 3 or 4 or 5 or 6 or 7. For instance, if it is 50 per cent it can be indicated by a tick mark (") as shown in Figure 4.1.

Each question within different variables of the interview schedule is framed after a close study of the previous research works, theories, models, interview schedules and pilot study.

Pilot Survey

A pilot survey was conducted on a cross-section of the respondents in Thiruvananthapuram district. Five non-gazetted women employees from each of two line departments, five workers from three unorganised sectors were randomly selected for the pilot survey. At the end of the survey, questions found irrelevant in the draft interview schedule were deleted and missing questions found vital were added. After conducting a thorough analysis on the topic, 'Employment, Income, Entitlement and Empowerment: A Case Study of Women in Selected Activities', the style of administering some questions was modified in order to avoid probable ambiguities pertaining to the meaning of the questions and to obtain more reliable, unbiased and accurate answers.

The Interview Schedule so reformed, is reframed and administered for the final collection of data. The full text of the Interview Schedule is given in *Appendix I.*

The Universe

The female non-gazetted employees of organised sectors and female workers of unorganised sectors in Thiruvananthapuram district form the population of the study. Thiruvanathapuram district is suggested because there is strong empirical evidence that the district has highest concentration of the working class people both in organised and unorganised sectors by virtue of being the state capital.

The Sample

From amongst the population, a sample of 400 respondents were selected for study, 200 of which were drawn from each of the organised and unorganised sectors. The sampling technique adopted for selection of sample is shown below:

Sampling Technique

The study considered a 'Purposive Sampling Technique' for selecting the women non-gazetted officersfrom organised sector (200) and women workers from unorganised sectors (200). Purposively, certain number of respondents were selected by classifying them into different groups. The groups includes age, educational qualification, occupational status, location, religion, occupational sectors and form of organisation. The selection process includes:

- 16 women from the age group of below 20, 144 from 20 – 35, 148 from 35-50 and 72 from the age group of above 50 years.
- 16 respondents from below primary education, 60 respondents having education between primary and SSLC, 136 from having

education between SSLC and Degree, and 188 of those having education of above degree.

- 32 respondents from Gazetted officers and 368 from Non-gazetted rank.
- 264 from those belongs to urban and 136 from rural belongings.
- 180 respondents belongs to Hindu, 88 from Muslims, 100 from Christians, and 32 from other religions.
- 80 respondents from those who are engaged in farm activities, 84 from hospitality, 68 from micro enterprises, 48 from solid waste management, 40 from health sector and 80 from education sectors.
- 72 from government organisations, 128 from non-government organisations, and 200 from unorgnised sectors.

Procedure of Analysis

Various items have been selected on the basis of average score of each item of the eight variables for developing the 'Women Empowerment Achievement Rating Schedule (WEARS)'. If the positive response on the item has higher average score values for organised sector than to unorganised sectors, such items are selected. This is because, it is assumed that the empowerment will formally be more in the case of non-gazetted women officers in organised sector and less in the case of women workers in the unorganised sector.

Before proceeding to analysis, exploration for checking data quality with Robust Estimation Test has been conducted to validate the collected data using histogram with normality test available in the computer software package – Statistical Package for Social Sciences (SPSS). Trimming of extreme values for a pragmatic trimmed mean has been done in some of the unavoidable cases without detrimental to the ethics of statistics.

In the first stage, scores and their percentage on total scores of the various selected variables of women empowerment are calculated. The women empowerment achievement scores and their percentage on total scores are also calculated. The calculated scores and their percentage on total scores of non-gazetted officers of organised sector and workers of unorganised sectors are evaluated. For the sake of authenticity and conceptual clarity, statistical tools such as arithmetic mean, standard deviation and coefficient of variation are also computed for each of the sub-variables (items) using SPSS computer software package.

In the second stage of analysis, using 'Multiple Regression Analysis' developed different predictive equations with different sets of selected independent variables. The selected independent variables are: (i) Accessibility and control over private properties [V_2], (ii) Accessibility and control over public properties [V_3], (iii) Control over income and employment [V_4], (iv) Control over decision on own body [V_5], (v) Independence on mobility [V_6], (vi) Accessibility and control over Politics [V_7], (vii) Accessibility and control over knowledge, information and proficiency [V_8], and (viii) Legal status and accessibility to legislature [V_9]. An attempt is made to frame a model of women empowerment in Kerala with the help of the predictor regression equations.

There are eight sets of predictor equations of different combinations of independent variables consisting of a total of 255 predictor equations as shown below:

Table 4.1: Details of Predictor Equations

Sl. No.	*Combination Group of Independent Variables*	nC_x	*Number of equations*
1.	One-Variable Predictor Equations	$8C_1$	8
2.	Two-Variable Predictor Equations	$8C_2$	28
3.	Three-Variable Predictor Equations	$8C_3$	56
4.	Four-Variable Predictor Equations	$8C_4$	70
5.	Five-Variable Predictor Equations	$8C_5$	56
6.	Six-Variable Predictor Equations	$8C_6$	28
7.	Seven-Variable Predictor Equations	$8C_7$	8
8.	Eight-Variable Predictor Equations	$8C_8$	1
	Total Predictor Equations		**255**

In each set of variable combinations, the best fit predictor equation is selected based on the highest value of multiple correlations (R) and multiple correlations square (R^2). The general model of predictor equation on women empowerment is shown below:

$$\hat{V}_{12} = \beta_0 + \qquad + \beta_2 \qquad + \dots\dots + \beta_n\, x_n + \varepsilon$$

Where, = $\hat{V}_{12}$ Women Empowerment (dependent variable); β_0 = Constant;

$\beta_1, \beta_2, \beta_2 \ldots\ldots \beta_n$ are the Beta Co-efficient of the respective independent variables; and

ε = Estimation Error

In the third stage of analysis, the nine experimental variables (one dependent and eight independent variables) were put to Factor Analysis. The factors are extracted using Principal Component Method rotated with Kaiser Varimax Rotation Method. The factor structures of non-gazetted officers of organised sectors and workers of unorganised sectors are compared with the factor structure of total sample. Statistical calculations are made through a computer software package (SPSS).

In the fourth stage of analysis is the computation of Women Empowerment Index on selected activities by taking into account the activities, sectors (organised and unorganised), rural and urban, religion, education and age.

In the fifth stage of analysis, framed hypothesis were tested through conducting Levene's Test for Equality of Variances and *t*–test for Equality of Means, Analysis of variance (ANOVA) – one way using SPSS. The test results are interpreted meaningfully and decisions are taken whether the null hypotheses are to be accepted or rejected.

The five stages of conducted analysis with decisions concerned are explained in Chapter 5 and 6.

5

Women Empowerment–Analysis of Variables and Model

This Chapter contains analysis on the various factors such as socio-economic background of women in selected activities, empowerment index on income, employment, entitlement of women in selected activities, various constituents leading to empowerment of women in the selected activities and the predictor equation for women empowerment. The presentation of analysis is made under four main heads as follows:

(a) Socio-economic factors and its influence on women empowerment in selected activities.

(b) Indexing of various socio-economic groups based on women empowerment relating to income, employment and entitlement in selected activities of women in Thiruvananthapuram district of Kerala.

(c) Variablewise analysis of nine (9) major variables selected to study the income, employment, entitlement and empowerment of women.

(d) Predictor equation model of the women empowerment.

(a) Socio-economic Factors and its Influence on Women Empowerment

Socio-economic variables have an impact on the study on the empowerment of women in Kerala. For this, the profile of the respondents selected at random is analysed by taking into account the seven (7) selected variables. These selected variables include:

1. Age; 2. Educational qualifications; 3. Nature of sector (Organised and Unorganised); 4. Job Status (Gazetted and Non-gazetted); 5. Location (Rural and Urban); 6. Religion; 7. Nature of activity (Farm activity, hospitality, Micro Enterprises, Solid Waste Management, Health and Education); and 8. Marital Status.

1. Age

The attitudinal change and the behavior is based on the age to which they belongs. So, for determining the status and development, it is important. The agewise classification of respondents are depicted in Table 5.1

Table 5.1: Age Wise Distribution of Respondents

Age Group	*Respondents*	*Percentage to Total*
Below 20	36	9
20-35	144	36
35-50	148	37
Above 50	72	18
Total	**400**	**100**

Source: SPSS output of Primary Data.

Age group of the respondents in the sample revealed (Table 5.1) that majority of the respondents are in the age group of 35 to 50 years (37 per cent). 144 respondents (36 per cent) of the respondents are in the age group of 20-35 years. Only 36 respondents (9 per cent) are in the age group of less than 20 years, and 72 respondents (18 per cent) are in the age group of above 50 years. It is concluded that a large majority of the respondents in the sample are in the age group of 20 to 50 years.

2. Educational Qualification

The qualification of respondents is another major variable used for knowing the status and development of women. It means that on account of higher education they are lenient and behave better and develop their status due to high knowledge and maturity. This, in turn, creates better development and status of women in Kerala.The qualificationwise category of respondents are furnished in Table 5.2.

Table 5.2

Educational Qualification	*Number of Respondents*	*Percentage to Total*
Below Primary	16	4
Primary – SSLC	60	15
SSLC-Degree	136	34
Above Degree	188	47
Total	**400**	**100**

Source: SPSS output of Primary Data

As is noticed from the Table 5.2 that 188 respondents (47 per cent) of the sample are educated above the graduation level, while 136 respondents (34 per cent) of them have an education level of above SSLC but below Degree. Only a few respondents from the sample, i.e., 16 respondents (4 per cent) having education at below primary and 60 respondents (15 per cent) have an education level of above primary but below SSLC. It is clear from the analysis on the qualification of the respondents that most of them have an education level of above degree.

3. Nature of Sector

The basic premise of the study rests in the sector in which they are working namely, Organised and Unorganised. For organised sector, there are organisations which are under the control of the government and non-governmental organisations. *In toto*, there are three groups namely, government organisations, non-governmental organisations and unorgnised sectors. The respondents falling under each category is shown in Table 5.3.

Table 5.3: Classification of Respondents on the Basis of Sector

Sector	*Number of Respondents*	*Percentage to Total*
Government Organisation	72	18
Non-Governmental Organisation	128	32
Unorganised	200	50
Total	**400**	**100**

Source: SPSS output of Primary Data.

As is noticed from Table 5.3 that a large majority of the respondents fall under unorganised sector, i.e., 200 respondents (50 per cent), 128 respondents (32 per cent) are working under non-governmental organisations and 72 respondents (18 per cent) are working in government organisations.

4. Job Status

Another important variable which determine the status of women in Kerala is their job status. The status of job may be either Gazetted or Non-gazetted. The classification of respondents on the basis of job status is noticed in Table 5.4

Table 5.4: Classification of Respondents on the Basis of Job Status

Status	*Number of Respondents*	*Percentage to Total*
Gazetted	32	8
Non-gazetted	368	·92
Total	**400**	**100**

Source: SPSS output of Primary Data.

It is seen from the Table 5.4 that 368 respondents (92 per cent) are working in the non-gazetted cadre nd only 32 respondents (8 per cent) are working in the gazetted post.

5. Location

The women empowerment to a greater extent is location-specific, hence is an important variable. The locationwise classification of respondents are given in Table 5.5.

Table 5.5: Classification of Respondents on the Basis of Location

Location	*Number of Respondents*	*Percentage to Total*
Urban	264	66
Rural	136	34
Total	**400**	**100**

Source: SPSS output of Primary Data.

It is seen from the Table 5.5 that 264 respondents (66 per cent) are residing in urban areas and only 136 respondents (34 per cent) are residing in the rural areas which leads to the conclusion that a large majority of the respondents in the sample are residing in urban areas

6. Religion

Another important variable which changes the attitude and behaviour of women is religion. Each and every religion has its own effect on building the culture of every person. The civilisation and culture of people will have an effect on creating or reducing the status and development. The religionwise classification of respondents are shown in Table 5.6.

Table 5.6: Religionwise Classification of Respondents

Religion	*Number of Respondents*	*Percentage to Total*
Hindu	180	45
Muslim	88	22
Christian	100	25
Others	32	8
Total	**400**	**100**

Source: SPSS output of Primary Data.

It is clear from Table 5.6 that 180 respondents (45 per cent) and 100 respondents (25 per cent) belong to Hindus and Christians respectively. 88 respondents (22 per cent) are from Muslim religion and only 32 respondents (8 per cent) belongs to other communities. It means that there is adequate representation of respondents from Hindu and Christian religion compared to Muslim religion.

7. Nature of Activity

Another important variable which determines women empowerment is the nature of activity carried out by them. The important activities performed by the women in Kerala are farm activities like lease land farming, organic cultivation and agricultural labourers in unorganised sector; hospitality industry or activities like conducting canteen, catering services and so on; micro enterprises; solid waste management; health sector; and education sector. The classification of respondents on the basis of nature of activity is shown in Table 5.7.

Table 5.7: Classification on the Basis of Nature of Activity

Nature of Activity	*Number of Respondents*	*Percentage to Total*
Farm Activities	80	20
Hospitality	84	21
Micro Enterprises	68	17
Solid Waste Management	48	12
Health Sector	40	10
Education Sector	80	20
Total	**400**	**100**

Source: SPSS out put of Primary Data.

As is noticed from Table 5.7 that 84 respondents (21 per cent) are engaged in health sector followed by 80 respondents (20 per cent) in farm activities and education sector each. There are 68 respondents (17 per cent) engaged in micro enterprises and 48 respondents (12 per cent) in solid waste management. Only 40 respondents (10 per cent) are engaged in the health sector. It is clear that a large majority of them are engaged in Hospitality, Farm and Education Sector.

8. Marital Status

Another variable taken for analysing the personal profile of women respondents is marital status. This also has an impact on the status, development and empowerment of women in Kerala in respect of income, employment, entitlement and empowerment in selected activities. The marital status of respondents in the sample are collected and presented in Table 5.8.

Table 5.8: Classification of Respondents on the Basis of Marital Status

Marital Status	*Number of Managers*	*Percentage to Total*
Unmarried	182	46
Married	218	54
Total	400	100

Source: SPSS output of Primary Data.

It is seen from Table 5.8 that 218 respondents (54 per cent) of the sample are married and only 182 respondents (46 per cent) in the sample are unmarried. In short, it is clear from the analysis that majority of the sample respondents are married and only a few are bachelors.

Now, the present study proceeds with analysing all the 400 respondents selected who were classified into 56 heterogeneous groups in conformity with their empowerment level as to Income, Employment and Entitlement based on their activity, education, organisation, status, location, and religion and have been properly ranked based on the empowerment index.

(b) Women Empowerment Index Based on Income, Employment and Entitlement in Selected Activities

The empowerment of women and their status will vary depending upon the location, activity, attainment of level of education, nature of organisation, nature of occupation, religion and age. The ranking details are shown in Table 5.9.

Table 5.9: Sectorwise, Activitywise Empowerment Index Ranking of Women Groups

Sl. No.	*Sector*	*Activity*	*Index*	*CF*	*Percentage to Total*
1.	Urban	GO/HEALTH/GO/E4	10	10	2.5
2.	Rural	GO/HEALTH/GO/E4	2	12	0.50
3.	Urban	GO/EDUCATION/GO/E4	8	20	2.00
4.	Rural	GO/EDUCATION/GO/E4,E3(1)	10	30	2.5
5.	Urban	GO/HOSPITAL/GO/E4	3	33	0.75
6.	Urban	GO/HEALTH/NG/E4	5	38	1.25
7.	Urban	GO/EDUCATION/NG/E4,E3(10)	17	55	4.25
8.	Rural	GO/HEALTH/NG/E3	5	60	1.25
9.	Rural	GO/EDUCATION/NG/E3	3	63	0.50
10.	Urban	GO/HOSPITAL/NG/E3	7	70	1.75
11.	Rural	GO/HOSPITAL/NG/E3	1	71	0.25
12.	Urban	NGO/HEALTH/NG/E4	4	75	1.00
13.	Urban	NGO/EDUCATION/E4	28	103	7.00
14.	Rural	NGO/HEALTH/E4	5	108	1.25
15.	Rural	NGO/EDUCATION/E4	6	114	1.50
16.	Urban	NGO/EDUCATION/E3	3	117	0.75
17.	Urban	NGO/HOSPITAL/E4	20	137	5.00
18.	Urban	NGO/HEALTH/E3	1	138	0.25

Sl. No.	*Sector*	*Activity*	*Index*	*CF*	*Percentage to Total*
19.	Urban	NGO/HOSPITAL/E3	5	143	1.25
20.	Urban	NGO/HOSPITAL/E2	2	145	0.50
21.	Rural	NGO/EDUCATION/E3	2	147	0.50
22.	Urban	NGO/EDUCATION/E2	1	148	0.25
23.	Urban	NGO/MICRO ENTERPRISE/E4	3	151	0.75
24.	Urban	NGO/MICRO ENTERPRISE/E3	9	160	2.25
25.	Urban	NGO/MICRO ENTERPRISE/E2	3	163	0.50
26.	Rural	NGO/MICRO ENTERPRISE/E4	5	168	1.25
27.	Rural	NGO/MICRO ENTERPRISE/E3	7	175	1.75
28.	Urban	NGO/FARMING /E1	1	176	0.25
29.	Urban	UNO/HEALTH/E4	3	179	0.75
30.	Urban	UNO/HEALTH/E3	7	186	1.75
31.	Urban	UNO/HOSPITAL/E4	20	206	5.00
32.	Urban	UNO/HOSPITAL/E3	15	221	3.75
33.	Urban	UNO/MICRO/E4	20	241	5.00
34.	Urban	UNO/MICRO/E3	10	251	2.50
35.	Rural	UNO/MICRO/E4	3	254	0.75
36.	Rural	UNO/MICRO/E3	3	257	0.75
37.	Rural	UNO/HOSPITAL/E4	2	259	0.50
38.	Urban	UNO/HOSPITAL/E2	5	264	1.25
39.	Rural	UNO/HOSPITAL/E3	3	267	0.75
40.	Rural	UNO/ MICRO /E2	3	270	0.75
41.	Rural	UNO/ MICRO /E1	1	271	0.25
42.	Rural	UNO/HOSPITAL/E2	1	272	0.25
43.	Urban	UNO/SOLID WASTE/E4	10	282	2.50
44.	Urban	UNO/SOLID WASTE/E3	15	297	3.75
45.	Urban	UNO/SOLID WASTE/E2	20	317	5.00
46.	Urban	UNO/SOLID WASTE/E1	4	321	1.00
47.	Urban	UNO/FARM/E2	3	324	0.75
48.	Urban	UNO/FARM/E1	2	326	0.50
49.	Rural	NGO/FARM/E4	4	330	1.00
50.	Rural	NGO/FARM/E3	10	340	2.50
51.	Rural	NGO/FARM/E2	8	348	2.00

Sl. No.	*Sector*	*Activity*	*Index*	*CF*	*Percentage to Total*
52.	Rural	NGO/FARM/E1	2	350	0.50
53.	Rural	UNO/FARM/E4	10	360	2.50
54.	Rural	UNO/FARM/E3	18	378	4.50
55.	Rural	UNO/FARM/E2	15	393	3.75
56.	Rural	NGO/FARM/E1	7	400	1.75
		Total	**400**		**100**

Source: SPSS output of Primary Data.

It is noticed from Table 5.9 that the highest women empowerment rank goes to the first 10 respondents (2.5 per cent) who are residing in urban areas and are serving in Health Department of the Government Organistions as Gazetted Officers (GO) with education level of above Degree (E4). Whereas the highest women empowerment rank goes to 2 respondents (0.5 per cent) who are residing in rural area and serving in Health Department (of the Government Organisations (GO) as Gazetted Officers (GO) with education level of above Degree.

The highest women empowerment rank goes to the 8 respondents (2 per cent) who are residing in urban area and serving in Education Department of the Government Organisations as Gazetted Officers with education level of above Degree. But the highest women empowerment rank goes to 10 respondents (2.5 per cent) who are residing in rural area and serving in Education Department of the Government Organisations as Gazetted Officers with education level of above Degree and 1 respondent with an education level between SSLC and Degree (E3).

The highest women empowerment rank goes to 3 respondents (0.75 per cent) who are residing in urban area and serving in Hospitality activities of the Government Organisations as Gazetted Officers with education level of above Degree.

The highest women empowerment rank goes to the first 5 respondents (1.25 per cent) who are residing in urban area and serving in Health Department of the government organisations as Non- Gazetted Officers (NGO) with education level of above Degree and 10 with an education level between SSLC and Graduation.

The highest women empowerment rank goes to the first 17 respondents (4.25 per cent) who are residing in urban area and serving in Education Department of the Government Organisations as Non-Gazetted Officers with education level of above Degree and 10 respondents (2.5 per cent) with an education level between SSLC and Degree. But the highest women empowerment rank goes to 5 respondents (1.25 per cent) who are residing in rural area and serving in Health Department of the Government Organisations as Non-gazetted Officers with education level between SSLC and Degree.

The highest women empowerment rank goes to the first 3 respondents (0.75 per cent) who are residing in rural area and serving in Educational activity of the government organisations as Non-gazetted Officers with education level between SSLC and Graduation.

The highest women empowerment rank goes to the first 7 respondents (1.75 per cent) who are residing in urban area and serving in Hospitality activity of the Government Organisations as Non-gazetted Officers with education level between SSLC and Degree. Whereas the highest women empowerment rank goes to only 4 respondents who are residing in rural area and serving in Hospitality activities of the Government Organisations as Non-gazetted Officers with education level between SSLC and Degree.

The highest women empowerment rank goes to 4 respondents (1 per cent) who are residing in urban area and serving in Health Department of the Non-government Organisations with education level of above Degree.

The highest women empowerment rank goes to 28 respondents (7 per cent) who are residing in urban area and serving in Education Department of the Non-government Organisations with education level of above Degree.

The highest women empowerment rank goes to 5 respondents (1.25 per cent) who are residing in rural area and serving in Health Department of the Non-government Organisations with education level of above Degree.

The highest women empowerment rank goes to 6 respondents (1.5 per cent) who are residing in rural area and serving in Education Department of the Non-government Organisations with education level of above Degree. But the highest women empowerment rank goes to 3 respondents (0.75 per cent) who are residing in urban area and serving in Education Department of the Non-government Organisations with education level between SSLC and Degree.

The highest women empowerment rank goes to 20 respondents (5 per cent) who are residing in urban area and serving in Hospitality activity of the Non-government Organisations with education level of above Degree. The highest women empowerment rank goes only to 1 respondent (0.25 per cent) who are residing in urban area and serving Health activities of the Non-government Organisations with education level between SSLC and Degree.

The highest women empowerment rank goes to 5 respondents (1.25 per cent) who are residing in urban area and serving Hospitality activities of the Non-government Organisations with education level between SSLC and Degree. The highest women empowerment rank goes only to 2 respondents (0.5 per cent) who are residing in urban area and serving Hospitality activities of the Non-government Organisations with education level between primary and SSLC.

The highest women empowerment rank goes to 2 respondents (0.5 per cent) who are residing in rural area and serving Educational activities of the Non-government Organisations with education level between SSLC and Degree. But highest women empowerment rank goes only to 1 respondent (0.25 per cent) who are residing in urban area and operating education of the Non-government Organisations with education level between primary and SSLC.

The highest women empowerment rank goes to 3 respondents (0.75 per cent) who are residing in urban area and operating micro enterprises of the non-government organisations with education level of above Degree. The highest women empowerment rank goes to 9 respondents (2.25 per cent) who are residing in urban area and operating micro enterprises of the non-government organisations with education level between SSLC and Degree. The highest women empowerment rank goes to the first 3 respondents (0.75 per cent) who are residing in urban area and operating micro enterprises of the non-government organisations with education level between primary and SSLC.

The highest women empowerment rank goes to the first 5 respondents (1.25 per cent) who are residing in rural area and operating micro enterprises of the Non-government Organisations with education level of above Degree. But highest women empowerment rank goes to 7 respondents (1.75 per cent) who are residing in rural area and operating micro enterprises of the Non-government Organisations with education level between SSLC and Degree.

The highest women empowerment rank goes to 1 respondent (0.25 per cent) who are residing in urban and operating Farm activities of the Non-government Oganisations with education level below primary.

The highest women empowerment rank goes to 3 respondents (0.75 per cent) who are residing in urban area and working in the Health Department of the unorganised sector with education level of above Degree. The highest women empowerment rank goes to 7 respondent (1.75 per cent) who are residing in urban area and operating Health Department of the unorganised sector with education level between SSLC and Degree.

The highest women empowerment rank goes to 20 respondents (5 per cent) who are residing in urban area and operating Hospitality activities of the unorganised sector with education level of above Degree. But the highest women empowerment rank goes to 15 respondents (3.75 per cent) who are residing in urban area and operating Hospitality activities of the unorganised sector with education level between SSLC and Degree.

The highest women empowerment rank goes to the first 20 respondents (5 per cent) who are residing in urban area and operating micro enterprise activities of the unorganised sector with education level of above Degree. The highest women empowerment rank goes to the first 10 respondents (2.5 per cent) who are residing in urban area and operating micro enterprise activities of the unorganised sector with education level SSLC and Degree.

The highest women empowerment rank goes to 3 respondents (0.75 per cent) who are residing in rural area and operating micro enterprise activities of the unorganised sector with education level of above Degree. The highest women empowerment rank goes to 3 respondents (0.75 per cent) who are residing in rural area and operating micro enterprise activities of the unorganised sector with education level SSLC and Degree. The highest women empowerment rank goes to the first 3 respondents (0.75 per cent) who are residing in rural area and operating Hospitality activities of the unorganised sector with education level between SSLC and Degree.

The highest women empowerment rank goes to 2 respondents (0.5 per cent) who are residing in rural area and operating Hospitality activities of the unorganised sector with education level of above Degree.

The highest women empowerment rank goes to 5 respondents (1.25 per cent) who are residing in urban area and operating Hospitality activities of the unorganised sector with education level between Primary and SSLC. Whereas the highest women empowerment rank goes to 3 respondents (0.75 per cent) who are residing in rural area and operating Hospitality activities of the unorganised sector (UOS) with education level between SSLC and Degree.

The highest women empowerment rank goes to the first 3 respondents (0.75 per cent) who are residing in rural area and operating micro enterprises in the unorganised sector with an education level between Primary and SSLC. But the highest women empowerment rank goes only to 1 respondent (0.25 per cent) who are residing in rural area and operating micro enterprises in the unorganised sector with an education level below Primary.

The highest women empowerment rank goes to 1 respondent (0.25 per cent) who is residing in rural area and operating Hospitality activities in the unorganised sector with an education level between Primary and SSLC.

The highest women empowerment rank goes to 10 respondents (2.5 per cent) who are residing in urban area and engaged in Solid Waste Management in the unorganised sector with education level of Degree and above. But the highest women empowerment rank goes to 15 respondents (3.75 per cent) who are residing in urban area and engaged in Solid Waste Management in the unorganised sector with education level between SSLC and Degree. Whereas the highest women empowerment rank goes to 20 respondents (5 per cent) who are residing in urban area and engaged in Solid Waste Management in the unorganised sector with education level between Primary and SSLC. The highest women empowerment rank goes to 4 respondents (1 per cent) who are residing in urban area and engaged in Solid Waste Management in the unorganised sector with education level below Primary.

The highest women empowerment rank goes to 3 respondents (0.75 per cent) who are residing in urban area and engaged in Farm activities in the unorganised sector with education level between Primary and SSLC. Whereas the highest women empowerment rank goes to the first 2 respondents (0.5 per cent) who are residing in urban area and engaged in Farm activities in the unorganised sector with education level below Primary.

The highest women empowerment rank goes to 4 respondents (1 per cent) who are residing in rural area and engaged in Farm activities in the Non-governmental Organisations with an education level of above Degree. But the highest women empowerment rank goes to the first 10 respondents (2.5 per cent) who are residing in rural area and engaged in Farm activities in the Non-governmental Organisations with an education level of between SSLC and Degree.

The highest women empowerment rank goes to 8 respondents (2 per cent) who are residing in rural area and engaged in Farm activities in the Non-governmental Organisations with an education level of between primary and SSLC. But the highest women empowerment rank goes only 2 respondents (0.5 per cent) who are residing in rural area and engaged in Farm activities in the Non-governmental Organisations with an education level of below primary.

The highest women empowerment rank goes to 10 respondents (2.5 per cent) who are residing in rural area and engaged in Farm activities in the unorganised sector with education level of above Degree. Whereas the highest women empowerment rank goes to the first 18 respondents (4.5 per cent) who are residing in rural area and engaged in Farm activities in the unorganised sector with education level between SSLC and Degree. The highest women empowerment rank goes to 15 respondents (3.75 per cent) who are residing in rural area and engaged in Farm activities in the unorganised sector with education level between Primary and SSLC. But the highest women empowerment rank goes to the first 7 respondents (1.75 per cent) who are residing in rural area and engaged in Farm activities in the unorganised sector with education level below primary.

To conclude, the women empowerment is high in those cases where women got higher education and also living in urban areas compared to rural areas. The empowerment of women among Gazetted Officers of the Government organisation with higher educational status is higher than those with lower education. In respect of activities selected like farm activities, hospitality activities, micro enterprises activities, solid waste management, health sector activities and activities in the education sector, the women empowerment is high only in those cases where they are placed in higher educational status.

The present study proceed further to look into the main and sub-variables for predicting a model for women empowerment.

(c) Variablewise Analysis of Income, Entitlement and Empowerment of Women in Kerala

The selected eight main variables and their sub-variables which determine women empowerment are :

1. Accessibility and Control over Private Properties (V_2).
2. Accessibility and Control over Public Properties (V_3).
3. Accessibility and Control over Income and Employment (V_4).
4. Control over Decision on Own Body (V_5).
5. Independence on Mobility (V_6).
6. Accessibility and Control over Politics (V_7).
7. Accessibility and Control over Knowledge, Information and Proficiency (V_8).
8. Legal Status and Accessibility to Legislature (V_9).

The itemwise analysis of each of the sub-variables of the main variable is made based on the average score expressed by the respondents in the sample and deviations are notified based on the Standard Deviation and Coefficient of Variation.

Main Variable I - Accessibility and Control Over Private Properties (V_2)

The Kerala Model of development owes its attributed success to the achievements in the areas of health and education where the contribution of women is particularly significant. The matriarchal system that prevailed among some of the dominant communities in the past, the progressive social movements, government policies, and a historically conducive climate are a few factors identified as contributors to the success of women in Kerala. The traditional matriarchal system gave women the freedom to access several services including education. The empowerment started when they got the right to access property of both private and public. For studying this variable, eleven sub-variables (11) are identified and analysed. They are:

1. Savings

Saving is the difference between income and expenditure or there is abstention from present consumption for a future use. Savings is an important variable which lead to surplus amount as income which can be utilised for their own purposes.

The item number 2.1 of the Table 5.10.1 is about savings which creates empowerment. Out of the 400 respondents interviewed, 76 respondents (19 per cent) have recorded their opinion at zero per cent and none of them recorded a level at 100 per cent. Savings leads to empowerment and as part of the accessibility and control over private property by recording a level at 20 to 40 per cent level by 220 (55 per cent), 84 respondents (21 per cent) recorded their level at 50 per cent and 20 respondents (6 per cent) recorded a level at a higher per cent of 60 to 80 per cent. The mean score of the opinion is 31 per cent with a standard deviation of 19 and a covariance of 61 per cent. The combined mean (52 per cent) which contribute to the main variable is only less and it indicates that its effect to the it is only 31 per cent.

2. Family Income

Another sub variable identified for accessibility to control over private properties is family income. One of the important factor which contribute to the earning of private property is the income from the family. In certain families, the only income available is the income from the head of the family. In some other cases, other family members including the spouse earn income and this leads to generation of income in the family which in turn contribute to acquiring of private property.

Item number 2.2 of the Table 5.10.1 gives the opinion on the Family income. 11 respondents (3 per cent) recorded their level of opinion at 20 per cent and less. 82 respondents (21 per cent) recorded their opinion at a level between 40 and 50 per cent. 290 respondents (73 per cent) recorded a level at 60 per cent. Only a minor number of respondents, 17 out of 400 (4 per cent), recorded their opinion at 80 per cent to 100 per cent level. The mean level of opinion recorded is 57 per cent with a standard deviation of 10 and covariance of 18 per cent. The mean level recorded is very high compared to the combined mean which is 52 per cent which gives information that family income leads to accessibility and control over private property which in turn leads to women empowerment.

3. Food

Food is an important dire necessity for people of every walk including women. The access to food depends on their own decision of decision of others.

Item number 2.3 of the Table 5.10.1 gives opinion on family income. 40 respondents (11 per cent) out of 400 respondents recorded their opinion in between zero per cent and 20 per cent. 115 respondents (29 per cent) recorded their opinion at a level at 40 per cent. 157 respondents (40 per cent) recorded their level between 50 and 60 per cent. Eighty-eight respondents recorded their opinion at 80 to 100 per cent range. The mean score of thelevel of opinion is 52 per cent with standard deviation of 21 and a covariance of 40 per cent. The combined mean is equal to the mean score which indicates that this is an important variable which contributes to the accessibility and control over private property.

4. Clothing

Another important dire necessity for life of people is clothing. The acquisition of this is also depend on the earnings. In those families where husband earns income and the decision to purchase is vested to him in another case, where wife also earns income, leads to acquisition by herself.

Item number 2.4 of the Table 5.10.1 depicts opinion on clothing. 21 respondents (5 per cent) recorded their level at 20 per cent and less. 54 respondents (14 per cent) out of 400 respondents recorded their level of opinion at 14 per cent. 112 respondents (28 per cent) recorded a level at 50. 119 respondents (30 per cent) out of 400 respondents recorded a level 60 per cent. 94 respondents (24 per cent) recorded a higher level at 80 per cent and above. The mean score of opinion is 57 per cent with a standard deviation of 17 and a covariance of 30 per cent. The mean score is higher than the combined mean of 52 per cent clearly indicates that this variable has a direct impact on accessibility and control over private property by the women.

5. Shelter

Another dire necessity of life is the shelter. Occupation of shelter—thatched, terrace or others—depends on the income of the occupant. It is also occupied either by husband or wife or both depending on their earnings.

Item number 2.5 of Table 5.10.1 is the opinion on Shelter. 78 respondents (19 per cent) recorded their level at 20 per cent and less. 182 respondents (46 per cent) recorded a level between 40 and 150 per cent. 112 respondents (28 per cent) recorded their level of opinion at 60 per cent. Only 28 respondents (7 per cent) recorded a level at 80 per cent and above. The mean score in this case is 47 per cent and standard deviation of 17 and a covariance of 37 per cent. Here the mean score is 47 per cent and is less than the combined mean of 52 per cent which shows that this variable is not so significant.

6. Accessibility to Housing Loans

In majority of the cases, the owners of houses usually construct their houses by borrowing from housing societies, nationalised commercial banks, or from private banks.

Item number 2.6 of the Table 5.10.1 is about the opinion of respondents on accessibility to Housing Loans. 26 respondents (7 per cent) of the respondents in the sample by recording their level of opinion at 20 per cent and less. 107 respondents (27 per cent) recorded a level at 40 per cent and 131 respondents (33 per cent) recorded a level at 50 per cent. 126 respondents (32 per cent) recorded a level at 60 per cent. Only 10 respondents (3 per cent) recorded a higher level at 80 per cent and above. The mean score recorded is 49 per cent and a standard deviation of 12 and a covariance of 25 per cent. The means score is less than the combined mean of 52 per cent which shows that this variable is not significant one as far as accessibility of private property by women is concerned.

7. Accessibility to Vehicle Loans

Nowadays vehicles are owned and used by both gender without any exception. Not only that there are sufficient facilities available for getting loans for purchase of vehicles, but alsothis facility added merit to women for acquiring private property.

Item number 2.7 of the Table 5.10.1 is the opinion of respondents on accessibility to vehicle loans. In this case, 59 respondents (15 per cent) recorded their level of opinion at 20 per cent and less. 273 respondents (68 per cent) recorded a level between 40 and 50 per cent. 61 respondents (15 per cent) recorded a level at 60 per cent. Only 17 respondents (2 per cent) recorded a level at 80 per cent and above. The mean score recorded is 46 per cent with a standard deviation of 13 per cent and a co-variance of 29 per cent. In this case also, the means score is less than the combined mean of 52 per cent and is not significant.

8. Accessibility to Consumption Loans

Now there is availability of loans for various purposes including consumption. By making use of this facility, the people consume more, especially women, that in turn leads to women empowerment.

Item number 2.8 of Table 5.10.1 is about the opinion on accessibility to consumption loans. 45 respondents (12 per cent) recorded their level of opinion at less than 40 per cent. 139 respondents (35 per cent) recorded level of 50 per cent and 168 respondents (42 per cent) recorded a level of 60 per cent. 48 respondents (13 per cent) recorded a level of 80 per cent and above. The mean level of opinion is 57 per cent with a standard deviation of 12 and a covariance of 22 per cent. The combined mean is 52 percent and is less than the mean score which means this variable contributes much towards accessibility to consumption loans.

9. Status and Property Laws

Another sub variable analysed is the Status and Property laws for looking into the the fact that whether property laws have any impact on accessibility and control over private property.

Item number 2.9 of Table 5.10.1 is the opinion of respondents on status and property laws. 37 respondents (10 per cent) recorded their opinion level at 20 per cent and less. 122 respondents out of 400 (31 per cent) recorded their level of opinion at 40 per cent and 94 respondents (24 per cent) recorded a level of 50 per cent. 107 respondents (27 per cent) recorded a level of 60 per cent. 40 respondents (10 per cent) recorded a higher level of 80 percent and above. The mean score recorded is 49 per cent with a standard deviation of 19 and a covariance of 38 per cent. The mean score is less than the combined mean which is 52 per cent which clearly indicates that this is not so significant.

10. Impact of Globalisation on Expenditure Pattern

Globalisation has an impact on the culture, standard of living, and generation of income. The pattern of consumption is increased due to globalisation, in general, and women, in particular.

Item number 2.10 of the Table 5.10.1 is about opinion on impact of globalisation on expenditure pattern. 13 respondents out of 400 (3 per cent) recorded a level less than 20 per cent. 62 respondents (16 per cent) and 170 respondents (43 per cent) recorded their opinion level at 40 per cent and 50 per cent respectively. 133 respondents (33 per cent) recorded a level at 60 per cent and 22 respondents (6 per cent) recorded a level at 80 per cent and none of them recorded a level at 100 per cent. The mean percentage level of opinion in this case is 52 per cent with a standard deviation of 11 and a covariance of 21. The combined mean is 52 which is equal to the mean score clearly indicating that there is impact on change in the expenditure pattern due to globalisation.

11. Role in Decision-making

The decision-making is an important variable in empowerment. For increasing their empowerment, women want to take decisions. The decisions on acquiring private property, vehicles, spending, and savings are basically included here.

Item number 2.11 of the Table 5.10.1 is about the opinion on role in decision- making. None of them recorded their level of opinion at 40 per cent and less. Only 2 respondents (1 per cent) recorded a level at 40 per cent. 75 respondents (19 per cent) and 117 respondents (29 per cent) recorded a level at 50 per cent and 60 per cent respectively. 184 respondents (46 per cent) recorded a level at 80 per cent and 22 respondents (6 per cent) recorded a level at cent per cent. The mean level of opinion recorded is 69 per cent with a Standard Deviation of 14 and a covariance of 21. The mean recorded level of opinion in this case is higher than that of combined mean which is 52 per cent which is a clear indication that this variable is important in women empowerment.

Main Variable II—Accessibility and Control Over Public Properties (V_3)

Historically Kerala has been quite different from the rest of the country in terms of the indicators of women's development In fact, Kerala has often been referred to as the "land of women" based on the sex ratio which is higher than men. The state has never had a female-male ratio below unity at any time in the century. The achievements in literacy and education have positively influenced the status of women in the state. This in turn enhances the power of taking decisions and making use of the common facilities available as public properties. This main variable is analysed with the help of nineteen (19) sub variables. They are:

1. Labour Issues in Bringing Water

For getting water from the common facility extended by the government is an important issue faced by the women in our state. Sometimes, they are using common pond or well that are available in certain areas only. The views of respondents on labour issues in bringing water is shown as item number 3.1 of Table 5.11.1. In this case 66 respondents (17 per cent) recorded a level of opinion at 20 per cent and less. 83 respondents (21 per cent) and 118 respondents (30 per cent) recorded their level of opinion at 40 per cent and 50 per cent respectively. 107 respondents (27 per cent) recorded a level at 60 per cent and 26

Table 5.10.1: Variable 1. Accessibility and Control Over Private Properties (Item No. 2.1 to 2.11)

Sl No	*Sub-Variables (Items)*	*Opinion Scores*								*Avg*	*SD*	*CV*
		0	*20*	*40*	*50*	*60*	*80*	*100*	*Total*			
1.	($V_{2.1}$) Savings	76 (19)	92 (23)	128 (32)	84 (21)	18 (5)	2 (1)	0 (0)	400 (100)	31	19	61
2.	($V_{2.2}$) Family income	1 (0)	10 (3)	36 (9)	46 (12)	290 (73)	16 (4)	1 (0)	400 (100)	57	10	18
3.	($V_{2.3}$) Food	14 (4)	26 (7)	115 (29)	91 (23)	66 (17)	76 (19)	12 (3)	400 (100)	52	21	40
4.	($V_{2.4}$) Clothing	4 (1)	17 (4)	54 (14)	112 (28)	119 (30)	90 (23)	4 (1)	400 (100)	57	17	30
5.	($V_{2.5}$) Shelter	5 (1)	73 (18)	64 (16)	118 (30)	112 (28)	27 (7)	1 (0)	400 (100)	47	17	37
6.	($V_{2.6}$) Accessibility to housing loans	0 (0)	26 (7)	107 (27)	131 (33)	126 (32)	8 (2)	2 (1)	400 (100)	49	12	25
7.	($V_{2.7}$) Accessibility to vehicle loans	0 (0)	59 (15)	81 (20)	192 (48)	61 (15)	5 (1)	2 (1)	400 (100)	46	13	29

Sl. No	*Sub-Variables (Items)*	*Opinion Scores*								*Avg*	*SD*	*CV*
		0	*20*	*40*	*50*	*60*	*80*	*100*	*Total*			
8.	($V_{2.8}$) Accessibility to consumption loans	0 (0)	2 (1)	43 (11)	139 (350	168 (42)	38 (10)	10 (3)	400 (100)	57	12	22
9.	($V_{2.9}$) Status and property laws	26 7	11 (3)	122 (31)	94 (24)	107 (27)	36 (9)	4 (1)	400 (100)	49	19	38
10.	($V_{2.10}$) Impact of Globalisation on expenditure pattern	0 (0)	13 (3)	62 (16)	170 (43)	133 (33)	22 (6)	0 (0)	400 (100)	52	11	21
11.	($V_{2.11}$) Role in decision-making	0 (0)	0 (0)	2 (1)	75 (19)	117 (29)	184 (46)	22 (6)	400 (100)	69	14	21

Source: SPSS output of Primary Data.
Figures in brackets shows percentage to total.

respondents (6 per cent) recorded a level at 80 per cent and above. The mean score in this case is 47 per cent with a standard deviation of 17 and a covariance of 36. The means score is less than the combined mean which is 51 per cent shows that its impact is only 47 per cent and not significant.

2. Labour Issues in Bringing Fuel

Another problem faced by women in getting the public property extended by the government is the issues connected with supplying of fuel. The level of opinion of respondents were collected and are tabulated as item number 3.2 of Table 5.11.1.

In this issue, 34 respondents (9 per cent) recorded a level of 20 per cent and less. 78 respondents (20 per cent) and 104 respondents (26 per cent) recorded their opinion level at 40 per cent and 50 per cent respectively. 99 respondents (25 per cent) recorded a level at 60 per cent and 85 respondents (21 per cent) recorded a high level of 80 per cent to 100 per cent. The mean recorded level of opinion in this case is 55 per cent with standard deviation of 18 and a covariance of 32 per cent. The mean score is higher than the combined mean which shows that this is a major issue which prevents in accessing the public property by women.

3. Problems Related to Availability of Water

Another serious problem faced by women in getting the services provided by the government is water. There are places where water is scarce. Availability of water adequately is an urgent necessity for women to improve their status. The opinion regarding this is depicted as item number 3.3 of Table 5.11.1.

In this case, 121 respondents (31 per cent) recorded a level at 20 per cent and less. 114 respondents (29 per cent) and 87 respondents (22 per cent) recorded a level of opinion between 40 and 50 per cent. 50 respondents (13 per cent) recorded a level at 60 per cent. Only 28 respondents (7 per cent) recorded a higher level at 80 per cent and cent percent. The mean score in this case is 41 per cent with a standard deviation of 19 and a co-variance of 46 per cent. The mean recorded level of opinion is less than the combined mean (51 cent) which means that this not so significant in empowering women.

4. Problems Related to Availability of Fuel

Availability of fuel is also an important issue confronted by women which affects their daily life. The views of respondents regarding this is shown as item number 3.4 of Table 5.11.1.

Fifty seven respondents (15 per cent) recorded their opinion level at 20 per cent and less than 69 respondents (17 per cent) and 106 respondents (27 per cent) recorded a level at 40 per cent and 50 per cent respectively. 105 respondents (27 per cent) recorded a level at 60 per cent. 56 respondents (14 per cent) and 7 respondents (2 per cent) recorded a level of 80 per cent and 100 per cent. The mean level of opinion recorded by respondents is 51 per cent with a standard deviation of 20 and covariance of 39 per cent. The combined mean is also 51 per cent which means that there exists problems in connection with the availability of fuel.

5. Problems Related to Availability of Sanitation

Another important variable which improves the status and development of women is the facilities available for sanitation. In terms of literacy, life expectancy, and mean age at marriage, women in Kerala score higher than any other state in the country. Kerala's achievement in human development is, in fact, the outcome of the better status of women in terms of education and health. The views of respondents regarding the availability of sanitation is shown as item number 3.5 of Table 5.11.1. 174 respondents (44 per cent) recorded their opinion level at 20 per cent and less than 96 respondents (24 per cent) and 77 respondents (19 per cent) recorded a level at 40 per cent and 50 per cent respectively. 45 respondents (11 per cent) recorded a level at 60 per cent. 5 respondents (1 per cent) and 3 respondents (1 per cent) recorded a level of 80 per cent and 100 per cent. The mean level of opinion recorded by respondents is 36 per cent with a standard deviation of 17 and covariance of 48 per cent. The combined mean is only 36 per cent which is less than the combined mean (51 per cent) which means that this is not a significant problem now as far as women in Kerala are concerned.

6. Problems Related to Kind of Health Issues

The female life expectancy at the national level was only 31.7 years, while the same was 42.3 years in Kerala. Thus, historically, a favourable ground was set for Kerala women while most of the Indian states were deplorably poor in this regard.

And the female life expectancy in Kerala exceeds that of the male, just as it does in the developed world. This is basically on account of the fact that they are health conscious and measures are initiated by the Government for protecting women by giving antenatal and postnatal care facilities.

The views of respondents regarding the problems related to kinds of health issues is shown as item number 3.6 of Table 5.11.1.

Fifty respondents (44 per cent) recorded their opinion level at 20 per cent and less. 73 respondents (18 per cent) and 108 respondents (27 per cent) recorded a level at 40 per cent and 50 per cent respectively. 103 respondents (26 per cent) recorded a level at 60 per cent. 56 respondents (14 per cent) and 10 respondents (3 per cent) recorded a level of 80 per cent and 100 per cent. The mean level of opinion recorded by respondents is 52 per cent with a standard deviation of 20 and covariance of 38 per cent. The combined mean is 52 per cent which is more than that of the combined means (51 per cent) which means that this is an important variable as far as access and control over public property are concerned.

7. Availability of Security

Kerala proves that economic development *per se* does not guarantee gender equality and that gender development is a pre-requisite for overall human development. Women's agency can create social justice - it is an integral part of the development process, not just an outcome of development. Securities are required for or accessing loans and also for getting facilities offered by the government and other agencies. The views of respondents on the availability of security is shown as item number 3.7 of Table 5.11.1.

In this case, 19 respondents (5 per cent) recorded their opinion level at 20 per cent and less. 43 respondents (11 per cent) and 90 respondents (23 per cent) recorded a level at 40 per cent and 50 per cent respectively. 110 respondents (28 per cent) recorded a level at 60 per cent. 122 respondents (31 per cent) and 16 respondents (4 per cent) recorded a level of 80 per cent and 100 per cent. The mean level of opinion recorded by respondents is 61 per cent with a standard deviation of 18 and covariance of 30 per cent. The combined mean is 61 per cent which is very high compared to the combined mean (51 per cent) which makes it clear that the security and its availability is prominent in obtaining public property by women in Kerala.

8. Expenditure on Security

Government is responsible for providing personal security to women especially for participating the functions and all. If it is not granted by the government, they are undertaken by them and spent on that. The views of respondents on expenditure on security is given as item number 3.8 of Table 5.11.1.

In this case, 138 respondents (34 per cent) recorded their opinion level at 20 per cent and less. 99 respondents (25 per cent) and 80 respondents (20 per cent) recorded a level at 40 per cent and 50 per cent respectively. 58 respondents (15 per cent) recorded a level at 60 per cent. 28 respondents (7 per cent) recorded a level of 80 per cent and above. The mean level of opinion recorded by respondents is 40 per cent with a standard deviation of 20 and covariance of 51 per cent. The combined mean is 40 per cent which is very low compared to the combined mean (51 per cent) which makes it clear that the expenditure on security is not a prominent one in accessibility and control over public property.

9. Food Security

Another important variable in obtaining public property is the food security. It is also the responsibility of the government to provide adequate food materials for their living at reasonably good quality food materials at less cost. The views of respondents are collected and is tabulated as item number number 3.9 of Table 5.11.1.

In this case, 41 respondents (11 per cent) recorded their opinion level at 20 per cent and less. 74 respondents (19 per cent) and 101 respondents (25 per cent) recorded a level of 40 per cent and 50 per cent respectively. 96 respondents (24 per cent) recorded a level of 60 per cent. 82 respondents (21 per cent) recorded a level of 80 per cent and 6 respondents (2 per cent) recorded a level of opinion at 100 per cent. The mean recorded level of opinion is 54 per cent with a standard deviation of 20 and a covariance of 37 per cent. The combined mean is 54 per cent which is higher than the combined mean (51 per cent) which makes it clear that the food security is a prominent one in accessibility and control over public property by women.

10. Calorie Expense

Calorie intake in an immediate necessity for safeguarding the health of everyone in general, and women in particular. Adequate materials must be provided or accessed by women for meeting the same and incur expenses relating thereto. The views of respondents were collected and are tabulated as item number 3.10 of Table 5.11.1.

Table 5.11.1 : Variable 1. Accessibility and Control Over Public Properties (Item No. 3.1 to 3.10)

Sl No	*Sub-Variables (Items)*	*Opinion Scores*								*Avg*	*SD*	*CV*
		0	*20*	*40*	*50*	*60*	*80*	*100*	*Total*			
1.	($V_{3.1}$) Labour issues in bringing water	11 (3)	55 (14)	83 ((21)	118 (30)	107 (27)	25 (6)	1 (0)	400 (100)	47	17	36
2.	($V_{3.2}$) Labour issues in bringing fuel	0 (0)	34 (9)	78 (20)	104 (26)	99 (25)	80 (20)	5 (1)	400 (100)	55	18	32
3.	($V_{3.3}$) Problems related to availability of water	10 (3)	111 (28)	114 (29)	87 (22)	50 (13)	25 (6)	3 (1)	400 (100)	41	19	46
4.	($V_{3.4}$) Problems related to availability of fuel	15 (4)	42 (11)	69 (17)	106 (27)	105 (26)	56 (14)	7 (2)	400 (100)	51	20	39
5.	($V_{3.5}$) Problems related to availability of sanitation	10 (3)	164 (41)	96 (24)	77 (19)	45 (11)	5 (1)	3 (1)	400 (100)	36	17	48
6.	($V_{3.6}$) Problems related to kinds of health issues	11 (3)	39 (10)	73 (18)	108 (27)	103 (26)	56 (14)	10 (3)	400 (100)	52	20	38
7.	($V_{3.7}$) Availability of security	2 (1)	17 (4)	43 (11)	90 (23)	110 (28)	122 (31)	16 (4)	400 (100)	61	18	30

Sl No	*Sub-Variables (Items)*	*Opinion Scores*								*Avg*	*SD*	*CV*
		0	*20*	*40*	*50*	*60*	*80*	*100*	*Total*			
8.	($V_{3.8}$) Expenditure on security	28 (7)	107 (27)	99 (25)	80 (20)	58 (15)	27 (7)	1 (0)	400 (100)	40	20	51
9.	($V_{3.9}$) Food security	14 (4)	27 (7)	74 (19)	101 (25)	96 (24)	82 (21)	6 (2)	400 (100)	54	20	37
10.	($V_{3.10}$) Calorie expense	10 (3)	29 (7)	95 (24)	131 (33)	111 (28)	23 (6)	1 (0)	400 (100)	49	15	31

Source: SPSS output of Primary Data.
Figures in brackets shows percentage to total.

In this case, 39 respondents (10 per cent) recorded their opinion level at 20 per cent and less. 95 respondents (24 per cent) and 131 respondents (33 per cent) recorded a level of 40 per cent and 50 per cent respectively. 111 respondents (28 per cent) recorded a level of 60 per cent. 23 respondents (6 per cent) recorded a level of 80 per cent and 1 respondent recorded a level of opinion at 100 per cent. The mean recorded level of opinion is 49 per cent with a standard deviation of 15 and a covariance of 31 per cent. The combined mean is 49 per cent which is lower than the combined mean (51 per cent) which means that calorie expense is not so important in accessibility and control over public property by women.

11. Nutritional Status

Another important variable which contributes to status and development of women for empowerment is the nutritional status. Nutritious food is important for improving the health and life expectancy of women in Kerala. Government takes measures for providing nutritious food to women during ante and post-natal care. The views of respondents on nutritional status is tabulated as item number 3.11 of Table 5.11.2.

In this case, 36 respondents (9 per cent) recorded their opinion level at 20 per cent and less. 55 respondents (14 per cent) and 101 respondents (25 per cent) recorded a level at 40 per cent and 50 per cent respectively. 108 respondents (27 per cent) recorded a level at 60 per cent. 89 respondents (22 per cent) recorded a level of 80 per cent and 11 respondents (3 per cent) recorded a level of opinion at 100 per cent. The mean recorded level of opinion is 56 per cent with a standard deviation of 20 and a covariance of 36 per cent. The combined mean is 56 per cent which is higher than the combined mean (51 per cent) which makes it clear that the nutritional status is a prominent one in accessibility and control over public property by women.

12. Non-acquisition of Primary Education Status

Today Kerala's female literacy is 88 per cent (54 per cent at the national level) and life expectancy is 72.4 years (60.4 years at the national level). Kerala's female literacy was four times higher than that of India. The first girls' school in the private sector of the state was established in 1819. In the following years, a Government Girls School (1859) and a training school for women teachers (1887) were opened. Statistics (from different human development reports) indicate that women have contributed more than men in the development of education programs and health sectors of the state. Kerala ranks first among the Indian states in terms of performance on the Human Development Index (HDI), Gender Equality Index (GEl) and Gender Empowerment Measure (GEM). The views of respondents on non-acquisition of primary education was collected and is tabulated as item number 3.12 of Table 5.11.2. In this case 47 respondents (12 per cent) recorded their opinion level at 20 per cent and less. 180 respondents (45 per cent) and 118 respondents (30 per cent) recorded a level of 20 per cent and 40 per cent respectively. 27 respondents (7 per cent) recorded a level of 60 per cent. 17 respondents (4 per cent) recorded a level of 60 per cent and 11 respondents (3 per cent) recorded a level of opinion at and above 80 per cent. The mean recorded level of opinion is 29 per cent with a standard deviation of 18 and a covariance of 63 per cent. The combined mean is 29 per cent which is lower than the combined mean (51 per cent) which makes it clear that the non acquisition of primary education is not a prominent one in accessibility and control over public property by women.

13. Child Welfare Services

Another important public property accessed by women is the child welfare services extended by the government from time to time. There are welfare schemes provided by government in the form of inoculation of polio vaccine to children from time to time, nutritional food and other medical aid through operation of Anganwadis or health care centres. The views of respondents on child welfare services are shown as item number 3.13 of Table 5.11.2. In this case, 34 respondents (8 per cent) recorded their opinion level at 20 per cent and less. 28 respondents (7 per cent) and 90 respondents (23 per cent) recorded a level of 40 per cent and 50 per cent respectively. 122 respondents (31 per cent) recorded a level of 60 per cent. 105 respondents (26 per cent) recorded a level of 80 per cent and 21 respondents (5 per cent) recorded a level of opinion at 100 per cent. The mean recorded level of opinion is 60 per cent with a standard deviation of 21 and a covariance of 35 per cent. The combined mean is 60 per cent which is higher than the combined mean (51 per cent) which makes it clear that the child welfare services is a prominent one in accessibility and control over public property by women.

14. Accessibility to Housing

Another notable variable in accessing and controlling of public property is the accessibility to housing. Housing is an important for safe residence to women. The views of respondents on it is depicted as item number 3.14 of Table 5.11.2. In this case, 28 respondents (7 per cent) recorded their opinion level at 20 per cent and less. 79 respondents (20 per cent) and 112 respondents (28 per cent) recorded a level at 40 per cent and 50 per cent respectively. 109 respondents (27 per cent) recorded a level of 60 per cent. 65 respondents (1 per cent) recorded a level of 80 per cent and 7 respondents (2 per cent) recorded a level of opinion at 100 per cent. The mean recorded level of opinion is 54 per cent with a standard deviation of 17 and a covariance of 31 per cent. The combined mean is 54 per cent which is higher than the combined mean (51 per cent) which makes it clear that the accessibility to housing is a prominent one in accessibility and control over public property by women.

15. Accessibility to Banking

Another important sub variable identified is the accessibility to banking. The development of banking accessibility is very important for women empowerment and avoiding of gender inequality. Accessing the government facilities and support requires bank account. The views of respondents on it are given as item number 3.15 of Table 5.11.2. In this case, 29 respondents (7 per cent) recorded their opinion level at 20 per cent and less. 37 respondents (9 per cent) and 79 respondents (20 per cent) recorded a level of 40 per cent and 50 per cent respectively. 124 respondents (31 per cent) recorded a level of 60 per cent. 103 respondents (26 per cent) recorded a level of 80 per cent and 28 respondents (7 per cent) recorded a level of opinion at 100 per cent. The mean recorded level of opinion is 61 per cent with a standard deviation of 21 and a covariance of 34 per cent. The combined mean is 61 per cent which is higher than the combined mean (51 per cent) which makes it clear that the accessibility to banking is very important one for the accessibility and control over public property by women.

16. Facilities to Other Basic Needs

This is another sub variable which leads to accessibility and control over public property. There are other facilities over and above the basic dire necessities of life such as the welfare measures for the development of women. The views of respondents on it are given as item number 3.16 of Table 5.11.2. In this case, 11 respondents (3 per cent) recorded their opinion level at 20 per cent and less. 34 respondents (9 per cent) and 73 respondents (18 per cent) recorded a level of 40 per cent and

50 per cent respectively. 118 respondents (30 per cent) recorded a level of 60 per cent. 128 respondents (32 per cent) recorded a level of 80 per cent and 36 respondents (9 per cent) recorded a level of opinion at 100 per cent. The mean recorded level of opinion is 65 per cent with a standard deviation of 19 and a covariance of 28 per cent. The combined mean is 65 per cent which is higher than the combined mean (51 per cent) which makes it clear that the facilities to other basic needs is a prominent sub variable in the accessibility and control over public property by women.

17. Accessibility to Loans

There are various schemes wherein loan facilities are extended by government through banks. For construction of houses, purchases of articles and vehicles. The views of respondents on it is given as item number 3.17 of Table 5.11.2. In this case, 41 respondents (11 per cent) recorded their opinion level at 20 per cent and less. 79 respondents (20 per cent) and 109 respondents (27 per cent) recorded a level at 40 per cent and 50 per cent respectively. 107 respondents (27 per cent) recorded a level of 60 per cent. 59 respondents (15 per cent) recorded a level of 80 per cent and 5 respondents (1 per cent) recorded a level of opinion at 100 per cent. The mean recorded level of opinion is 52 per cent with a standard deviation of 18 and a covariance of 34 per cent. The combined mean is 52 per cent which is higher than the combined mean (51 per cent) which makes it clear that the accessibility to loans is a prominent sub variable in the accessibility and control over public property by women.

18. Accessibility to Electricity

Another important facility offered by government is the electricity that is accessed by people and is a public property. The views of respondents on it are shown as item number 3.18 of Table 5.11.2. In this case, 8 respondents (2 per cent) recorded their opinion level at 20 per cent and less. 47 respondents (12 per cent) and 101 respondents (25 per cent) recorded a level of 40 per cent and 50 per cent respectively. 128 respondents (32 per cent) recorded a level of 60 per cent. 109 respondents (27 per cent) recorded a level of 80 per cent and 7 respondents (2 per cent) recorded a level of opinion at 100 per cent. The mean recorded level of opinion is 60 per cent with a standard deviation of 16 and a covariance of 26 per cent. The combined mean is 60 per cent which is higher than the combined mean (51 per cent) which means that the accessibility to electricity is also a prominent sub variable in the accessibility and control over public property by women.

19. Accessibility to Technical Education

In addition to the normal education, there are institutions run by the government for extending technical education solely to women. Women Poly Technical and Engineering Colleges are examples in this regard. The views of respondents on accessibility to technical education is given as item number 3.19 of Table 5.11.2. In this case, 59 respondents (15 per cent) recorded their opinion level at 20 per cent and less. 75 respondents (19 per cent) and 128 respondents (32 per cent) recorded a level at 40 per cent and 50 per cent respectively. 85 respondents (21 per cent) recorded a level at 60 per cent. 53 respondents (14 per cent) recorded a level of 80 per cent and above. The mean recorded level of opinion is 49 per cent with a standard deviation of 19 and a covariance of 38 per cent. The combined mean is 49 per cent which is lower than the combined mean (51 per cent) which means that the accessibility to technical education is not a significant sub variable in the accessibility and control over public property by women.

Main Variable III - Control Over Income and Employment (V_4)

Women are often in a disadvantaged position in comparison to men in labour markets around the world. Increased access to labour markets for women has great potential as a contribution to economic development, but only if the work in which women are engaged is decent and productive. Women are too often trapped in insecure employment situations with low productivity and low earnings. Since women are overrepresented in the unorganised sector where the conditions of work are insecure and wages are low with hardly any non-wage benefits. The economic crisis makes the achievement of a path towards sustainable and socially equitable growth and decent work for all increasingly more difficult and underlines the concerns over the social impacts of globalisation for women. Gender equality should be a key principle in any policy response as the effects of the crisis go beyond the scope of women in the world of work.

In Kerala, the problem of economic crisis was aggravated for women workers since large numbers of them are engaged in traditional industries which have historically been dependent on exports. One of the means by which women generate income is through employment. The working women population is comparatively less in Kerala even though they are well educated.

Table 5.11.2 : Variable 1. Accessibility and Control Over Public Properties (Item No.3.11 to 3.19)

Sl No	*Sub Variables(Items)*	*Opinion Scores*								*Mean*	*SD*	*CV*
		0	*20*	*40*	*50*	*60*	*80*	*100*	*Total*			
11.	($V_{3.11}$) Nutritional status	11 (3)	25 (6)	55 (14)	101 (25)	108 (27)	89 (22)	11 (3)	400 (100)	56	20	36
12.	($V_{3.12}$) Non-acquisition of primary education	47 (12)	180 (45)	118 (30)	27 (7)	17 (4)	5 (1)	6 (2)	400 (100)	29	18	63
13.	($V_{3.13}$) Child welfare services	13 (3)	21 (5)	28 (7)	90 (23)	122 (31)	105 (26)	21 (5)	400 (100)	60	21	35
14.	($V_{3.14}$) Accessibility to housing	1 (0)	27 (7)	79 (20)	112 (28)	109 (27)	65 (16)	7 (2)	400 (100)	54	17	31
15.	($V_{3.15}$) Accessibility to banking	8 (2)	21 (5)	37 (9)	79 (20)	124 (31)	103 (26)	28 (7)	400 (100)	61	21	34

Sl. No.	*Sub-Variables (Items)*	*Opinion Scores*								*Mean*	*SD*	*CV*
		0	*20*	*40*	*50*	*60*	*80*	*100*	*Total*			
16.	($V_{3.16}$) Accessibility to other basic needs	1 (0)	10 (3)	34 (9)	73 (18)	118 (30)	128 (32)	36 (9)	400 (100)	65	19	28
17.	($V_{3.17}$) Accessibility to loans	6 (2)	35 (9)	79 (20)	109 (27)	107 (27)	59 (15)	5 (1)	400 (100)	52	18	34
18.	($V_{3.18}$) Accessibility to electricity	1 (0)	7 (2)	47 (12)	101 (25)	128 (32)	109 (27)	7 (2)	400 (100)	60	16	26
19.	($V_{3.19}$) Accessibility to Technical Education	13 (3)	46 (12)	75 (19)	128 (32)	85 (21)	51 (13)	2 (1)	400 (100)	49	19	38

Source: SPSS output of Primary Data.
Figures in brackets shows percentage to total.

The social influences of women's work are also quite extensive. Work opportunities outside home reduce the economic dependence of women on men, and in turn, increase her economic command within the family.

Women's earning give them access to and control over an independent income, which would make their economic contribution visible and high.

The main variable control over income and employment is analysed with the help of nineteen (19) sub variables. They are:

1. Work done which Carry Wages

The women in Kerala are engaging in tasks for getting wages. The wages available to them are also comparatively lower than those of men. The views of respondents on work done which carry wages is given as item number 4.1 of the Table 5.12.1. As far as this variable is concerned, 41 respondents (10 per cent) recorded their level of opinion at 20 per cent and less. 110 respondents marked their level of opinion at 40 per cent. 148 respondents (37 per cent) recorded their level of opinion at 50 per cent. But 94 respondents (24 per cent) marked a level at 60 per cent. Only 7 respondents (2 per cent) marked a level at 80 per cent and none of them recorded a level at cent per cent. The mean recorded level of opinion is 46 per cent with a standard deviation of 15 and a covariance of 33 per cent. The mean score in this case is less than the combined mean (50 per cent) which means this is not significant variable contributing much to the main variable.

2. Work done which Carry no Wages

As far as women are concerned, they are undertaking numerous tasks in the house without any wages. These are work which in daily life are undertaken for managing the house as a housewife. The views of respondents on work done which carry no wages is shown as item number 4.2 of the Table 5.12.1.

In this case, 32 respondents (8 per cent) recorded their level of opinion at 20 per cent and less. 76 respondents (19 per cent) and 109 respondents (27 per cent) marked their level of opinion at 40 per cent and 50 per cent. 108 respondents (27 per cent) recorded their level of opinion at 60 per cent. But only 61 respondents (15 per cent) marked a level of 80 per cent and 14 respondents (2 per cent) marked a level of 100 per cent. The mean recorded level of opinion is 54 per cent with a standard deviation of 19 and a covariance of 34 per cent. The mean score in this case is higher than combined mean (50 per cent) which means this is a prominent variable contributing much to the main variable.

3. Self-reliance in the Decision-making Process

Women in Kerala are self-reliant in decision-making in every walk of their life. In Kerala, they are taking decision regarding the purchase of articles, properties, vehicles, deposits of the savings, investment, politics, starting of business, employment and management of situations. All these decisions are taken independently. The views of respondents on self-reliance in the decision-making process is depicted as item number 4.3 of the Table 5.12.1.

In this case, 51 respondents (13 per cent) recorded their level of opinion at 20 per cent and less. 85 respondents (21 per cent) and 106 respondents (27 per cent) marked their level of opinion at 40 per cent and 50 per cent. 109 respondents (27 per cent) recorded their level of opinion at 60 per cent. 47 respondents (12 per cent) marked a level at 80 per cent and only 2 respondents (1 per cent) marked a level at 100 per cent. The mean recorded level of opinion is 50 per cent with a standard deviation of 18 and a covariance of 37 per cent. The mean score in this case is equal to the combined mean (50 per cent) which means this is a prominent variable contributing much to the main variable.

4. Time Spent on Different Jobs and Rest

Women in Kerala are dedicated to their family work for efficient management of the house. Working women in this regard are faced a lot than the housewives. The views of respondents on time spent on different jobs and rest is noticed as item number 4.4 of the Table 5.12.1.

In this case, 57 respondents (15 per cent) recorded their level of opinion at 20 per cent and less. 69 respondents (21 per cent) and 106 respondents (27 per cent) marked their level of opinion at 40 per cent and 50 per cent. 105 respondents (26 per cent) recorded their level of opinion at 60 per cent. 56 respondents (14 per cent) marked a level of 80 per cent and only 7 respondents (2 per cent) marked a level of 100 per cent. The mean recorded level of opinion is 51 per cent with a standard deviation of 20 and a covariance of 39 per cent. The mean score in this case exceeds the combined mean (50 per cent) which means this is a prominent variable contributing much to the main variable.

5. Utilisation of Wages Earned/Spent

The amount of earnings from employment is either spent by her own decision or a joint decision with her husband and other family members. The amount earned is sometimes spent in full or in part or there is no spending. The views of respondents on it are given as item number 4.5 of the Table 5.12.1.

In this case, 131 respondents (33 per cent) recorded their level of opinion at 20 per cent and less. 99 respondents (25 per cent) and 90 respondents (23 per cent) marked their level of opinion at 40 per cent and 50 per cent respectively. 65 respondents (16 per cent) recorded their level of opinion at 60 per cent. 15 respondents (4 per cent) marked a level of 80 per cent and none of them recorded a level of cent per cent. The mean recorded level of opinion is 40 per cent with a standard deviation of 17 and a covariance of 42 per cent. The mean score in this case is less than the combined mean (50 per cent) which means this is not main contributory factor to the main variable.

6. Utilisation of Wages Earned is Handed Over

The amount of earnings of women from employment is handed over to her husband or father or other elder members of the family and not spent directly. The views of respondents on it are shown as item number 4.6 of the Table 5.12.1.

In this case, 26 respondents (7 per cent) recorded their level of opinion at 20 per cent and less. 48 respondents (12 per cent) and 103 respondents (26 per cent) marked their level of opinion at 40 per cent and 50 per cent. 169 respondents (42 per cent) recorded their level of opinion at 60 per cent. 50 respondents (13 per cent) marked a level of 80 per cent and 4 respondents (1 per cent) recorded a level of cent per cent. The mean recorded level of opinion is 55 per cent with a standard deviation of 16 and a covariance of 28 per cent. The mean score in this case is higher than the combined mean (50 per cent) which means this is the main contributory factor to the mean variable.

7. The Degree of Decision-making Power on Family Expenditure

The degree of decision-making power on family expenditure is also enquired into and collected opinion from the respondents and are tabulated as item number 4.7 of Table 5.12.1.

124 respondents (31 per cent) recorded their level of opinion at 20 per cent and less. 70 respondents (18 per cent) and 73 respondents

(18 per cent) marked their level of opinion at 40 per cent and 50 per cent respectively. 44 respondents (11 per cent) recorded their level of opinion at 60 per cent. 76 respondents (19 per cent) marked a level of 80 per cent and 13 respondents (3 per cent) recorded a level of cent per cent. The mean recorded level of opinion is 47 per cent with a standard deviation of 24 and a covariance of 52 per cent. The mean score in this case is less compared to the combined mean (50 per cent) which means this is not the main contributory factor to the mean variable.

8. Share of Women's Income in Family Expenditure

Family expenditure is met by those who are earning income in the family. All members are earning means the expenditure is less because it is proportionately met by all. In the case of the single earner, who is a women, more amount is spent towards family expenditure. The opinion on share of income of women towards meeting of the expenditure of the family is collected and is presented as item number 4.8 of Table 5.12.1.

In this case, 134 respondents (34 per cent) recorded their level of opinion at 20 per cent and less. 78 respondents (20 per cent) and 47 respondents (12 per cent) marked their level of opinion at 40 per cent and 50 per cent. 96 respondents (24 per cent) recorded their level of opinion at 60 per cent. 45 respondents (11 per cent) marked a level at 80 per cent and none of them recorded a level of cent per cent. The mean recorded level of opinion is 43 per cent with a standard deviation of 21 and a covariance of 50 per cent. The mean score in this case is less than the combined mean (50 per cent) which means this is not the main contributory factor to the mean variable.

9. Expenditure on Personal Needs

Those who are earning income by themselves can spent accordingly for meeting their personal needs. The views of respondents on expenditure on personal needs is given as item number 4.9 of Table 5.12.1.

In this case, 34 respondents (8 per cent) recorded their level of opinion at 20 per cent and less. 28 respondents (7 per cent) and 90 respondents (23 per cent) marked their level of opinion at 40 per cent and 50 per cent. 122 respondents (31 per cent) recorded their level of opinion at 60 per cent. 105 respondents (26 per cent) marked a level of 80 per cent and 21 respondents (5 per cent) recorded a level at cent per cent. The mean recorded level of opinion is 60 per cent with a

Table 5.12.1: Variable III – Control Over Income and Employment (Item Number 4.1 to 4.10)

Sl. No.	*Sub-Variables (Items)*	*Opinion Scores*								*Avg*	*SD*	*CV*
		0	*20*	*40*	*50*	*60*	*80*	*100*	*Total*			
1.	($V_{4.1}$) Work done which carry wages	21 (5)	20 (5)	110 (28)	148 (37)	94 (24)	7 (2)	0 (0)	400 (100)	46	15	33
2.	($V_{4.2}$) Work done which carry no wages	5 (1)	27 (7)	76 (19)	109 (27)	108 (27)	61 (15)	14 (4)	400 (100)	54	19	34
3.	($V_{4.3}$) Self-reliance in the decision-making process	14 (4)	37 (9)	85 (21)	106 (27)	109 (27)	47 (12)	2 (1)	400 (100)	50	18	37
4.	($V_{4.4}$) Time spent on different jobs and rest	15 (4)	42 (11)	69 (17)	106 (27)	105 (26)	56 (14)	7 (2)	400 (100)	51	20	39
5.	($V_{4.5}$) Utilisation of Wages earned (spent)	4 (1)	127 (32)	99 (25)	90 (23)	65 (16)	15 (4)	0 (0)	400 (100)	40	17	42
6.	($V_{4.6}$) Utilisation of Wages earned (handed over)	4 (1)	22 (6)	48 (12)	103 (26)	169 (42)	50 (13)	4 (1)	400 (100)	55	16	28
7.	($V_{4.7}$) The degree of decision- making power in family expenditure	11 (3)	113 (28)	70 (18)	73 (18)	44 (11)	76 (19)	13 (3)	400 (100)	47	24	52
8.	($V_{4.8}$) Share of woman's income in family expenditure	15 (4)	119 (30)	78 (20)	47 (12)	96 (24)	45 (11)	0 (0)	400 (100)	43	21	50

Sl. No.	*Sub-Variables (Items)*	*Opinion Scores*								*Avg*	*SD*	*CV*
		0	*20*	*40*	*50*	*60*	*80*	*100*	*Total*			
9.	($V_{4.9}$) Expenditure on personal needs	13 (3)	21 (5)	28 (7)	90 (23)	122 (31)	105 (26)	21 (5)	400 (100)	60	21	35
10.	($V_{4.10}$) Accessibility to income generating jobs	0 (0)	15 (4)	64 (16)	92 (23)	103 (26)	86 (22)	40 (10)	400 (100)	61	20	32
11.	($V_{4.11}$) Level of independence for selection of streams of study	0 (0)	2 (1)	23 (6)	74 (19)	87 (22)	163 (41)	51 (13)	400 (100)	70	18	25
12.	($V_{4.12}$) Level of independence for selection of jobs	8 (2)	34 (9)	96 (24)	109 (27)	136 (34)	17 (4)	0 (0)	400 (100)	49	15	31
13.	($V_{4.13}$) Wage difference	0 (0)	2 (1)	33 (8)	62 (16)	123 (31)	146 (37)	34 (9)	400 (100)	67	17	25
14.	($V_{4.14}$) Relationship of woman's job with education	6 (2)	104 (26)	132 (33)	97 (24)	40 (10)	20 (5)	1 (0)	400 (100)	41	17	41
15.	($V_{4.15}$) Relationship of woman's job with land holding	23 (6)	114 (29)	114 (29)	85 (21)	45 (11)	17 (4)	2 (1)	400 (100)	38	19	49

Sl. No.	Sub-Variables (Items)	Opinion Scores								Avg	SD	CV
		0	20	40	50	60	80	100	Total			
16.	($V_{4.16}$) Relationship of woman's job with men's job status	48 (12)	162 (41)	125 (31)	47 (12)	18 (5)	0 (0)	0 (0)	400 (100)	29	16	56
17.	($V_{4.17}$) Access and control over trade and commerce (who sells, at what cost, at what location, etc.)	8 (2)	75 (19)	121 (30)	119 (30)	72 (18)	5 (1)	0 (0)	400 (100)	43	15	35
18.	($V_{4.18}$) Intervention in new products' market (what to sell, what to buy)	9 (2)	174 (44)	117 (29)	40 (10)	15 (4)	3 (1)	42 (11)	400 (100)	39	25	65
19.	($V_{4.19}$) Participation (role) of women in trade unions	1 (0)	12 (3)	46 (12)	84 (21)	125 (31)	125 (31)	7 (2)	400 (100)	61	17	27

Source: SPSS Output of Primary Data.
Figures in brackets shows percentage to total.

standard deviation of 21 and a covariance of 35 per cent. The mean score in this case is higher than the combined mean (50 per cent) which means this is the main contributory factor to the mean variable.

10. Accessibility to Income Generating Jobs

Women in Kerala are earning income by engaging jobs in house, businesses, factories, fields, employment in government or private and by means of operating micro enterprises. In Kerala, there is ample scope for earning income through employment whether public or private or starting businesses. The views of respondents on accessibility to income generating jobs is given as item number 4.10 of Table 5.12.1.

In this case, 19 respondents (4 per cent) recorded their level of opinion at 20 per cent and none of them recorded a level of zero. 64 respondents (16 per cent) and 92 respondents (23 per cent) marked their level of opinion at 40 per cent and 50 per cent respectively. 103 respondents (26 per cent) recorded their level of opinion at 60 per cent. 86 respondents (22 per cent) marked a level of 80 per cent and 40 respondents (10 per cent) recorded a level of cent per cent. The mean recorded level of opinion is 61 per cent with a standard deviation of 20 and a covariance of 32 per cent. The mean score in this case is higher than the combined mean (50 per cent) which means this is the main contributory factor to the mean variable.

11. Level of Independence for Selection of Streams of Study

In majority of the cases, the stream of study is selected by their parents, and in certain cases, only the women choose a study. Now, a large majority of the girls have their own preference in studies so that they select a branch of study independently. The views of respondents on it are noted as item number 4.11 of Table 5.12.2.

In this case, only 2 respondents (1 per cent) recorded their level of opinion at 20 per cent and none of them recorded a level of zero. 23 respondents (6 per cent) and 74 respondents (19 per cent) marked their level of opinion at 40 per cent and 50 per cent. 87 respondents (22 per cent) recorded their level of opinion at 60 per cent. 163 respondents (41 per cent) marked a level of 80 per cent and 51 respondents (13 per cent) recorded a level of cent per cent. The mean recorded level of opinion is 70 per cent with a standard deviation of 18 and a covariance of 25 per cent. The mean score in this case is higher than the combined mean (50 per cent) which means this the main contributory factor to the mean variable.

12. Level of Independence for Selection of Jobs

As far as independence for selection jobs are concerned, the preference is much less because getting a job is not as easy in Kerala. Yet in majority of the cases, women have preference in selecting a job independently. On account of globalisation, chances are wide open; so, the degree of independence in selecting jobs is very high in Kerala. The opinion of respondents on it is depicted as item number 4.12 of Table 5.12.2.

There are 42 respondents (11 per cent) who recorded their level of opinion at 20 per cent and less. 96 respondents (24 per cent) and 109 respondents (27 per cent) marked their level of opinion at 40 per cent and 50 per cent respectively. 136 respondents (34 per cent) recorded their level of opinion at 60 per cent. 17 respondents (4 per cent) marked a level of 80 per cent and none of them recorded a level of cent per cent. The mean recorded level of opinion is 49 per cent with a standard deviation of 15 and a covariance of 31 per cent. The mean score in this case is low when compared to the combined mean (50 per cent) which means the respondents are of the opinion that there is less chance for selection of jobs independently.

13. Wage Difference

The state had a work force of around 83 lakhs of which 19 lakhs are women workers. The labour community in Kerala mainly consists of those who are engaged in the informal sector (loading and unloading, casual work, construction work, brick making and self-employment), traditional industries (coir, cashew, handloom and Beedi), IT industry, units in export promotion zones and those who are seasonally employed. Depending upon the nature and type of work, the wages differ accordingly. The wages given to women in the informal sector is lesser when compared to men employees. The views of respondents on wage difference is shown as item number 4.13 of Table 5.12.2.

Only 2 respondents (1 per cent) recorded their level of opinion at 20 per cent and none of them recorded a level at zero. 33 respondents (8 per cent) and 62 respondents (16 per cent) marked their level of opinion at 40 per cent and 50 per cent respectively. 123 respondents (31 per cent) recorded their level of opinion at 60 per cent. 146 respondents (37 per cent) marked a level of 80 per cent and 34 respondents (9 per cent) recorded a level of cent per cent. The mean recorded level of opinion is 67 per cent with a standard deviation of 17 and a covariance of 25 per cent. The mean score in this case is very high when compared to the combined mean (50 per cent) which means the respondents are of the opinion that there exists a very high difference in wages.

14. Relationship of Women's Job with Education

The views of respondents were gathered to look into the women's job with education and is presented as item number 4.14 of Table 5.12.2. In this case, 110 respondents (28 per cent) recorded their level of opinion at 20 per cent and less. 132 respondents (33 per cent) and 97 respondents (24 per cent) marked their level of opinion at 40 per cent and 50 per cent. 40 respondents (10 per cent) recorded their level of opinion at 60 per cent. 20 respondents (10 per cent) marked a level at 80 per cent and 1 respondent recorded a level of cent per cent. The mean recorded level of opinion is 41 per cent with a standard deviation of 17 and a covariance of 41 per cent. The mean score in this case is very low than combined mean (50 per cent) which means the respondents are of the opinion that there is no such correlation exists in between women's job and education.

15. Relationship of Women's Job with Land Holding

Women have the entitlement right to acquire and control over properties. Whenever, women have sufficient income from jobs, they acquire and hold land or land and buildings. The views of respondents are shown as item number 4.15 of Table 5.12.2.

In this case, 137 respondents (35 per cent) recorded their level of opinion at 20 per cent and less. 114 respondents (29 per cent) and 85 respondents (21 per cent) marked their level of opinion at 40 per cent and 50 per cent respectively. 45 respondents (11 per cent) recorded their level of opinion at 60 per cent. 17 respondents (4 per cent) marked a level of 80 per cent and 2 respondents (1 per cent) recorded a level of cent per cent. The mean recorded level of opinion is 38 per cent with a standard deviation of 19 and a covariance of 49 per cent. The mean score in this case is very low than the combined mean (50 per cent) which means that no such correlation exists between women's job and land holdings.

16. Relationship of Women's Job Status with that of Men's Job

The status of women's job with that of men's job was also looked into and the opinion of respondents were gathered and depicted as item number 4.16 of Table 5.12.2.

In the case of status of women's job with that of men's job 210 respondents (53 per cent) recorded their level of opinion at 20 per cent and less. 125 respondents (31 per cent) and 47 respondents (12 per cent) marked their level of opinion at 40 per cent and 50 per cent respectively. 18 respondents (5 per cent) recorded their level of opinion at 60 per cent and none of them recorded at level at 80 per cent and above. The mean recorded level of opinion is 29 per cent with a standard deviation of 16 and a covariance of 56 per cent. The mean score in this case is very low than than the combined mean (50 per cent) which means that no correlation exists between status of women's job with that of men's job.

17. Access and Control Over Trade and Commerce

As far as trade and commerce is concerned, what role is played by women is also enquired into. It covers who is selling the product, at what price they are selling, and also what to buy. Even in rural areas, they obtain earnings by means of selling of whatever articles available with us and used the money for daily spending. The opinion in this regard is shown as item number 4.17 of Table 5.12.2.

In this case, 83 respondents (21 per cent) recorded their level of opinion at 20 per cent and less. 121 respondents (30 per cent) and 119 respondents (30 per cent) marked their level of opinion at 40 per cent and 50 per cent respectively. 72 respondents (18 per cent) recorded their level of opinion at 60 per cent. Only one respondent, marked a level of 80 per cent and none of them marked at 100 per cent.The mean recorded level of opinion is 43 per cent with a standard deviation of 15 and a covariance of 35 per cent. The mean score in this case is very low compared to combined mean (50 per cent) which means that this is not a significant variable contributing much to the main variable.

18. Intervention in New Products Market

The role of women in the invention of new products markets is also looked into by examining the kind of intervention such as to sell and what to buy. The collected data is presented as item number 4.18 of Table 5.12.2.

In this case, 183 respondents (46 per cent) recorded their level of opinion at 20 per cent and less. 117 respondents (29 per cent) and 40 respondents (10 per cent) marked their level of opinion at 40 per cent and 50 per cent. 15 respondents (4 per cent) recorded their level of opinion at 60 per cent. Only 3 respondents (1 per cent) marked a level

Table 5.12.2: Variable IV – Control Over Income and Employment (Item Number 4.11 to 4.19)

Sl No	*Sub-Variables (Items)*	*Opinion Scores*								*Avg*	*SD*	*CV*
		0	*20*	*40*	*50*	*60*	*80*	*100*	*Total*			
1.	($V_{4.11}$) Level of independence for selection of streams of study	0 (0)	2 (1)	23 (6)	74 (19)	87 (22)	163 (41)	51 (13)	400 (100)	70	18	25
2.	($V_{4.12}$) Level of independence for selection of jobs	8 (2)	34 (9)	96 (24)	109 (27)	136 (34)	17 (4)	0 (0)	400 (100)	49	15	31
3.	($V_{4.13}$) Wage difference	0 (0)	2 (1)	33 (8)	62 (16)	123 (31)	146 (37)	34 (9)	400 (100)	67	17	25
4.	($V_{4.14}$) Relationship of woman's job with education	6 (2)	104 (26)	132 (33)	97 (24)	40 (10)	20 (5)	1 (0)	400 (100)	41	17	41
5.	($V_{4.15}$) Relationship of woman's job with land holding	23 (6)	114 (29)	114 (29)	85 (21)	45 (11)	17 (4)	2 (1)	400 (100)	38	19	49
6.	($V_{4.16}$) Relationship of woman's job with men's job status	48 (12)	162 (41)	125 (31)	47 (12)	18 (5)	0 (0)	0 (0)	400 (100)	29	16	56

Sl No	*Sub-Variables (Items)*	*Opinion Scores*								*Avg*	*SD*	*CV*
		0	*20*	*40*	*50*	*60*	*80*	*100*	*Total*			
7.	($V_{4.17}$) Access and control over trade and commerce (who sell, at what cost, at what location etc.)	8 (2)	75 (19)	121 (30)	119 (30)	72 (18)	5 (1)	0 (0)	400 (100)	43	15	35
8.	($V_{4.18}$) Intervention in new products' market (what is to sell, what to buy)	9 (2)	174 (44)	117 (29)	40 (10)	15 (4)	3 (1)	42 (11)	400 (100)	39	25	65
9.	($V_{4.19}$) Participation (role) of women in trade unions	1 (0)	12 (3)	46 (12)	84 (21)	125 (31)	125 (31)	7 (2)	400 (100)	61	17	27

Source: SPSS output of Primary Data.
Figures in brackets shows percentage to total.

of 80 per cent and 42 of them (11 per cent) marked at 100 per cent.The mean recorded level of opinion is 39 per cent with a standard deviation of 25 and a covariance of 65 per cent. The mean score in this case is very low compared to combined mean (50 per cent) which means that this is not a significant variable contributing much to the main variable.

19. Participation or Role of Women in Trade Unions

Almost all people in Kerala are politically conscious in general, and women in particular. They belong to any one political party and are active in politics on account of decentralised planning. In the case of jobs also, they join any of the unions affiliated to party politics. The collected data is presented as item number 4.19 of Table 5.12.2.

In this case, 13 respondents (3 per cent) recorded their level of opinion at 20 per cent and less. 46 respondents (12 per cent) and 84 respondents (21 per cent) marked their level of opinion at 40 per cent and 50 per cent. 125 respondents (31 per cent) recorded their level of opinion at 60 per cent. 125 respondents (31 per cent) marked a level of 80 per cent and only 7 of them (2 per cent) marked at 100 per cent.The mean recorded level of opinion is 61 per cent with a standard deviation of 17 and a covariance of 27 per cent. The mean score in this case is very high compared to combined mean (50 per cent) which means that this is a significant variable contributing much to the main variable.

Main Variable V – Control on the Decision on Own Body

The women today need to set free from slavery or others strict or unfair control so as to enable them to lead a better life which, in turn, accords them a better status. The variables include freedom to take decision on their marriage, giving birth to child, sexual intercourse with partner and also avoidance of tortures in work place, torture by spouse, rape, and mental and physical hazards. This main variable is analysed with the help of Ten (10) sub variables as follows:

1. Freedom for Taking Decision on Marriage

In Kerala, the marriages are arranged by their parents or elders sometimes with the consent of the women or without their consent. In certain circumstances, they themselves select their partners. In certain religions, marriages are arranged even at an early age where they are not prepared for marriage and lacks maturity. In the present globalised era, marriages takes place with the consent of the parties concerned especially in the state of Kerala. The views of respondents on freedom for taking decision on marriage are shown as item number 5.1 of Table 5.13.1.

In the case of freedom for taking decision on marriage, 5 respondents (1 per cent) recorded their level of opinion at 20 per cent and less. 9 respondents (2 per cent) and 82 respondents (21 per cent) marked their level of opinion at 40 per cent and 50 per cent. 105 respondents (26 per cent) recorded their level of opinion at 60 per cent. 122 respondents (31 per cent) marked a level of 80 per cent and 77 of them (19 per cent) marked at 100 per cent.The mean recorded level of opinion is 71 per cent with a standard deviation of 19 and a covariance of 27 per cent. The mean score in this case is very low than combined mean (49 per cent) which means that the respondents argued that there is sufficient freedom for taking decision on marriage.

2. Control over the Decisions on Child Birth

Population and its control is an urgent necessity as far as India, in general, and Kerala, in particular are concerned due to high density of population. There is a need for consensus between husband and wife or life partners in respect of giving birth to child. Based on considering their status, income, education and the economy as a whole, a decision should be taken to child bearing and also with the consent of the life partner women. The opinion of respondents on freedom for control over the decisions on child birth is shown as item number 5.2 of Table 5.13.1.

In this case, 2 respondents (1 per cent) recorded their level of opinion at 20 per cent and less. 23 respondents (6 per cent) and 74 respondents (19 per cent) marked their level of opinion at 40 per cent and 50 per cent. 87 respondents (26 per cent) recorded their level of opinion at 60 per cent. Whereas 163 respondents (41 per cent) marked a level at 80 per cent and 51 of them (13 per cent) marked at 100 per cent.The mean recorded level of opinion is 70 per cent with a standard deviation of 18 and a covariance of 25 per cent. The mean score in this case is very high as 70 per cent compared to combined mean of 49 per cent which indicates that the respondents argued that there is sufficient control over the decisions on child birth.

3. Freedom on Decision on Sexual Intercourse with the Partner

For leading a better life, and also for bettering the women status and development requires sufficient freedom for decision on sexual intercourse with their partner. The opinion of respondents on freedom for control over the decisions on child birth is shown as item number 5.3 of Table 5.13.1.

In this case, 131 respondents (33 per cent) recorded their level of opinion at 20 per cent and less. 99 respondents (25 per cent) and 90 respondents (23 per cent) marked their level of opinion at 40 per cent and 50 per cent. 65 respondents (16 per cent) recorded their level of opinion at 60 per cent. Whereas only 15 respondents (4 per cent) marked a level of 80 per cent and none of them marked a level at 100 per cent.The mean recorded level of opinion is 40 per cent with a standard deviation of 17 and a covariance of 42 per cent. The mean score in this case is very low as 40 per cent than combined mean of 49 per cent which indicates that the respondents argued that there is no freedom on decisions on sexual intercourse with the partner.

4. Physical and Mental Torture Like Rape

Subtle forms which may include sexual innuendoes, inappropriate sexual gestures, and propositions for dates or sexual favour, blatant forms like, leering, pinching, grabbing, hugging, patting, brushing against and touching are extreme behaviour amounting to attempted rape and rape. Rape is one of the most reprehensible crimes and is often unreported. The views of respondents on it are shown as item number 5.4 of Table 5.13.1.

In this case, 166 respondents (41 per cent) recorded their level of opinion at 20 per cent and less. 108 respondents (27 per cent) and 70 respondents (12 per cent) marked their level of opinion at 40 per cent and 50 per cent respectivley. 47 respondents (12 per cent) recorded their level of opinion at 60 per cent. Whereas only 9 respondents (2 per cent) marked a level of 80 per cent and none of them marked a level of 100 per cent. The mean recorded level of opinion is 37 per cent with a standard deviation of 16 and a covariance of 44 per cent. The mean score in this case is very low as 37 per cent which is less than the combined mean of 49 per cent which indicates that the respondents are not agreed with the physical and mental torture like rape.

5. Physical and Mental Torture Like Caste – Religion-based Atrocities

There are atrocities happening among the downtrodden groups of communities. Sexual harassment is the lot, not only of the relatively less powerful and, therefore, more vulnerable sections, but high profile and glamorous occupations also receive more than their share of unwanted male attention. Kerala women are not an exception to discrimination on the basis of gender, caste and class. The views of respondents on it are shown as item number 5.5 of Table 5.13.1.

In this case, 149 respondents (38 per cent) recorded their level of opinion at 20 per cent and less. 112 respondents (28 per cent) and 45 respondents (11 per cent) marked their level of opinion at 40 per cent and 50 per cent respectively. 87 respondents (22 per cent) recorded their level of opinion at 60 per cent. Whereas only 7 respondents (2 per cent) marked a level of 80 per cent and none of them marked a level at 100 per cent. The mean recorded level of opinion is 38 per cent with a standard deviation of 18 and a covariance of 49 per cent. The mean score in this case is very low as 38 per cent which is less than the combined mean of 49 per cent which indicates that this is not a significant variable contributing much to the main variable.

6. Physical and Mental Torture like Sexual Harassment at Work Place

Although many women harbour fear of the potential rapist who may be lurking behind bushes or in dark alleyways, the greatest threat of sexual or physical harm to women is actually from people women know, usually an acquaintance, a co-worker, or an intimate partner. The opinion of respondents on it are shown as item number 5.6 of Table 5.13.1.

In this case, 24 respondents (6 per cent) recorded their level of opinion at 20 per cent and less. 40 respondents (10 per cent) and 119 respondents (30 per cent) marked their level of opinion at 40 per cent and 50 per cent respectively. 163 respondents (41 per cent) recorded their level of opinion at 60 per cent. Whereas 53 respondents (13 per cent) marked a level of 80 per cent and a meager number (one) of respondents marked a level of 100 per cent. The mean recorded level of opinion is 55 per cent with a standard deviation of 14 and a covariance of 26 per cent. The mean score in this case is very high as 55 per cent which is higher than the combined mean of 49 per cent which indicates that this is a significant variable contributing much to the main variable.

7. Physical and Mental Torture by Spouse

There is physical and mental torture from spouse that hinders women in leading a better life. The extent of crimes against women are rising and the most common and most severe forms of crime against women is domestic violence perpetrated by husband. Violence against women is not only a manifestation of sex inequality, but also serves to maintain the unequal balance of power. The opinion of respondents on it is shown as item number 5.7 of Table 5.13.1.

In this case, 104 respondents (27 per cent) recorded their level of opinion at 20 per cent and less. 65 respondents (16 per cent) and 104 respondents (26 per cent) marked their level of opinion at 40 per cent and 50 per cent. 86 respondents (22 per cent) recorded their level of opinion at 60 per cent. Whereas 41 respondents (10 per cent) marked a level of 80 per cent and none of them recorded a level at 100 per cent. The mean recorded level of opinion is 45 per cent with a standard deviation of 20 and a covariance of 45 per cent. The mean score in this case is very low pegged at 45 per cent which is higher than the combined mean of 49 per cent which indicates that this is not a significant variable contributing much to the main variable.

8. Physical and Mental Torture by Close Relative

There are also happenings of physical and mental torture from close relatives which hinder the development and status of women in Kerala. The opinion of respondents on it is shown as item number 5.8 of Table 5.13.1.

In this case, 140 respondents (36 per cent) recorded their level of opinion at 20 per cent and less. 96 respondents (24 per cent) and 72 respondents (18 per cent) marked their level of opinion at 40 per cent and 50 per cent. 70 respondents (22 per cent) recorded their level of opinion at 60 per cent. Whereas 21 respondents (5 per cent) marked a level of 80 per cent and a meager number (one) recorded a level of 100 per cent. The mean recorded level of opinion is 39 per cent with a standard deviation of 20 and a covariance of 51 per cent. The mean score in this case is very low pegged at 39 per cent which is higher than the combined mean of 49 per cent which indicates that this is not a significant variable contributing much to the main variable.

1. Societal Attitude on Women Status

Women occupy a prominent role in the society of Kerala. Now they are having almost equal position to that of men by possessing almost all the rights for improving their status. There is a need to build up a gender sensitive social environment, to look into laws pertaining to sexual assault on women, property rights of women and support for divorced women. The opinion of respondents on it are shown as item number 5.9 of Table 5.13.1.

In this case, 133 respondents (34 per cent) recorded their level of opinion at 20 per cent and less. 76 respondents (9 per cent) and 47 respondents (12 per cent) marked their level of opinion at 40 per cent and 50 per cent. 97 respondents (24 per cent) recorded their level of opinion at 60 per cent. Whereas 46 respondents (12 per cent) marked a level of 80 per cent and a meager number (one) recorded a level of 100 per cent. The mean recorded level of opinion is 43 per cent with a standard deviation of 22 and a covariance of 50 per cent. The mean score in this case is very low, at 43 per cent, which is lower than the combined mean of 49 per cent which indicates that this is not a significant variable contributing much to the main variable.

2. Societal Attitude on Women Sexuality

Kerala is widely considered a model state in India and abroad in terms of social development in spite of its comparatively low per capita income levels. Kerala women are still influenced largely by the religious and social images imposed upon them for centuries. The stereotype ideals of women have reduced them to a level of physical, mental, and spiritual subjugation. Women sexuality in Kerala is based on the customs, traditions and religious beliefs depending on the system of culture and civilisation. The opinion of respondents on it is shown as item number 5.10 of Table 5.13.1.

In this case, 71 respondents (18 per cent) recorded their level of opinion at 20 per cent and less. 79 respondents (20 per cent) and 89 respondents (22 per cent) marked their level of opinion at 40 per cent and 50 per cent. 99 respondents (25 per cent) recorded their level of opinion at 60 per cent. Whereas 58 respondents (15 per cent) marked a level of 80 per cent and 4 respondents (1 per cent) recorded a level of 100 per cent. The mean recorded level of opinion is 50 per cent with a standard deviation of 19 and a covariance of 38 per cent. The mean score in this case is very low as 50 per cent which is lower than the combined mean of 49 per cent which indicates that this is a significant variable contributing much to the main variable.

Table 5.13.1: Variable V – Control on Decision on Own Body (Item Number 5.1 to 5.10)

Sl No	*Sub-Variables (Items)*	*Opinion Scores*								*Avg*	*SD*	*CV*
		0	*20*	*40*	*50*	*60*	*80*	*100*	*Total*			
1.	($V_{5.1}$) Freedom for taking decision on marriage	0 (0)	5 (1)	9 (2)	82 (21)	105 (26)	122 (31)	77 (19)	400 (100)	71	19	27
2.	($V_{5.2}$) Control over the decisions on child birth	0 (0)	2 (1)	23 (6)	74 (19)	87 (22)	163 (41)	51 (13)	400 (100)	70	18	25
3.	($V_{5.3}$) Freedom on decision on sexual intercourse with the partner	4 (1)	127 (32)	99 (25)	90 (23)	65 (16)	15 (4)	0 (0)	400 (100)	40	17	42
4.	($V_{5.4}$) Physical and mental torture like rape	1 (0)	165 (41)	108 (27)	70 (18)	47 (12)	9 (2)	0 (0)	400 (100)	37	16	44
5.	($V_{5.5}$) Physical and mental torture like caste-religion based atrocities	22 (6)	127 (32)	112 (28)	45 (11)	87 (22)	7 (2)	0 (0)	400 (100)	38	18	49
6.	($V_{5.6}$) Physical and mental torture like sexual harassment at work place	0 (0)	24 (6)	40 (10)	119 (30)	163 (41)	53 (13)	1 (0)	400 (100)	55	14	26

Sl No	*Sub-Variables (Items)*	*Opinion Scores*								*Avg*	*SD*	*CV*
		0	*20*	*40*	*50*	*60*	*80*	*100*	*Total*			
7.	($V_{5.7}$) Physical and mental torture by spouse	18 (5)	86 (22)	65 (16)	104 (26)	86 (22)	41 (10)	0 (0)	400 (100)	45	20	45
8.	($V_{5.8}$) Physical and mental torture by close relative	26 (7)	114 (29)	96 (24)	72 (18)	70 (18)	21 (5)	1 (0)	400 100	39	20	51
9.	($V_{5.9}$) Societal attitude on women status	14 (4)	119 (30)	76 (19)	47 (12)	97 (24)	46 (12)	1 (0)	400 (100)	43	22	50
10.	($V_{5.10}$) Societal attitude on women sexuality	1 (0)	70 (18)	79 (20)	89 (22)	99 (25)	58 (15)	4 (1)	400 (100)	50	19	38

Source: SPSS output of Primary Data.
Figures in brackets shows percentage to total.

Main Variable VI – Autonomy on Mobility

One of the important factor responsible for human development and the development of women status is the free mobility. The trend in migration from Kerala to other countries of the world is increasing. There is high rate of migration in Kerala to other countries especially Gulf countries is from Malappuram District. For mobility, there is a need for autonomy in such decisions. Now, we are living in a global village where there is free flow of goods and services so also human beings. The main variable autonomy on mobility as far as women is concerned is analysed with the help of eleven (11) sub variables.

1. Freedom for Mobility in Single

Mobility may be single or in group (family). Now in the globalised era there is free mobility of labourers from elsewhere in the world for employment irrespective of whether men or women. The opinion of respondents on it is given as item number 6.1 of Table 5.14.1.

In this case 66 respondents (16 per cent) recorded their level of opinion at 20 per cent and less. 107 respondents (27 per cent) and 81 respondents (20 per cent) marked their level of opinion at 40 per cent and 50 per cent. 92 respondents (23 per cent) recorded their level of opinion at 60 per cent. Whereas 32 respondents (8 per cent) marked a level of 80 per cent and 22 respondents (6 per cent) recorded a level of 100 per cent. The mean recorded level of opinion is 50 per cent with a standard deviation of 20 and a covariance of 41 per cent. The mean score is equal the combined mean of 50 per cent which indicates that there is freedom for mobility in single.

2. Freedom for Mobility with Women Companion

Women's mobility is more so when there is a companion than remaining singly. The level of opinion on the freedom for mobility with women companion is shown as item number 6.2 of Table 4.14.1. The views of respondents on it are noted as item number 6.2 of Table 5.14.1.

In this case, 14 respondents (3 per cent) recorded their level of opinion at 20 per cent and less. 16 respondents (4 per cent) and 66 respondents (17 per cent) marked their level of opinion at 40 per cent and 50 per cent. 137 respondents (34 per cent) recorded their level of opinion at 60 per cent. Whereas 135 respondents (34 per cent) marked a level at 80 per cent and 32 respondents (8 per cent) recorded a level at 100 per cent. The mean recorded level of opinion is 66 per cent with a standard deviation of 18 and a covariance of 27 per cent. The mean score is higher than the combined mean of 50 per cent which indicates that there is freedom for mobility is more when there is a women companion.

3. Freedom for Mobility with Men Companion

The mobility of women when there is men companion was also examined and opinion have been obtained and is presented as item number 6.3 of Table 5.14.1.

There are 8 respondents (2 per cent) who recorded their level of opinion at 20 per cent and none of them recorded at zero. 29 respondents (7 per cent) and 67 respondents (17 per cent) marked their level of opinion at 40 per cent and 50 per cent. 131 respondents (33 per cent) recorded their level of opinion at 60 per cent. 135 respondents (34 per cent) marked a level of 80 per cent and 30 respondents (8 per cent) recorded a level of 100 per cent. The mean recorded level of opinion is 66 per cent with a standard deviation of 17 and a covariance of 27 per cent. The mean score is higher than the combined mean of 50 per cent which indicates that there is freedom for mobility is more when there is a men companion.

4. Freedom for Mobility in Day Time

Another important factor responsible for the mobility of women in Kerala is the timings. The mobility of women is more during the day time than at night. The opinion of respondents on it is shown as item number 6.4 of Table 5.14.1.

There are 23 respondents (6 per cent) who recorded their level of opinion at 20 per cent and less. 32 respondents (8 per cent) and 92 respondents (23 per cent) marked their level of opinion at 40 per cent and 50 per cent respectively. 133 respondents (33 per cent) recorded their level of opinion at 60 per cent. 103 respondents (31 per cent) marked a level at 80 per cent and 17 respondents (4 per cent) recorded a level of 100 per cent. The mean recorded level of opinion is 60 per cent with a standard deviation of 19 and a covariance of 31 per cent. The mean score is higher than the combined mean of 50 per cent which indicates that freedom for mobility is more during day time.

5. Freedom for Mobility at Night

As far as women in Kerala is concerned, there is less mobility at night. The opinion of respondents on it is shown as item number 6.5 of Table 5.14.1.

In this case, 114 respondents (29 per cent) recorded their level of opinion at 20 per cent and less. 106 respondents (27 per cent) and 80 respondents (20 per cent) marked their level of opinion at 40 per cent and 50 per cent. 61 respondents (15 per cent) recorded their level of opinion at 60 per cent. 31 respondents (8 per cent) marked a level of 80 per cent and only 8 respondents (2 per cent) recorded a level of 100 per cent. The mean recorded level of opinion is 43 per cent with a standard deviation of 21 and a covariance of 50 per cent. The mean score is lower than the combined mean of 50 per cent which indicates that there is less mobility at night.

6. Lack of Freedom for Mobility due to Caste–Religion

There is less mobility for women in Kerala basically as they belong to a particular caste or religion. In Kerala, the custom and tradition of the Muslim women, especially in Malabar areas, or those wearing purdah, prevents the free mobility of women. The views of respondents on it is noted as item number 6.2 of Table 5.14.1.

In this case, 91 respondents (23 per cent) recorded their level of opinion at 20 per cent and less. 97 respondents (24 per cent) and 69 respondents (17 per cent) marked their level of opinion at 40 per cent and 50 per cent. 86 respondents (22 per cent) recorded their level of opinion at 60 per cent. Whereas 29 respondents (7 per cent) marked a level of 80 per cent and 28 respondents (7 per cent) recorded a level of 100 per cent. The mean recorded level of opinion is 46 per cent with a standard deviation of 26 and a covariance of 55 per cent. The mean score is lower than the combined mean of 50 per cent which indicates that there is no prevention on account being a women and belongs to a particular religion or case.

7. Lack of Freedom for Mobility due to Special Conditions

Another important factor responsible for preventing or for slow down of the process of mobility is on account of certain incidents or conditions. For example, there is less mobility to widows. The views of respondents on it are shown as item number 6.7 of Table 5.14.1.

In this case, 48 respondents (12 per cent) recorded their level of opinion at 20 per cent and less.70 respondents (18 per cent) and 90 respondents (23 per cent) marked their level of opinion at 40 per cent and 50 per cent. 94 respondents (24 per cent) recorded their level of opinion at 60 per cent. 78 respondents (20 per cent) marked a level of 80 per cent and 20 respondents (5 per cent) recorded a level at 100 per cent. The mean recorded level of opinion is 55 per cent with a standard deviation of 22 and a covariance of 39 per cent. The mean score is higher than the combined mean of 50 per cent which indicates that there is adequate mobility when special conditions are prevailing.

8. Lack of Freedom for Mobility due to Special Personal Issues

Another important problem which hinders the mobility of women in general is the personal issues confronted during periods and other issues such as pregnancy. The opinion of respondents on it is shown as item number 6.8 of Table 5.14.1.

There are 150 respondents (37 per cent) who recorded their level of opinion at 20 per cent and less. 68 respondents (17 per cent) and 95 respondents (24 per cent) marked their level of opinion at 40 per cent and 50 per cent respectivley. 74 respondents (19 per cent) recorded their level of opinion at 60 per cent. 13 respondents (3 per cent) marked a level at 80 per cent and none of them recorded a level of cent per cent. The mean recorded level of opinion is 71 per cent with a standard deviation of 17 and a covariance of 24 per cent. The mean score is higher than the combined mean of 50 per cent which indicates that there is freedom for mobility even when there exist special personal issues.

9. Lack of Freedom for Mobility due to Local Customs

There are certain incidents such as local customs and traditions which prevent the freedom of mobility of women in Kerala especially in the case of Tribes and all. The opinion of respondents on it is given as item number 6.9 of Table 5.14.1.

In this case, 150 respondents (37 per cent) recorded their level of opinion at 20 per cent and less. 68 respondents (17 per cent) and 95 respondents (24 per cent) marked their level of opinion at 40 per cent and 50 per cent. 74 respondents (19 per cent) recorded their level of opinion at 60 per cent. 13 respondents (3 per cent) marked a level of 80 per cent and none of them recorded a level of 100 per cent. The mean recorded level of opinion is 37 per cent with a standard deviation of 22 and a covariance of 59 per cent. The mean score is less than the combined mean of 50 per cent which indicates that there is no such prevention as far as the respondents are concerned.

10. Lack of Freedom for Mobility due to Women Status

The mobility of women depends on the status of living. Those who are at the helm of affairs move faster than those at the lower strata. Basically, the mobility depends on the earnings and the chance. Women who are in a high position have larger amount of money, many contacts and plenty of chances which constitute as various determining factors of mobility. The views of respondents on it are depicted as item number 6.10 of Table 5.14.1.

In this case, there are 190 respondents (47 per cent) recorded their level of opinion at 20 per cent and less. 94 respondents (24 per cent) and 75 respondents (19 per cent) marked their level of opinion at 40 per cent and 50 per cent respectivley. 36 respondents (9 per cent) recorded their level of opinion at 60 per cent. Only 5 respondents (1 per cent) marked a level of 80 per cent and none of them recorded a level of cent per cent. The mean recorded level of opinion is 30 per cent with a standard deviation of 21 and a covariance of 70 per cent. The mean score is very less compared to combined mean of 50 per cent which indicates that this not a significant variable which contributes to the main variable.

11. Lack of Freedom for Mobility due to Places of Worship

There is another factor which is responsible for women mobility and that is the place of worship. Sometimes peoples reside in a place surrounding to a place of worship. In that case, they won't go anywhere other than this place of worship. The opinion of respondents on it are shown as item number 6.11 of Table 5.14.1.

In this case, 266 respondents (67 per cent) recorded their level of opinion at 20 per cent and less. 70 respondents (18 per cent) and 46 respondents (12 per cent) marked their level of opinion at 40 per cent and 50 per cent respectively. Where as only 16 respondents (4 per cent) recorded their level of opinion at 60 per cent and 2 respondents (1 per cent) marked a level of 80 per cent. Here, none of them recorded a level of 100 per cent. The mean recorded level of opinion is 22 per cent with a standard deviation of 20 and a covariance of 87 per cent. The mean score is very less compared to combined mean of 50 per cent which means that there is no such prevention as far the respondents are concerned.

Table 5.14.1: Variable VI – Autonomy on Mobility (Item Number 6.1 to 6.11)

Sl No	*Sub-Variables (Items)*	*Opinion Scores*								*Avg*	*SD*	*CV*
		0	*20*	*40*	*50*	*60*	*80*	*100*	*Total*			
1.	($V_{6.1}$) Freedom for mobility in single	1 (0)	65 (16)	107 (27)	81 (20)	92 (23)	32 (8)	22 (6)	400 (100)	50	20	41
2.	($V_{6.2}$) Freedom for mobility with women companion	1 (0)	13 (3)	16 (4)	66 (17)	137 (34)	135 (34)	32 (8)	400 (100)	66	18	27
3.	($V_{6.3}$) Freedom for mobility with men companion	1 (0)	7 (2)	29 (7)	67 (17)	131 (33)	135 (34)	30 (8)	400 (100)	66	17	27
4.	($V_{6.4}$) Freedom for mobility in day time	8 (2)	15 (4)	32 (8)	92 (23)	133 (33)	103 (26)	17 (4)	400 (100)	60	19	31
5.	($V_{6.5}$) Freedom for mobility in night	23 (6)	91 (23)	106 (27)	80 (20)	61 (15)	31 (8)	8 (2)	400 (100)	43	21	50
6.	($V_{6.6}$) Lack of freedom for mobility due to caste-religion issues being women	45 (11)	46 (12)	97 (24)	69 (17)	86 (22)	29 (7)	28 (7)	400 (100)	46	26	55
7.	($V_{6.7}$) Lack of freedom for mobility due to special conditions such as being widow*	9	39	70	90	94	78	20	400	55	22	39
		2	10	18	23	24	20	5	100			

Sl No	*Sub-Variables (Items)*	*Opinion Scores*								*Avg*	*SD*	*CV*
		0	*20*	*40*	*50*	*60*	*80*	*100*	*Total*			
8.	($V_{6.8}$) Lack of freedom for mobility due to special conditions such as menses periods	0 (0)	0 (0)	6 (2)	60 (15)	139 (35)	131 (33)	64 (16)	400 (100)	71	17	24
9.	($V_{6.9}$) Lack of freedom for mobility due to local customs	61 (15)	89 (22)	68 (17)	95 (24)	74 (19)	13 (3)	0 (0)	400 (100)	37	22	59
10.	($V_{6.10}$) Lack of freedom for mobility due to women status	93 (23)	97 (24)	94 (24)	75 (19)	36 (9)	5 (1)	0 (0)	400 (100)	30	21	70
11.	($V_{6.11}$) Lack of freedom for mobility due to places of worship	130 (33)	136 (34)	70 (18)	46 (12)	16 (4)	2 (1)	0 (0)	400 (100)	22	20	87

Source: SPSS output of Primary Data.
Figures in brackets shows percentage to total.

VII. Main Variable – Autonomy Over Politics

In Kerala, the women's participation in politics is low and no difference is noticed from the rest of the country. On the contrary, going by the numbers in which they turn out for electioneering and to cast vote in various elections, women's participation can quite justifiably bedescribed as active and the proportion of votes cast by women has improved. Still, the proportion of women among those contesting the elections and getting elected has tended to be extremely small. The Kerala Assembly during 2009 unanimously passed two bills—the Kerala Panchayati Raj (Second Amendment) Bill, 2009 and the Kerala Municipality (Amendment) Bill, 2009—that will reserve 50 per cent seats in local bodies for women. In the forthcoming polls to the local governments in Kerala that are slated to take place in September 2010, 50 per cent of seats would go to women and in the running of local-self government institutions. Women would get to head 50 per cent of the Standing Committees of the local bodies. The mainn variable—women autonomy over politics—is analysed with the help of twelve (12) sub variables which are stated below:

1. Participation in the Capacity as Voter in General Elections

Women who were not active in politics in the past are so even today. Some of them enter into politics based on the motivation and pressure either by their husband or other prominent persons working in party politics in that area. But, they usually cast votes in the general elections. The opinion of respondents on it is shown as item number 7.1 of Table 5.15.1. In this case, none of them recorded a level of 40 per cent and less. Only 7 respondents (2 per cent), recorded their level of opinion at 50 per cent. 83 respondents (21 per cent) marked their level of opinion at 60 per cent. A large majority of them recorded a high level of 80 per cent and above. There are 178 respondents (45 per cent) who recorded their level of opinion at 80 per cent. So also, 132 respondents (33 per cent) marked a level at cent per cent. The mean recorded level of opinion noticed is 82 per cent with a standard deviation of 15 and a covariance of 18 per cent. The mean score is very high compared to combined mean of 55 per cent which means that the respondents are of the opinion that they are active in participating general elections as a voter and not more than that.

2. Participation in the Capacity of Candidate in General Elections

There is political empowerment to women by extending 50 per cent reservation in seats of the grassroots institutions. It is now mandatory so that they contest in such elections and govern the institutions by means of political empowerment. There are incidents where women contest as a candidate for election based on the reservation in the legislative assembly. The views of respondents on it are shown as item number 7.2 of Table 5.15.1.

In this case, none of them recorded a level of zero but only 9 respondents (2 per cent) recorded their level of opinion at 20 per cent. 24 respondents (6 per cent) recorded their level of opinion at 40. 62 respondents (16 per cent) marked their level of opinion at 50 per cent. And 92 respondents (23 per cent) recorded a level of 60 per cent. A large majority of them recorded a high level of 80 per cent and above. There are 105 respondents (26 per cent) who recorded their level of opinion at 80 per cent. So also, 108 respondents (27 per cent) marked a level of cent per cent. The mean recorded level of opinion noticed is 72 per cent with a standard deviation of 21 and a covariance of 30 per cent. The mean score is very high compared to combined mean of 55 per cent which means that the respondents are of the opinion that they are contesting as a candidate while participating in general elections.

1. Freedom to Cast Vote as per Own Decision

In respect of casting of votes, the women have the freedom of exercising their own decision. It means that they are not accepting the recommendation for casting vote in favour of a political party. The opinion of respondents on it is depicted as item number 7.3 of Table 5.15.1.

In this case, 21 respondents (6 per cent) recorded their level of opinion at 20 per cent and less. 48 respondents (12 per cent) recorded their level of opinion at 40. 108 respondents (27 per cent) marked their level of opinion at 50 per cent and 108 respondents (27 per cent) recorded a level of 60 per cent. There are 93 respondents (23 per cent) recorded their level of opinion at 80 per cent. So also, 22 respondents (6 per cent) marked a level at cent per cent. The mean recorded level of opinion noticed is 60 per cent with a standard deviation of 19 and a covariance of 32 per cent. The mean score is higher than the combined mean of 55 per cent which means that the respondents are of the opinion that women have exercised their votes by their own decisions and were not influenced by others pressure.

2. Membership in Political Parties

Women are not active in politics and hence they do not take membership in political parties. In the case of employees, they are active in unions which are affiliated to certain political parties. In such cases, they take membership in such political parties and are sometimes active also. As far as non-working women are concerned, they neither active in politics nor they take membership in political parties. The views of respondents on it are shown as item number 7.4 of Table 5.15.1.

In this case, a large majority of the respondents marked their level of opinion at 40 per cent and less. 110 respondents (28 per cent) marked their level of opinion at 20 per cent and less. 113 respondents (28 per cent) marked their level of opinion at 40 per cent and 97 respondents (27 per cent) recorded a level of 50 per cent. There are 54 respondents (14 per cent) who recorded their level of opinion at 60 per cent. 22 respondents (6 per cent) marked a level of 80 per cent and 4 respondents (1 per cent) marked their level of opinion at cent per cent. The mean recorded level of opinion noticed is 42 per cent with a standard deviation of 18 and a covariance of 44 per cent. The mean score is less than the combined mean of 55 per cent which means that the respondents are of the opinion that women do not have membership in party politics.

3. Membership in Community Organisations

Kudumbasree introduced several innovative programmes for the financial, economic and social upliftment of poor women by organising them into community-based structures like Neighbourhood groups. Kudumbasree promotes thrift mobilisation by setting up Thrift and Credit Societies at Neighbourhood Group level to encourage the poor to save and to provide them cost-effective and easy credit. Thrift and credit societies facilitate easy and timely credit to the unreached. The amount of loan and the priority of disbursement are decided by the Neighbourhood Groups. The repayment is collected weekly during the routine Neighbourhood meetings. Kudumbasree has organised community-based organisations (CBOs) of the poor in the state. Community Development Societies (CDS) act as delivery system for various centrally sponsored urban poverty reduction programmes. Almost all women in Kerala in one way or the other are members of the community-based organisations for getting benefits for the development and improvement in status through economic empowerment. The views of respondents on it are shown as item number 7.5 of Table 5.15.1.

In this case, 112 respondents (28 per cent) recorded their level of opinion at 20 per cent and less. 92 respondents (23 per cent) recorded their level of opinion at 40 per cent. 63 respondents (16 per cent) marked their level of opinion at 50 per cent and 60 respondents (15 per cent) recorded a level of 60 per cent. There are 61 respondents (15 per cent) recorded their level of opinion at 80 per cent. 12 respondents (3 per cent) marked a level of cent per cent. The mean recorded level of opinion noticed is 47 per cent with a standard deviation of 23 and a covariance of 48 per cent. The mean score is less than the combined mean of 55 per cent which means that the respondents are of the opinion that all of them are not involved in community-based organisations.

4. Approach of Political Parties towards Women

The approaches of political parties on women were also enquired into and the views were collected and tabulated as item number 7.6 of Table 5.15.1. In this case, 122 respondents (31 per cent) recorded their level of opinion at 20 per cent and less. 106 respondents (27 per cent) recorded their level of opinion at 40 per cent. 96 respondents (24 per cent) marked their level of opinion at 50 per cent and 49 respondents (12 per cent) recorded a level of 60 per cent. Only 27 respondents (7 per cent) recorded a high level of 80 per cent and above. The mean recorded level of opinion noticed is 41 per cent with a standard deviation of 20 and a covariance of 49 per cent. The mean score is less than the combined mean of 55 per cent which means that the respondents are of the opinion that the treatment of political parties to women is not appreciable.

5. Reservation of Seats for Women in Election to Parliament

For giving political empowerment to women, in general, and Kerala, in particular, provision of reservation of seats for election to the parliament exists. The views of respondents on it are shown as item number 7.7 of Table 5.15.1.

Only 9 respondents (2 per cent) marked their level of opinion at 20 per cent and less. 13 respondents (3 per cent) marked their level of opinion at 40 per cent. 27 respondents (7 per cent) marked their level of opinion at 50 per cent and 83 respondents (21 per cent) recorded a level at 60 per cent. There are 198 respondents (50 per cent) recorded their level of opinion at 80 per cent. Also 70 respondents (18 per cent) marked a level at cent per cent. The mean recorded level of opinion noticed is 75 per cent with a standard deviation of 18 and a covariance of 24 per cent. The mean score is higher than the combined mean of 55 per cent which indicates that the respondents were very much satisfied with the pattern of reservation extended to parliament election.

6. Reservation of Seats for Women in Election to Legislative Assembly

For giving political empowerment to women, provision has been made of reservation of seats for election to the legislative assembly. The views of respondents on it are given as item number 7.8 of Table 5.15.1.

Only 20 respondents (5 per cent) marked their level of opinion at 20 per cent and less. 54 respondents (14 per cent) marked their level of opinion at 40 per cent. 91 respondents (23 per cent) marked their level of opinion at 50 per cent and 143 respondents (36 per cent) recorded a level of 60 per cent. There were 87 respondents (22 per cent) who recorded their level of opinion at 80 per cent. Only 5 respondents (1 per cent) marked a level of cent per cent. The mean recorded level of opinion noticed is 58 per cent with a standard deviation of 16 and a covariance of 28 per cent. The mean score is higher than the combined mean of 55 per cent which indicates that the respondents were very much satisfied with the pattern of reservation extended to legislative assembly.

7. Reservation of Seats for Women in Election to Local Government

The Eighth Plan period saw a revolutionary amendment to the Constitution of India, which provided for the reservation of one-third of the seats in Panchayati Raj institutions and urban local self-governing bodies such as, municipalities and corporations, for women. The 73rd and 74th Constitutional amendments, which made this reservation possible, are considered as a democratic revolution in the history of women's empowerment in India and Kerala. Only 1/3rd of the seats were reserved to women in local government at the initial phase of the introduction of the Peoples Plan Campaign during the IXth Plan and now 50 per cent of the seats are reserved for women in local bodies. The opinion of respondents on it is given as item number 7.9 of Table 5.15.1.

In this case, 88 respondents (22 per cent) marked their level of opinion at 20 per cent and less. 82 respondents (21 per cent) marked their level of opinion at 40 per cent. 99 respondents (25 per cent) marked their level of opinion at 50 per cent and 92 respondents (23 per cent) recorded a level of 60 per cent. Only 38 respondents (10 per cent) recorded their level of opinion at 80 per cent and none of them recorded a level of cent per cent. The mean recorded level of opinion noticed is 56 per cent with a standard deviation of 19 and a covariance of 42 per cent. The mean score is higher than the combined mean of 55 per cent which indicates that the respondents are very much satisfied with the pattern of reservation extended to local bodies in Kerala.

8. The Method of Participation of Women

There are various methods by which women participate in different activities for their development as well as development of the economy as a whole. The methods include participation through community based organisations, setting-up of micro enterprises through micro credit and finance operations, through Self Help Groups, Area Development Society, Neighbourhood Groups, and participation in governance of local bodies. The opinion of respondents on it is given as item number 7.10 of Table 5.15.1.

In this case, 24 respondents (6 per cent) marked their level of opinion at 20 per cent and less while 49 respondents (12 per cent) marked their level of opinion at 40 per cent. 98 respondents (25 per cent) marked their level of opinion at 50 per cent and 127 respondents (32 per cent) recorded a level of 60 per cent. 98 respondents (25 per cent) recorded their level of opinion at 80 per cent and only 4 respondents (1 per cent) marked their level at cent per cent. The mean recorded level of opinion noticed was 58 per cent with a standard deviation of 17 and a covariance of 30 per cent. The mean score is higher than the combined mean of 55 per cent which indicates that the respondents were very much satisfied with the method of participation for the attainment of political autonomy.

9. Nominations of Women to Corporations/Boards

Like that of reservation of seats for women in legislature, parliament and local bodies, there are nominations to statutory corporations and boards. The views of respondents regarding this are shown as item number 7.11 of Table 5.15.1.

Table 5.15. : Variable VII– Political Autonomy (Item Number 7.1 to 7.12)

Sl. No.	*Sub-Variables (Items)*	*Opinion Scores*								*Avg*	*SD*	*CV*
		0	*20*	*40*	*50*	*60*	*80*	*100*	*Total*			
1.	($V_{7.1}$) Participation in the capacity as voter in general elections	0 (0)	0 (0)	0 (0)	7 (2)	83 (21)	178 (45)	132 (33)	400 (100)	82	15	18
2.	($V_{7.2}$) Participation in the capacity as candidate in general elections	0 (0)	9 (2)	24 (6)	62 (16)	92 (23)	105 (26)	108 (27)	400 (100)	72	21	30
3.	($V_{7.3}$) Freedom to caste vote as per own decision	3 (1)	18 (5)	48 (12)	108 (27)	108 (27)	93 (23)	22 (6)	400 (100)	60	19	32
4.	($V_{7.4}$) Membership in political parties	10 (3)	100 (25)	113 (28)	97 (24)	54 (14)	22 (6)	4 (1)	400 (100)	42	18	44
5.	($V_{7.5}$) Membership in community organisations	4 (1)	108 (27)	92 (23)	63 (16)	60 (15)	61 (15)	12 (3)	400 (100)	47	23	48
6.	($V_{7.6}$) Approach of political parties towards women	19 (5)	103 (26)	106 (27)	96 (24)	49 (12)	18 (5)	9 (2)	400 (100)	41	20	49
7.	($V_{7.7}$) Reservation of seats for women in election to parliament	0 (0)	9 (2)	13 (3)	27 (7)	83 (21)	198 (50)	70 (18)	400 (100)	75	18	24

Sl. No.	*Sub-Variables (Items)*	*Opinion Scores*								*Avg*	*SD*	*CV*
		0	*20*	*40*	*50*	*60*	*80*	*100*	*Total*			
8.	($V_{7.8}$) Reservation of seats for women in election to Legislative Assembly	0 (0)	20 (5)	54 (14)	91 (23)	143 (36)	87 (22)	5 (1)	400 (100)	58	16	28
9.	($V_{7.9}$) Reservation of seats for women in election to Local Government	15 (4)	73 (18)	82 (21)	99 (25)	92 (23)	38 (10)	1 (0)	400 (100)	46	19	42
10.	($V_{7.10}$) The method of participation of women	4 (1)	20 (5)	49 (12)	98 (25)	127 (32)	98 (25)	4 (1)	400 (100)	58	17	30
11.	($V_{7.11}$) Nominations of women to Corporations/Boards	7 (2)	104 (26)	100 (25)	87 (22)	66 (17)	27 (7)	9 (2)	400 (100)	44	20	46
12.	($V_{7.12}$) Nominations or women to political party chief	26 (7)	140 (35)	120 (30)	52 (13)	33 (8)	19 (5)	10 (3)	400 (100)	37	21	58

Source: SPSS output of Primary Data.
Figures in brackets shows percentage to total.

In this case, 121 respondents (28 per cent) marked their level of opinion at 20 per cent and less. Whereas 100 respondents (25 per cent) marked their level of opinion at 40 per cent. 87 respondents (22 per cent) marked their level of opinion at 50 per cent and 66 respondents (17 per cent) recorded a level of 60 per cent. Only 27 respondents (7 per cent) recorded their level of opinion at 80 per cent and 9 respondents (2 per cent) marked their level at cent per cent. The mean recorded level of opinion noticed is 44 per cent with a standard deviation of 20 and a covariance of 46 per cent. The mean score is less than the combined mean of 55 per cent which indicates that the respondents were not satisfied with the method of participation for the attainment of political autonomy.

10. Nominations of Women as Chief of Party Politics

Sometimes women are nominated as chief of political parties. The views of respondents were collected and are presented as item number 7.12 of Table 5.15.1.

In this case, 166 respondents (42 per cent) marked their level of opinion at 20 per cent and less whereas 120 respondents (30 per cent) marked their level of opinion at 40 per cent. 52 respondents (13 per cent) marked their level of opinion at 50 per cent and 33 respondents (8 per cent) recorded a level of 60 per cent. 19 respondents (5 per cent) recorded their level of opinion at 80 per cent and only 10 respondents (3 per cent) marked their level at cent per cent. The mean recorded level of opinion noticed is 37 per cent with a standard deviation of 21 and a covariance of 58 per cent. The mean score is less than the combined mean of 55 per cent which indicates that the respondents were not satisfied with the nomination as chief of political parties for attainment of political autonomy.

VIII. Main Variable – Professional Autonomy in Knowledge and Information

Women's autonomy, though, is conditioned largely by gender stratification and hierarchy in the society; education also can enhance autonomy in several respects. For instance, education can lead to knowledge autonomy, because educated women have wider world view, a greater sense of alternative lifestyles, and a greater ability to question authority. Similarly, education can lead to decision-making autonomy since an educated women is more confident of her ability to make a decision or voice an opinion, and more likely to insist on participating in family discussions. Another dimension of autonomy is physical autonomy, since educated women have more contact with the outside world. Education also enhances women's economic autonomy by improving access to and control over economic resources. Degree of autonomy enjoyed by women in a society is perhaps the most effective measure of empowerment. Women's autonomy is likely to have significant impact on society by altering women's relative control over household resources, and by influencing their attitudes and abilities. This main variable is analysed with the help of ten (10) sub variables. They are:

1. Women's Participation in Gram Sabha

Gram sabha is the deciding body of every ward in a Panchayat. It is the meeting of the beneficiaries in each of the wards. That the participation of women in Gram sabha is more than that of men is a notable feature in Kerala. In many cases, they came as the families delegated them rather than on their own free will. Women mainly constitute the beneficiary groups and are normally concentrated in the subject groups like women welfare, sanitation or drinking water. This in turn creates a feeling that they are also a part of a public action. In the initial periods, all members actively participated in the Gram sabha for transacting business there but during the second phase onwards, there were dropout on account of the fact that they lost faith in it. The opinion of respondents was collected and is presented as item number 8.1 of Table 5.16.1.

In this case 98 respondents (24 per cent) marked their level of opinion at 20 per cent and less. Whereas 30 respondents (8 per cent) and 77 respondents (19 per cent) marked their level of opinion at 40 per cent and 50 per cent respectively. 134 respondents (34 per cent) marked their level of opinion at 60 per cent and 61 respondents (15 per cent) recorded a level of 80 per cent. None of them recorded a level of above 80 per cent. The mean recorded level of opinion noticed is 48 per cent with a standard deviation of 23 and a covariance of 48 per cent. The mean score was less than the combined mean of 51 per cent which indicates that the participation was not up to the mark.

2. Women's Participation in Community Organisations

There are different community organisations formed for protecting the interest and welfare of the women community in Kerala. Almost all of them are under the Kudumbasree, a mission undertaken by Government of Kerala for eradicating the poverty at its root.

Area development societies, CDS, Neighbourhood Groups and SHGs are the type of organisations operated for implementing various programmes of the Central and State Government. The views of respondents on it is shown as item number 8.2 of Table 5.16.1.

In this case, 129 respondents (32 per cent) marked their level of opinion at 20 per cent and less. Whereas 93 respondents (23 per cent) and 84 respondents (21 per cent) marked their level of opinion at 40 per cent and 50 per cent respectively. 57 respondents (14 per cent) marked their level of opinion at 60 per cent and 37 respondents (9 per cent) recorded a level at 80 per cent. None of them recorded a level of above 80 per cent. The mean score in this case is 41 per cent with a standard deviation of 21 and a covariance of 51 per cent. The mean score is less than the combined mean of 51 per cent which indicates that the participation in community organisation is not remarkably good.

3. Ability to Bring up Own Interests

Another important sub variable used for knowing the professional autonomy in knowledge and information is ability to bring up own interests. The views of respondents on it are shown as item number 8.3 of Table 5.16.1.

In this case 111 respondents (28 per cent) marked their level of opinion at 20 per cent and less. Whereas 96 respondents (24 per cent) and 74 respondents (19 per cent) marked their level of opinion at 40 per cent and 50 per cent respectively. 43 respondents (11 per cent) marked their level of opinion at 60 per cent and 54 respondents (14 per cent) recorded a level at 80 per cent. Only 22 respondents (6 per cent) marked a level at cent per cent. The mean score in this case is 47 per cent with a standard deviation of 23 and a covariance of 49 per cent. The mean score is less than the combined mean of 51 per cent which indicates that this variable is not a significant contributory factor to the main variable.

4. Ability to Bring up Consensus-building

Professional autonomy in knowledge and information is required for creating ability to bring up consensus-building. The opinion of respondents regarding this was enquired into and is presented as item number 8.4 of Table 5.16.1.

There were 12 respondents (4 per cent) who marked their level of opinion at 20 per cent and less. Whereas 43 respondents (11 per cent) and 72 respondents (18 per cent) marked their level of opinion at 40 per cent and 50 per cent respectively. 128 respondents (32 per cent) marked their level of opinion at 60 per cent and 121 respondents (30 per cent) recorded a level of 80 per cent. Only 24 respondents (6 per cent) marked a level of cent percent. The mean recorded level of opinion in this case is 63 per cent with a standard deviation of 19 and a covariance of 30 per cent. The mean score exceeds the combined mean of 51 per cent which indicates that professional autonomy in knowledge and information is needed for creating ability to bring up consensus-building.

5. Ability of Bargaining

For increasing the bargaining capacity of women, it requires sufficient information and knowledge. The professional autonomy in knowledge and information improves the bargaining capacity of women which in turn leads to better status and development. The views of respondents regarding this was enquired into and collected opinion levels are presented as item number 8.5 of Table 5.16.1.

Only 43 respondents (11 per cent) marked their level at zero per cent. 26 respondents (7 per cent) and 31 respondents (8 per cent) marked their level of opinion at 20 per cent and 40 per cent respectively. 74 respondents (19 per cent) marked their level of opinion at 50 per cent and 142 respondents (36 per cent) recorded a level of 60 per cent. 84 respondents (21 per cent) marked a level of 80 per cent and none of them recorded a level of cent per cent. The mean recorded level of opinion in this case is 52 per cent with a standard deviation of 24 and a covariance of 47 per cent. The mean score exceeds the combined mean of 51 per cent which indicates that professional autonomy in knowledge and information create the ability of bargaining.

6. Power of Women's Associations

There are various women's associations in Kerala for protecting and safeguarding the interests of women. They are Mahila Mandals, Kerala State Women's Development Corporation, Kerala Women's Commission, and so on. On account of the power and strength of the women's associations, their ability to control and prevent violence and crimes against women is possible on one hand and gain on status, development and empowerment of women in Kerala on the other. The opinion of respondents on it was enquired into and collected and is presented as item number 8.6 of Table 5.16.1.

Only 18 respondents (5 per cent) marked their level of opinion at 20 per cent and less. 43 respondents (11 per cent) marked their level of opinion at 40 per cent and 90 respondents (23 per cent) recorded a level of 50 per cent. 110 respondents (28 per cent) marked a level of 60 per cent and 122 respondents marked their opinion level at 80 per cent. Only 16 respondents (4 per cent) marked a very high level at 100 per cent. The mean recorded level of opinion in this case is 61 per cent with a standard deviation of 18 and a covariance of 30 per cent. The mean score exceeds the combined mean of 51 per cent which indicates that professional autonomy in knowledge and information is obtained through women's associations.

7. Women's Participation in Big Organisations

Women's participation is not extended to the state or country but it extends all over the world. Because of their participation at the world level, their freedom and power are so widened that it, in turn, lead to high status and empowerment. The views of respondents on it were collected and are tabulated as item number 8.7 of Table 5.16.1.

In this, 165 respondents (42 per cent) marked their level of opinion at 20 per cent and less. 88 respondents (22 per cent) marked their level of opinion at 40 per cent and 75 respondents (19 per cent) recorded a level of 50 per cent. 60 respondents (15 per cent) marked a level of 60 per cent. Only 12 respondents (3 per cent) marked their opinion level at 80 per cent and above. The mean recorded level of opinion in this case is 37 per cent with a standard deviation of 18 and a covariance of 49 per cent. The mean score is less than the combined mean of 51 per cent which indicates that the women's participation in big organisation is not satisfactory.

8. Women's Participation in Big Networks

Women's participation in big networks was also enquired into and opinions of respondents were obtained. The information so collected is presented as item number 8.8 of Table 5.16.1.

Only 25 respondents (6 per cent) marked their level of opinion at 20 per cent and less. 38 respondents (10 per cent) marked their level of opinion at 40 per cent and 101 respondents (25 per cent) recorded a level of 50 per cent. 126 respondents (32 per cent) marked a level of 60 per cent. Whereas 110 respondents (28 per cent) marked their opinion level at 80 per cent and none of them recorded a level of cent per cent. The mean recorded level of opinion in this case is 58 per cent with a standard deviation of 17 and a covariance of 30 per cent. The mean score exceed the combined mean of 51 per cent is a clear indication that women's participation in big networks is satisfactory.

9. Women's Membership in Women's Associations

For strengthening power of the weaker sections, associations or unions are organised. Its main purpose is to get power and strength through collective action. In avoiding the difficulties they face in their daily life and also for improving their status and empowerment, they become part of the women associations in Kerala. The information so collected is presented as item number 8.9 of Table 5.16.1.

None of the respondents recorded a level at zero and 127 respondents (32 per cent) marked their level of opinion at 20 per cent. 113 respondents (28 per cent) marked their level of opinion at 40 per cent and 36 respondents (9 per cent) recorded a level of 50 per cent. 17 respondents (4 per cent) marked a level at 60 per cent. Whereas 47 respondents (12 per cent) marked their opinion level at 80 per cent and 60 of them recorded a level of cent per cent. The mean recorded level of opinion in this case is 49 per cent with a standard deviation of 28 and a covariance of 58 per cent. The fact that mean score is less than the combined mean of 51 per cent is a clear indication that women's membership in associations is not a satisfactory one.

10. Women's Membership in Information Centres like Library

Women today are educated and aware about their own power, duties and responsibilities. They gain information through education at higher levels. So also, they gather information from the library and other knowledge centres. Their opinion on the extent of information and knowledge gathered by them through visiting these centres are tabulated and presented as item number 8.10 of Table 5.16.1.

In this case, 51 respondents (13 per cent) recorded a levels of 20 per cent and less. 71 respondents (18 per cent) marked their level of opinion at 40 per cent and 109 respondents (27 per cent) recorded a level of 50 per cent. 106 respondents (27 per cent) marked a level of 60 per cent. Whereas 57 respondents (14 per cent) marked their opinion level at 80 per cent. Only 6 respondents (2 per cent) recorded a level of cent per cent. The mean recorded level of opinion in this case is 51 per cent with a standard deviation of 20 and a covariance of 39 per cent. The mean score is equal to combined mean of 51 per cent is a clear indication that women's membership in information centres is a satisfactory one.

Table 5.16.1: Variable VIII – Professional Autonomy in Knowledge and Information (Item Number 8.1 to 8.10)

Sl. No.	*Sub-Variables (Items)*	*Opinion Scores*								*Mean*	*SD*	*CV*
		0	*20*	*40*	*50*	*60*	*80*	*100*	*Total*			
1.	($V_{8.1}$) Women's participation in Gram sabha	37 (9)	61 (15)	30 (8)	77 (19)	134 (34)	61 (15)	0 (0)	400 (100)	48	23	48
2.	($V_{8.2}$) Women's participation in Community organisations	28 (7)	101 (25)	93 (23)	84 (21)	57 (14)	37 (9)	0 (0)	400 (100)	41	21	51
3.	($V_{8.3}$) Ability to bring up own interests	2 (1)	109 (27)	96 (24)	74 (19)	43 (11)	54 (14)	22 (6)	400 (100)	47	23	49
4.	($V_{8.4}$) Ability to bring up consensus-building	6 (2)	6 (2)	43 (11)	72 (18)	128 (32)	121 (30)	24 (6)	400 (100)	63	19	30
5.	($V_{8.5}$) Ability of bargaining	43 (11)	26 (7)	31 (8)	74 (19)	142 (36)	84 (21)	0 (00	400 (100)	52	24	47
6.	($V_{8.6}$) Power of women's associations	2 (1)	17 (4)	43 (11)	90 (23)	110 (28)	122 (31)	16 (4)	400 (100)	61	18	30

Sl. No.	Sub-Variables (Items)	Opinion Scores								Mean	SD	CV
		0	20	40	50	60	80	100	Total			
7.	($V_{8.7}$) Women's participation in big organisations	10 (3)	155 (39)	88 (22)	75 (19)	60 (15)	9 (2)	3 (1)	400 (100)	37	18	49
8.	($V_{8.8}$) Women's participation in big network	5 (1)	20 (5)	38 (10)	101 (25)	126 (32)	110 (28)	0 (0)	400 (100)	58	17	30
9.	($V_{8.9}$) Women's membership in women's associations	0 (0)	127 (32)	113 (28)	36 (9)	17 (4)	47 (12)	60 (15)	400 (100)	49	28	58
10.	($V_{8.10}$) Women's membership in information centres like library	16 (4)	35 (9)	71 (18)	109 (27)	106 (27)	57 (14)	6 (2)	400 (100)	51	20	39

Source: SPSS output of Primary Data.
Figures in brackets shows percentage to total.

IX. Main Variable - Legal Status and Accessibility to Legislature

The much publicised Kerala Model of Development with the help of social statistics asserts that women in Kerala enjoy a higher status when compared to their counterparts in other parts of India. The matrilineal social structures and lack of organised social opposition to women's education and social and economic advancement contributed to women's progress. The indicators that contributed to higher status of Kerala women include: favourable sex ratio, higher age at marriage, higher medical attention, material quality of life index, infant mortality rate and number of children. In spite of all these factors established as positive and true, crimes against women in Kerala have been increasing at an alarming rate and this points towards the question of legal status of its women. Kerala is a place where rules and regulations are widely circulated through different media. Generally, it is regarded that people know about the laws affecting their life. It is important to note that in the Constitutional law of India and subsequent laws and legislations enacted by the State Governments, gender equality is given high priority. The main variable is analysed with eight (8) sub variables.

1. The Attitude of Legislative Forums Towards Women

The legislative forums in Kerala take measures for maintaining the effectiveness of law in force. The attitude of legislative forum towards women were examined and views of respondents on it were collected and these are tabulated as item number 9.1 of Table 5.17.1.

Only 24 respondents (6 per cent) marked their level of opinion at 20 per cent and less. 50 respondents (13 per cent) marked their level of opinion at 40 per cent and 112 respondents (28 per cent) recorded a level of 50 per cent. 82 respondents (21 per cent) marked a level of 60 per cent. Whereas 89 respondents (22 per cent) marked their opinion level at 80 per cent and 43 respondents recorded a level of cent per cent. The mean recorded level of opinion in this case is 61 per cent with a standard deviation of 21 and a covariance of 34 per cent. The mean score is higher than the combined mean of 46 per cent which shows that the attitude of legal forums towards women in Kerala is favourable.

2. Women's Awareness on Laws Concerned with Women and their Rights

The women in Kerala are well educated so that they are well aware of the laws concerning their rights which are necessary for maintaining their status. The women's legal awareness for keeping their rights was looked into and opinions have been collected and are presented as item number 9.2 of Table 5.17.1.

In this case, 62 respondents (16 per cent) marked their level of opinion at 20 per cent and less. 54 respondents (14 per cent) marked their level of opinion at 40 per cent and 117 respondents (29 per cent) recorded a level of 50 per cent. 106 respondents (27 per cent) marked a level of 60 per cent. Whereas 56 respondents (14 per cent) marked their opinion level at 80 per cent. Only 5 respondents (1 per cent) recorded a level of cent per cent. The mean recorded level of opinion in this case is 51 per cent with a standard deviation of 19 and a covariance of 19 per cent. The mean score is higher than the combined mean of 46 per cent which shows that the women in Kerala are legally aware about protecting of their rights.

3. Women's Awareness on their Rights

Awareness about their own rights is important precondition for knowing the status of women, in general, and Kerala, in particular. The opinion of respondents on it was collected and is presented as item number 9.3 of Table 5.17.1.

In this case, 71 respondents (18 per cent) marked their level of opinion at 20 per cent and less. 71 respondents (18 per cent) marked their level of opinion at 40 per cent and 88 respondents (22 per cent) recorded a level at 50 per cent. 95 respondents (24 per cent) marked a level of 60 per cent. Whereas 63 respondents (16 per cent) marked their opinion level at 80 per cent. Only 12 respondents (3 per cent) recorded a level of cent per cent. The mean recorded level of opinion in this case is 51 per cent with a standard deviation of 21 and a covariance of 42 per cent. The mean score is higher than the combined mean of 51 per cent which shows that the women in Kerala are aware about their rights.

4. The Decision on the Violation of Women's Rights

The violation of women's rights was also look into and opinion on it was collected. The collected opinion is tabulated as item number 9.4 of Table 5.17.1.

A large majority of the respondents in the sample recorded their level at 40 per cent and less. 186 respondents (47 per cent) marked their level of opinion at 20 per cent and less and 109 respondents (27 per cent) marked their level of opinion at 40 per cent. 75 respondents (19 per cent) recorded a level of 50 per cent. 28 respondents (7 per cent) marked a level at 60 per cent. Whereas only 2 respondents marked their opinion level at 80 per cent and above. The mean recorded level of opinion in this case is 31 per cent with a standard deviation of 18 and a covariance of 59 per cent. The mean score is higher than the combined mean of 46 per cent which shows that the there is no question of violation of a women's rights.

5. The Decision on the Violation of Atrocities against Women

Development literature often correlates higher levels of education with the incidence of violence against women. Female education can play critical role in reducing violence against women and enhancing their control over their own bodies. The opinion of respondents on it is presented as item number 9.5 of Table 5.17.1.

In this case, a large majority of the respondents marked their opinion level at 40 per cent and less. 137 respondents (35 per cent) marked their level of opinion at 20 per cent and less. 108 respondents (27 per cent) marked their level of opinion at 40 per cent. 101 respondents (25 per cent) recorded a level at 50 per cent and 49 respondents (12 per cent) marked a level of 60 per cent. Whereas only 5 respondents (1 per cent) marked their opinion level at 80 per cent and none of them recorded a level above 80 per cent. The mean recorded level of opinion in this case is 37 per cent with a standard deviation of 18 and a covariance of 49 per cent. The mean score is lower than the combined mean of 46 per cent which shows that this variable is not contributing much to the main variable.

6. Accessibility and Experience with the Police set-up

The police force in the State gives protection to women whenever there is a question of crime and violence against women as part of controlling the law and order situation. The accessibility of the police force and the experience with them for solving any issue relating to women that arises are examined and views of respondents are collected. The collected opinion is presented as item number 9.6 of Table 5.17.1.

In this case also, large majority of the respondents marked their opinion level at 40 per cent and less. 129 respondents (32 per cent) marked their level of opinion at 20 per cent and less. 106 respondents (27 per cent) marked their level of opinion at 40 per cent. 66 respondents (25 per cent) recorded a level of 50 per cent and 74 respondents (19 per cent) marked a level of 60 per cent. Whereas only 25 respondents (7 per cent) marked their opinion level at 80 per cent and above. The mean recorded level of opinion in this case is 40 per cent with a standard deviation of 22 and a covariance of 55 per cent. The mean score is lower than the combined mean of 46 per cent which shows that this variable is not contributing much to the main variable.

7. Accessibility and Experience with the Court of Law

The judiciary checks the effective working of the law in force. They look into whether the justice provided to women as per Constitution is available or not. The accessibility and experience with the court of law was enquired into and opinion collected is presented as item number 9.7 of Table 5.17.1.

In this case also, large majority of the respondents marked their opinion level at 40 per cent and less. 111 respondents (28 per cent) marked their level of opinion at 20 per cent and less. 82 respondents (21 per cent) marked their level of opinion at 40 per cent. 84 respondents (21 per cent) recorded a level of 50 per cent and 92 respondents (23 per cent) marked a level of 60 per cent. Whereas only 31 respondents (8 per cent) marked their opinion level at 80 per cent and above. The mean recorded level of opinion in this case is 43 per cent with a standard deviation of 21 and a covariance of 49 per cent. The mean score is lower than the combined mean of 46 per cent which shows that this variable is not contributing much to the main variable.

8. Accessibility and Experience with Women's Commission

In Kerala, Women's Commission was constituted in the year 1996 with a basic aim of improving the status of women and to enquire into unfair practices affecting women. All the activities and programmes of the Commission are intended to uplift their status and for empowering them. The opinion of respondents on it was collected and is presented as item number 9.8 of Table 5.17.1.

In this case, 68 respondents (18 per cent) marked their level of opinion at 20 per cent and less. 76 respondents (19 per cent) marked their level of opinion at 40 per cent and 94 respondents (24 per cent)

Table 5.17.1: IX – Main Variable – Legal Status and Accessibility to Legislature (Item Number 9.1 to 9.8)

Sl No	*Sub-Variables (Items)*	*Opinion Scores*								*Avg*	*SD*	*CV*
		0	*20*	*40*	*50*	*60*	*80*	*100*	*Total*			
1.	($V_{9.1}$)The attitude of legislative forums towards women	1 (0)	23 (6)	50 (13)	112 (28)	82 (21)	89 (22)	43 (11)	400 (100)	61	21	34
2.	($V_{9.2}$) Women's awareness on laws concerned with women and their rights	8 (2)	54 (14)	54 (14)	117 (29)	106 (27)	56 (14)	5 (1)	400 (100)	51	19	38
3.	($V_{9.3}$) Women's awareness on their rights	8 (2)	63 (16)	71 (18)	88 (22)	95 (24)	63 (16)	12 (3)	400 (100)	51	21	42
4.	($V_{9.4}$) The decisions on the violation of women's rights	56 (14)	130 (33)	109 (27)	75 (19)	28 (7)	1 (0)	1 (0)	400 (100)	31	18	59
5.	($V_{9.5}$) The decisions on the violation of atrocities against women	34 (9)	103 (26)	108 (27)	101 (25)	49 (12)	5 (1)	0 (0)	400 (100)	37	18	49
6.	($V_{9.6}$) Accessibility and experience with the police set-up	37 (9)	92 (23)	106 (27)	66 (17)	74 (19)	15 (4)	10 (3)	400 (100)	40	22	55
7.	($V_{9.7}$) Accessibility and experience with the court of law	30 (8)	81 (20)	82 (21)	84 (21)	92 (23)	28 (7)	3 (1)	400 (100)	43	21	49
8.	($V_{9.8}$) Accessibility and experience with the women's commission	10 (3)	58 (15)	76 (19)	94 (24)	106 (27)	31 (8)	25 (6)	400 (100)	51	22	43

Source: SPSS output of Primary Data.
Figures in brackets shows percentage to total.

recorded a level of 50 per cent. 106 respondents (27 per cent) marked a level of 60 per cent. Whereas 31 respondents (8 per cent) marked their opinion level at 80 per cent. Only 25 respondents (6 per cent) recorded a level of cent per cent. The mean recorded level of opinion in this case is 51 per cent with a standard deviation of 22 and a covariance of 43 per cent. The mean score is higher than the combined mean of 46 per cent which shows that the accessibility and experience with the Women' Commission in Kerala is high.

(d) Predictor Equation of the Women Empowerment

From the analysis on the main variables and sub-variables of the opinion levels recorded by the respondents, the present study proceed with by forming a predictor equation model for the Employment, Income, Entitlement and Empowerment of women in Kerala by considering eight independent and one dependent variable. Here, the extent of influence of independent variable on dependent variable in relation to the women empowerment are examined (Regression Analysis).

The itemwise analysis of the eight (8) independent variables on women empowerment gives a detailed item wise picture of the opinion of the respondents. The Multiple Regression Analysis with different combinations of independent variables with the dependent variables is used to frame a Predictive Model for women empowerment in Kerala.

The dependent variable is the women empowerment which is systematically expressed as **'V_{10}'** and independent variables are: Accessibility and Control over Private Properties (V_2), Accessibility and Control over Public Properties (V_3), Control Over Income and Employment (V_4), Control on the Decision on Own Body (V_5), Autonomy on Mobility (V_6), Autonomy over Politics (V_7), Professional Autonomy in Knowledge and Information (V_8) and Legal Status and Accessibility to Legislature (V_9) and Personal Profile (V_1) expressed as 'V_2', 'V_3', 'V_4', 'V_5', 'V_6', 'V_7', 'V_8', and 'V_9' respectively.

The different combinations of Independent Variables consisting of One (1) Independent Variable, Two (2) Independent Variables, Three (3) Independent Variables, Four (4) Independent Variables, Five (5) Independent Variables, Six (6) Independent Variables, Seven (7) Independent Variables and Eight (8) Independent Variables equations are framed.

All the Predictor Equations made on the basis of Combination Method i.e., nC_x Method. Where, n = Total number of Variables ; C = Combination, x = number of success (variables) in each combination.

In One variable Predictor Equation, there are Eight (8) Combination of Variables ($5C_1$ = 8); In Two Variable Predictor Equation there are Twenty Eight (28) combination of variables ($5C_2$=28); In Three Variable Predictor Equation there are Fifty Six (56) combination of Variables ($5C_3$=56); In Four Variable Predictor Equation there are Seventy (70) Combination of Variables ($5C_4$= 70); In Five Variable Predictor Equation there are Fifty Six (56) Combination of Predictor Equation.($5C_5$=56); In Six Variable Predictor Equation there are Twenty Eight (28) Combination of Predictor Equation.($5C_6$=28); In Seven Variable Predictor Equation there are Eight (8) Combination of Predictor Equation.($5C_7$=8); In Eight Variable Predictor Equation there is One (1) Combination of Predictor Equation.($5C_8$=1)

Altogether there are Two Hundred and Fifty Five (255) Combination of equations in eight (8) Predictor Equation groups and from each such group of variables, the best Fit Predictor Equation is selected.

The selection of the Best Fit Predictor equation is based on the combination of independent variables on the Dependent Variable (Women Empowerment). There can be many combinations as there are independent variables. Hence, there are eight (8) groups of combinations of variables each, and from each group, that combination with the highest Multiple Correlation (R) and Correlation Square (R^2) is selected. The general predictor equation based upon independent variable is given below:

$$V_{10} = \beta_0 + \beta_2 v_2 + \beta_3 v_3 + \beta_4 v_4 + \beta_5 v_5 + \beta_6 v_6 + \beta_7 v_7 + \beta_8 v_8 + \beta_9 v_9 + \varepsilon$$

Where, V_{10} = Women Empowerment (Dependent Variable); β_0 = Constant, $\beta_2 v_2$, $\beta_3 v_3$, $\beta_4 v_4$, $\beta_5 v_5$, $\beta_6 v_6$, $\beta_7 v_7$, $\beta_8 v_8$, $\beta_9 v_9$ are the respective variables; Beta Co efficient (β); and ε = Error of the Estimate

One Variable, Two Variable, Three Variable, Four Variable, Five Variable, Six Variable, Seven Variable, Eight Variable are explained below under each head:

1. One Variable Predictor Equation

In one variable predictor equation there are eight (8) combination of equations for each set. The Correlation (R) and Correlation square (R^2) of each such combination is stated in Table 5.18.1. All the correlation of the various equations is statistically significant when compared with table values.

Table 5.18.1: One Variable Predictor Equation

Sl. No.	*Variables*	*Predictor Equations*	*R*	*R^2*
1.	V_2	$\widehat{V_{10}} = 42.8 + 0.15V_2 + 2.80$	0.32	0.10
2.	V_3	$\widehat{V_{10}} = 32.8 + 0.35V_3 + 2.40$	0.58	0.34
3.	V_4	$\widehat{V_{10}} = 28.2 + 0.45V_4 + 2.11$	0.70	0.49
4.	V_5	$\widehat{V_{10}} = 40.1 + 0.23V_5 + 2.49$	0.53	0.28
5.	V_6	$\widehat{V_{10}} = 44.3 + 0.13V_6 + 2.82$	0.29	0.09
6.	V_7	$\widehat{V_{10}} = 36.4 + 0.26V_7 + 2.33$	0.61	0.38
7.	V_8	$\widehat{V_{10}} = 48.6 + 0.04V_8 + 2.93$	0.12	0.01
8.	V_9	$\widehat{V_{10}} = 42.0 + 0.19V_9 + 2.50$	0.49	0.24

Source: SPSS (Statistical Package for Social Sciences) Output of Analysis of Primary Data.

Table No. 5.18.1 reveals that the best fit one variable predictor independent variable is the control over Income and Employment (V_4), since it has the highest correlation of 0.70 and correlation square of 0.49 with the independent variable women empowerment (V_{10}) among all other combinations. The best fit equations with the independent variable superior relationship 'V_4' is:

$$\widehat{V_{10}} = \beta_0 + \beta_4 V_4 + \varepsilon$$

After the calculation of the constant, the Beta coefficient of the variable $\mathbf{X_3}$ and the standard error, the best fit one variable predictor equation is:

$$= \mathbf{28.2 + 0.45V_4 + 2.11}$$

2. Two Variable Predictor Equation

In the two variable predictor equation, there are twenty eight (28) combinations of independent variable with dependent variables. The Correlation(R) and Correlation square (R^2) each of such combinations is given in Table 5.18.2.

The Table 4.18.2 reveals that the best fit two variable predictor equation is the combination of the variable in connection with women empowerment is control over Income and Employment (V_4), and Autonomy over Politics (V_7) ; since it has the highest Correlation (0.82) and Correlation square (0.70) with the dependent variable Women Empowerment (V_{10}). Control over Income and Employment (V_4), and Autonomy over Politics (V_7), The best fit equation is:

$$= \beta_0 + \beta_4 V_4 + \beta_7 X_7 + \varepsilon$$

After the calculation of the constant, the beta coefficient of the variable V_4 and V_7, and the standard error, the best fit two variable predictor equation is:

$$= 22.0 + 0.37V4 + 0.19V7 + 1.70$$

Table 5.18.2: Two Variable Predictor Equations

Sl. No.	*Variables*	*Predictor Equations*	*R*	R^2
1.	V2, V3	$\widehat{V_{10}} = 25.4 + 0.15V2 + 0.35V3 + 2.22$	0.66	0.43
2.	V2, V4	$\widehat{V_{10}} = 21.0 + 0.14V2 + 0.45V4 + 1.92$	0.76	0.58
3.	V2, V5	$\widehat{V_{10}} = 31.8 + 0.16V2 + 0.23V5 + 2.30$	0.63	0.39
4.	V2, V6	$\widehat{V_{10}} = 39.7 + 0.12V2 + 0.09V6 + 2.19$	0.39	0.14
5.	V2, V7	$\widehat{V_{10}} = 30.0 + 0.13V2 + 0.25V7 + 2.19$	0.67	0.45
6.	V2, V8	$\widehat{V_{10}} = 41.0 + 0.15V2 + 0.04V8 + 2.78$	0.34	0.11
7.	V2, V9	$\widehat{V_{10}} = 33.3 + 0.16V2 + 0.19V9 + 2.36$	0.60	0.36
8.	V3, V4	$\widehat{V_{10}} = 22.8 + 0.20V3 + 0.35V4 + 1.92$	0.76	0.58
9.	V3, V5	$\widehat{V_{10}} = 24.9 + 0.32V3 + 0.20V5 + 1.95$	0.75	0.56
10.	V3, V6	$\widehat{V_{10}} = 25.0 + 0.36V3 + 0.14V6 + 2.19$	0.67	0.45
11.	V3, V7	$\widehat{V_{10}} = 25.1 + 0.27V3 + 0.21V7 + 1.93$	0.76	0.57
12.	V3, V8	$\widehat{V_{10}} = 30.0 + 0.35V3 + 0.05V8 + 2.35$	0.60	0.37
13.	V3, V9	$\widehat{V_{10}} = 28.6 + 0.30V3 + 0.15V9 + 2.13$	0.69	0.48
14.	V4, V5	$\widehat{V_{10}} = 25.9 + 0.37V4 + 0.13V5 + 1.94$	0.75	0.57
15.	V4, V6	$\widehat{V_{10}} = 22.9 + 0.44V4 + 0.11V6 + 1.97$	0.74	0.55
16.	V4, V7	$\widehat{V_{10}} = 22.0 + 0.37V4 + 0.19V7 + 1.70$	0.82	0.70
17.	V4, V8	$\widehat{V_{10}} = 26.8 + 0.45V4 + 0.03V8 + 2.10$	0.70	0.49
18.	V4, V9	$\widehat{V_{10}} = 26.1 + 0.39V4 + 0.11V9 + 1.95$	0.75	0.56
19.	V5, V6	$\widehat{V_{10}} = 34.0 + 0.23V5 + 0.12V6 + 2.35$	0.61	0.37

Sl. No.	*Variables*	*Predictor Equations*	*R*	*R^2*
20.	V5, V7	$\bar{V}_{10}$ = 31.3 + 0.17V5 + 0.21V7 + 2.05	0.72	0.52
21.	V5, V8	$\bar{V}_{10}$ = 37.8 + 0.23V5 + 0.04V8 + 2.47	0.55	0.30
22.	V5, V9	$\bar{V}_{10}$ = 37.4 + 0.17V5 + 0.12V9 + 2.35	0.60	0.36
23.	V6,V7	$\bar{V}_{10}$ = 31.1 + 0.11V6 + 0.25V7 + 2.20	0.67	0.44
24.	V6,V8	$\bar{V}_{10}$ = 41.9 + 0.13V6 + 0.04V8 + 2.79	0.32	0.10
25.	V6,V9	$\bar{V}_{10}$ = 34.3 + 0.15V6 + 0.20V9 + 2.37	0.60	0.35
26.	V7,V8	$\bar{V}_{10}$ = 34.3 + 0.27V7 + 0.04V8 + 2.30	0.63	0.39
27.	V7,V9	$\bar{V}_{10}$ = 31.9 + 0.22V7 + 0.14V9 + 2.07	0.71	0.51
28.	V8,V9	$\bar{V}_{10}$ = 39.5 + 0.05V8 + 0.19V9 + 2.53	0.51	0.26

Source: SPSS (Statistical Package for Social Sciences) Output Analysis of Primary Data.

1. Three Variable Predictor Equations

In three variable predictor equations there are fifty six (56) combinations of independent variables. The Correlation (R) and Correlation square (R^2) of each of such combinations is given in Table 5.18.3.

Table 5.18.3: Three Variable Predictor Equations

Sl. No.	*Variables*	*Predictor Equations*	*R*	*R^2*
1.	V2, V3, V4	$\bar{V}_{10}$ = 15.6 + 0.14V2 + 0.20V3 + 0.35V4 + 1.71	0.82	0.67
2.	V2, V3, V5	$\bar{V}_{10}$ = 17.0 + 0.15V2 + 0.31V3 + 0.21V5 + 1.70	0.82	0.67
3.	V2, V3, V6	$\bar{V}_{10}$ = 21.0 + 0.11V2 + 0.36V3 + 0.12V6 + 2.09	0.71	0.50
4.	V2, V3, V7	$\bar{V}_{10}$ = 18.7 + 0.13V2 + 0.27V3 + 0.20V7 + 1.76	0.80	0.65
5.	V2, V3, V8	$\bar{V}_{10}$ = 22.4 + 0.15V2 + 0.35V3 + 0.05V8 + 2.18	0.68	0.46
6.	V2, V3, V9	$\bar{V}_{10}$ = 20.4 + 0.16V2 + 0.29V3 + 0.15V9 + 1.89	0.77	0.60
7.	V2, V4, V5	$\bar{V}_{10}$ = 18.3 + 0.15V2 + 0.37V4 + 0.14V5 + 1.71	0.82	0.62
8.	V2, V4, V6	$\bar{V}_{10}$ = 18.5 + 0.12V2 + 0.44V4 + 0.03V6 + 1.85	0.78	0.61
9.	V_2, V_4, V_7	$\bar{V}_{10}$ = 15.7 + 0.13V_2 + 0.37V_4 + 0.18V_7 + 1.50	0.86	0.74
10.	V2, V4, V8	$\bar{V}_{10}$ = 19.7 + 0.14V2 + 0.44V4 + 0.03V8 + 1.91	0.76	0.58

Sl. No.	*Variables*	*Predictor Equations*	*R*	R^2
11.	V2, V4, V9	$\bar{V}_{10} = 18.3 + 0.15V2 + 0.38V4 + 0.12V9 + 1.71$	0.82	0.67
12.	V2, V5, V6	$\bar{V}_{10} = 28.9 + 0.13V2 + 0.23V5 + 0.09V6 + 2.22$	0.66	0.43
13.	V2, V5, V7	$\bar{V}_{10} = 24.3 + 0.14V2 + 0.17V5 + 0.20V7 + 1.86$	0.78	0.60
14.	V2, V5, V8	$\bar{V}_{10} = 29.7 + 0.16V2 + 0.23V5 + 0.04V8 + 2.27$	0.64	0.41
15.	V2, V5, V9	$\bar{V}_{10} = 28.7 + 0.16V2 + 0.17V5 + 0.13V9 + 2.13$	0.69	0.48
16.	V2, V6, V7	$\bar{V}_{10} = 27.4 + 0.10V2 + 0.09V6 + 0.25V7 + 2.12$	0.70	0.49
17.	V2, V6, V8	$\bar{V}_{10} = 37.5 + 0.12V2 + 0.10V6 + 0.04V8 + 2.71$	0.40	0.16
18.	V2, V6, V9	$\bar{V}_{10} = 29.3 + 0.13V2 + 0.11V6 + 0.20V9 + 2.25$	0.65	0.42
19.	V2, V7, V8	$\bar{V}_{10} = 28.1 + 0.13V2 + 0.25V7 + 0.04V8 + 2.16$	0.68	0.47
20.	V2, V7, V9	$\bar{V}_{10} = 24.7 + 0.14V2 + 0.21V7 + 0.15V9 + 1.88$	0.77	0.60
21.	V2, V8, V9	$\bar{V}_{10} = 31.0 + 0.61V2 + 0.04V8 + 0.20V9 + 2.33$	0.61	0.38
22.	V3, V4, V5	$\bar{V}_{10} = 19.8 + 0.22V3 + 0.26V4 + 0.14V5 + 1.69$	0.82	0.67
23.	V3, V4, V6	$\bar{V}_{10} = 16.3 + 0.22V3 + 0.34V4 + 0.13V6 + 1.72$	0.83	0.66
24.	V3, V4, V7	$\bar{V}_{10} = 18.1 + 0.16V3 + 0.29V4 + 0.17V7 + 1.54$	0.85	0.73
25.	V3, V4, V8	$\bar{V}_{10} = 20.0 + 0.21V3 + 0.35V4 + 0.04V8 + 1.89$	0.77	0.59
26.	V3, V4, V9	$\bar{V}_{10} = 21.2 + 0.19V3 + 0.30V4 + 0.10V9 + 1.77$	0.80	0.64
27.	V3, V5, V6	$\bar{V}_{10} = 17.4 + 0.33V3 + 0.20V5 + 0.14V6 + 1.70$	0.82	0.67
28.	V3, V5, V7	$\bar{V}_{10} = 20.6 + 0.26V3 + 0.16V5 + 0.17V7 + 1.62$	0.84	0.70
29.	V3, V5, V8	$\bar{V}_{10} = 21.6 + 0.33V3 + 0.20V5 + 0.06V8 + 1.88$	0.77	0.59
30.	V3, V5, V9	$\bar{V}_{10} = 24.2 + 0.30V3 + 0.16V5 + 0.08V9 + 1.87$	0.77	0.60
31.	V3, V6, V7	$\bar{V}_{10} = 18.5 + 0.29V3 + 0.13V6 + 0.20V7 + 1.73$	0.81	0.66
32.	V3, V6, V8	$\bar{V}_{10} = 21.1 + 0.37V3 + 0.15V6 + 0.06V8 + 2.12$	0.70	0.48
33.	V3, V6, V9	$\bar{V}_{10} = 19.8 + 0.31V3 + 0.16V6 + 0.16V9 + 1.84$	0.78	0.62
34.	V3, V7, V8	$\bar{V}_{10} = 22.1 + 0.28V3 + 0.21V7 + 0.05V8 + 1.88$	0.77	0.60
35.	V3, V7, V9	$\bar{V}_{10} = 22.7 + 0.24V3 + 0.19V7 + 0.12V9 + 1.73$	0.81	0.66

Sl. No.	*Variables*	*Predictor Equations*	*R*	R^2
36.	V3, V8, V9	$\bar{V}_{10} = 15.2 + 0.31V3 + 0.06V8 + 0.15V9 + 2.06$	0.72	0.51
37.	V4, V5, V6	$\bar{V}_{10} = 20.6 + 0.37V4 + 0.13V5 + 0.12V6 + 1.78$	0.80	0.64
38.	V4, V5, V7	$\bar{V}_{10} = 20.9 + 0.32V4 + 0.10V5 + 0.17V7 + 1.59$	0.84	0.71
39.	V4, V5, V8	$\bar{V}_{10} = 24.3 + 0.40V4 + 0.13V5 + 0.03V8 + 1.92$	0.76	0.59
40.	V4, V5, V9	$\bar{V}_{10} = 25.1 + 0.35V4 + 0.10V5 + 0.08V9 + 1.86$	0.78	0.60
41.	V4, V6, V7	$\bar{V}_{10} = 17.3 + 0.36V4 + 0.11V6 + 0.18V7 + 1.54$	0.85	0.73
42.	V4, V6, V8	$\bar{V}_{10} = 21.2 + 0.44V4 + 0.12V6 + 0.03V8 + 1.95$	0.75	0.57
43.	V4, V6, V9	$\bar{V}_{10} = 20.0 + 0.37V4 + 0.13V6 + 0.13V9 + 1.75$	0.81	0.65
44.	V4, V7, V8	$\bar{V}_{10} = 20.5 + 0.36V4 + 0.19V7 + 0.03V8 + 1.68$	0.82	0.68
45.	V4, V7, V9	$\bar{V}_{10} = 20.9 + 0.32V4 + 0.17V7 + 0.09V9 + 1.57$	0.85	0.72
46.	V4, V8, V9	$\bar{V}_{10} = 24.4 + 0.38V4 + 0.04V8 + 0.12V9 + 1.92$	0.76	0.58
47.	V5, V6, V7	$\bar{V}_{10} = 26.0 + 0.17V5 + 0.11V6 + 0.21V7 + 1.90$	0.76	0.58
48.	V5, V6, V8	$\bar{V}_{10} = 31.3 + 0.23V5 + 0.13V6 + 0.05V8 + 2.31$	0.62	0.39
49.	V5, V6, V9	$\bar{V}_{10} = 30.4 + 0.16V5 + 0.14V6 + 0.13V9 + 2.16$	0.68	0.46
50.	V5, V7, V8	$\bar{V}_{10} = 29.0 + 0.17V5 + 0.21V7 + 0.43V8 + 2.02$	0.73	0.53
51.	V5, V7, V9	$\bar{V}_{10} = 29.6 + 0.12V5 + 0.20V7 + 0.10V9 + 1.94$	0.75	0.57
52.	V5, V8, V9	$\bar{V}_{10} = 34.9 + 0.17V5 + 0.05V8 + 0.12V9 + 2.32$	0.62	0.38
53.	V6, V7, V8	$\bar{V}_{10} = 28.6 + 0.12V6 + 0.25V7 + 0.05V8 + 2.17$	0.68	0.42
54.	V6, V7, V9	$\bar{V}_{10} = 25.5 + 0.13V6 + 0.21V7 + 0.15V9 + 1.88$	0.77	0.59
55.	V6, V8, V9	$\bar{V}_{10} = 31.3 + 0.15V6 + 0.05V8 + 0.20V9 + 2.33$	0.62	0.38
56.	V7, V8, V9	$\bar{V}_{10} = 29.4 + 0.22V7 + 0.05V8 + 0.14V9 + 2.03$	0.73	0.53

Source: SPSS (Statistical Package for Social Sciences) Output Analysis of Primary Data.

Table 5.18.3 reveals that the best fit three variable predictor equation is the combination with the Accessibility and Control Over Private Property (V_2), Control Over Income and Employment (V_4) and Autonomy over Politics (V_7). Since it has the highest Correlation value of.0.86 and Correlation square of 0.74 with the dependent variable Women Empowerment ($\bar{\bar{V}}_{10}$). The best fit equation with the independent variable Accessibility and Control Over Private Property (V_2), Control Over Income and Employment (V_4) and Autonomy over Politics (V_7)

$$\bar{\bar{V}}_{10} = \beta_0 + \beta_2 V_{2+} \beta_4 V_4 + \beta_7 X_7 + \epsilon$$

After the calculation of constant, the beta co-efficient of variables V_2, V_4 and V_7 and the standard error, the best fit three variable predictor equation for the problems of managers is:

$$\bar{\bar{V}}_{10} = 15.7 + 0.13V_2 + 0.37V_4 + 0.18V_7 + 1.50$$

4. Four Variable Predictor Equations

In this variable Predictor Equation, there are seventy (70) combinations of independent variables. The Correlation (R) and Correlation Square (R^2) of each of such combination are given in Table 5.18.4.

Table 5.18.4: Four Variable Predictor Equations

Sl. No.	*Variables*	*Predictor Equations*	*R*	*R2*
1.	V2,V3,V4,V5	$\bar{\bar{V}}_{10}$ = 12.2 + 0.15V2 + 0.22V3 + 0.25V4 + 0.15V5 + 1.41	0.88	0.77
2.	V2,V3,V4,V6	$\bar{\bar{V}}_{10}$ = 12.3 + 0.11V2 + 0.22V3 + 0.34V4 + 0.10V6 + 1.59	0.84	0.71
3.	V2,V3,V4,V7	$\bar{\bar{V}}_{10}$ = 11.8 + 0.13V2 + 0.16V3 + 0.29V4 + 0.17V7 + 1.31	0.90	0.80
4.	V2,V3,V4,V8	$\bar{\bar{V}}_{10}$ = 13.7 + 0.14V2 + 0.21V3 + 0.34V4 + 0.04V8 + 1.68	0.82	0.68
5.	V2,V3,V4,V9	$\bar{\bar{V}}_{10}$ = 13.6 + 0.15V2 + 0.19V3 + 0.29V4 + 0.11V9 + 1.50	0.86	0.74
6.	V2,V3,V5,V6	$\bar{\bar{V}}_{10}$ = 13.0 + 0.12V2 + 0.33V3 + 0.20V5 + 0.11V6 + 1.55	0.85	0.73

Sl. No.	*Variables*	*Predictor Equations*	*R*	R^2
7.	V2,V3,V5,V7	$\bar{V}_{10} = 13.5 + 0.14V2 + 0.26V3 + 0.17V5 + 0.16V7 + 1.40$	0.89	0.79
8.	V2,V3,V5,V8	$\bar{V}_{10} = 13.9 + 0.15V2 + 0.32V3 + 0.21V5 + 0.05V8 + 1.63$	0.83	0.69
9.	V2,V3,V5,V9	$\bar{V}_{10} = 15.9 + 0.16V2 + 0.29V3 + 0.16V5 + 0.09V9 + 1.60$	0.84	0.71
10.	V2,V3,V6,V7	$\bar{V}_{10} = 15.0 + 0.10V2 + 0.29V3 + 0.10V6 + 0.20V7 + 1.63$	0.84	0.70
11.	V2,V3,V6,V8	$\bar{V}_{10} = 12.5 + 0.11V2 + 0.37V3 + 0.12V6 + 0.06V8 + 2.03$	0.73	0.53
12.	V2,V3,V6,V9	$\bar{V}_{10} = 15.5 + 0.12V2 + 0.30V3 + 0.13V6 + 0.16V9 + 1.71$	0.82	0.67
13.	V2,V3,V7,V8	$\bar{V}_{10} = 15.9 + 0.13V2 + 0.28V3 + 0.20V7 + 0.05V8 + 1.70$	0.81	0.67
14.	V2,V3,V7,V9	$\bar{V}_{10} = 15.6 + 0.14V2 + 0.24V3 + 0.18V7 + 0.12V9 + 1.50$	0.86	0.74
15.	V2,V3,V8,V9	$\bar{V}_{10} = 17.2 + 0.15V2 + 0.30V3 + 0.06V8 + 0.16V9 + 1.83$	0.79	0.62
16.	V2,V4,V5,V6	$\bar{V}_{10} = 15.9 + 0.12V2 + 0.36V4 + 0.14V5 + 0.08V6 + 1.62$	0.84	0.70
17.	V2,V4,V5,V7	$\bar{V}_{10} = 14.3 + 0.14V2 + 0.31V4 + 0.10V5 + 0.16V7 + 1.34$	0.89	0.79
18.	V2,V4,V5,V8	$\bar{V}_{10} = 16.9 + 0.15V2 + 0.36V4 + 0.14V5 + 0.03V8 + 1.69$	0.82	0.68
19.	V2,V4,V5,V9	$\bar{V}_{10} = 17.1 + 0.15V2 + 0.34V4 + 0.10V5 + 0.09V9 + 1.60$	0.84	0.71
20.	V2,V4,V6,V7	$\bar{V}_{10} = 13.4 + 0.11V2 + 0.36V4 + 0.08V6 + 0.18V7 + 1.41$	0.88	0.77
21.	V2,V4,V6,V8	$\bar{V}_{10} = 17.0 + 0.12V2 + 0.44V4 + 0.09V6 + 0.03V8 + 1.83$	0.79	0.62

Sl. No.	Variables	Predictor Equations	R	R^2
22.	V2,V4,V6,V9	$\bar{V}_{10}$ = 15.3 + 0.12V2 + 0.37V4 + 0.10V6 + 0.13V9 + 1.59	0.84	0.71
23.	V2,V4,V7,V8	$\bar{V}_{10}$ = 14.3 + 0.13V2 + 0.36V4 + 0.18V7 + 0.03V8 + 1.47	0.88	0.75
24.	V2,V4,V7,V9	$\bar{V}_{10}$ = 14.0 + 0.14V2 + 0.32V4 + 0.17V7 + 0.10V9 + 1.32	0.89	0.79
25.	V2,V4,V8,V9	$\bar{V}_{10}$ = 16.8 + 0.15V2 + 0.38V4 + 0.03V8 + 0.12V9 + 1.68	0.82	0.68
26.	V2,V5,V6,V7	$\bar{V}_{10}$ = 21.7 + 0.11V2 + 0.17V5 + 0.08V6 + 0.20V7 + 1.78	0.80	0.68
27.	V2,V5,V6,V8	$\bar{V}_{10}$ = 26.4 + 0.13V2 + 0.23V5 + 0.09V6 + 0.05V8 + 2.18	0.67	0.45
28.	V2,V5,V6,V9	$\bar{V}_{10}$ = 25.2 + 0.13V2 + 0.16V5 + 0.10V6 + 0.13V9 + 2.02	0.73	0.53
29.	V2,V5,V7,V8	$\bar{V}_{10}$ = 22.2 + 0.14V2 + 0.17V5 + 0.20V7 + 0.04V8 + 1.83	0.79	0.62
30.	V2,V5,V7,V9	$\bar{V}_{10}$ = 22.2 + 0.15V2 + 0.12V5 + 0.19V7 + 0.10V9 + 1.72	0.81	0.66
31.	V2,V5,V8,V9	$\bar{V}_{10}$ = 26.3 + 0.16V2 + 0.04V5 + 0.13V8 + 0.12V9 + 2.09	0.71	0.50
32.	V2,V6,V7,V8	$\bar{V}_{10}$ = 25.1 + 0.10V2 + 0.09V6 + 0.25V7 + 0.04V8 + 2.09	0.71	0.50
33.	V2,V6,V7,V9	$\bar{V}_{10}$ = 21.3 + 0.11V2 + 0.10V6 + 0.21V7 + 0.16V9 + 1.76	0.80	0.64
34.	V2,V6,V8,V9	$\bar{V}_{10}$ = 26.5 + 0.12V2 + 0.12V6 + 0.05V8 + 0.20V9 + 2.21	0.66	0.44
35.	V2,V7,V8,V9	$\bar{V}_{10}$ = 22.4 + 0.14V2 + 0.21V7 + 0.04V8 + 0.15V9 + 1.84	0.78	0.61
36.	V3,V4,V5,V6	$\bar{V}_{10}$ = 13.2 + 0.24V3 + 0.24V4 + 0.15V5 + 0.13V6 + 1.44	0.87	0.76

Sl. No.	*Variables*	*Predictor Equations*	*R*	*R^2*
37.	V3,V4,V5,V7	$\bar{V}_{10} = 16.5 + 0.18V3 + 0.23V4 + 0.11V5 + 0.15V7 + 1.38$	0.89	0.76
38.	V3,V4,V5,V8	$\bar{V}_{10} = 17.3 + 0.23V3 + 0.25V4 + 0.15V5 + 0.05V8 + 1.64$	0.83	0.69
39.	V3,V4,V5,V9	$\bar{V}_{10} = 19.5 + 0.21V3 + 0.25V4 + 0.12V5 + 0.07V9 + 1.63$	0.83	0.70
40.	V3,V4,V6,V7	$\bar{V}_{10} = 12.4 + 0.18V3 + 0.28V4 + 0.12V6 + 0.17V7 + 1.32$	0.89	0.79
41.	V3,V4,V6,V8	$\bar{V}_{10} = 13.6 + 0.23V3 + 0.33V4 + 0.13V6 + 0.05V8 + 1.67$	0.83	0.68
42.	V3,V4,V6,V9	$\bar{V}_{10} = 14.0 + 0.21V3 + 0.28V4 + 0.14V6 + 0.12V9 + 1.49$	0.86	0.75
43.	V3,V4,V7,V8	$\bar{V}_{10} = 16.0 + 0.17V3 + 0.29V4 + 0.17V7 + 0.04V8 + 1.50$	0.86	0.74
44.	V3,V4,V7,V9	$\bar{V}_{10} = 17.2 + 0.16V3 + 0.26V4 + 0.16V7 + 0.08V9 + 1.42$	0.88	0.77
45.	V3,V4,V8,V9	$\bar{V}_{10} = 18.8 + 0.20V3 + 0.29V4 + 0.05V8 + 0.11V9 + 1.72$	0.81	0.66
46.	V3,V5,V6,V7	$\bar{V}_{10} = 13.8 + 0.28V3 + 0.16V5 + 0.13V6 + 0.16V7 + 1.36$	0.89	0.79
47.	V3,V5,V6,V8	$\bar{V}_{10} = 13.4 + 0.34V3 + 0.20V5 + 0.15V6 + 0.06V8 + 1.60$	0.84	0.71
48.	V3,V5,V6,V9	$\bar{V}_{10} = 16.0 + 0.31V3 + 0.15V5 + 0.15V6 + 0.09V9 + 1.58$	0.85	0.72
49.	V3,V5,V7,V8	$\bar{V}_{10} = 17.4 + 0.27V3 + 0.16V5 + 0.17V7 + 0.05V8 + 1.55$	0.85	0.73
50.	V3,V5,V7,V9	$\bar{V}_{10} = 20.0 + 0.25V3 + 0.13V5 + 0.17V7 + 0.07V9 + 1.55$	0.85	0.72
51.	V3,V5,V8,V9	$\bar{V}_{10} = 20.7 + 0.30V3 + 0.16V5 + 0.06V8 + 0.08V9 + 1.80$	0.79	0.63

Sl. No.	*Variables*	*Predictor Equations*	*R*	R^2
52.	V3,V6,V7,V8	$\bar{V}_{10} = 14.8 + 0.30V3 + 0.13V6 + 0.20V7 + 0.06V8 + 1.65$	0.83	0.69
53.	V3,V6,V7,V9	$\bar{V}_{10} = 15.1 + 0.26V3 + 0.14V6 + 0.17V7 + 0.13V9 + 1.45$	0.87	0.76
54..	V3,V6,V8,V9	$\bar{V}_{10} = 15.6 + 0.32V3 + 0.16V6 + 0.07V8 + 0.16V9 + 1.75$	0.81	0.65
55.	V3,V7,V8,V9	$\bar{V}_{10} = 19.5 + 0.25V3 + 0.18V7 + 0.06V8 + 0.12V9 + 1.66$	0.83	0.64
56.	V4,V5,V6,V7	$\bar{V}_{10} = 16.1 + 0.31V4 + 0.10V5 + 0{,}11V6 + 0.17V7 + 1.41$	0.89	0.77
57.	V4,V5,V6,V8	$\bar{V}_{10} = 18.6 + 0.36V4 + 0.14V5 + 0.12V6 + 0.04V8 + 1.75$	0.81	0.65
58.	V4,V5,V6,V9	$\bar{V}_{10} = 19.1 + 0.34V4 + 0.09V5 + 0.13V6 + 0.10V9 + 1.67$	0.83	0.69
59.	V4,V5,V7,V8	$\bar{V}_{10} = 19.3 + 0.31V4 + 0.10V5 + 0.17V7 + 0.04V8 + 1.56$	0.85	0.72
60.	V4,V5,V7,V9	$\bar{V}_{10} = 20.4 + 0.30V4 + 0.07V5 + 0.17V7 + 0.07V9 + 1.52$	0.86	0.74
61.	V4,V5,V8,V9	$\bar{V}_{10} = 23.3 + 0.34V4 + 0.10V5 + 0.04V8 + 0.08V9 + 1.85$	0.78	0.62
62.	V4,V6,V7,V8	$\bar{V}_{10} = 15.4 + 0.36V4 + 0.11V6 + 0.19V7 + 0.04V8 + 1.51$	0.86	0.74
63.	V4,V6,V7,V9	$\bar{V}_{10} = 15.4 + 0.31V4 + 0.12V6 + 0.17V7 + 0.10V9 + 1.35$	0.89	0.79
64.	V4,V6,V8,V9	$\bar{V}_{10} = 17.8 + 0.37V4 + 0.13V6 + 0.04V8 + 0.13V9 + 1.71$	0.82	0.67
65.	V4,V7,V8,V9	$\bar{V}_{10} = 19.1 + 0.32V4 + 0.18V7 + 0.04V8 + 0.10V9 + 1.54$	0.85	0.73
66.	V5,V6,V7,V8	$\bar{V}_{10} = 23.3 + 0.17V5 + 0.12V6 + 0.21V7 + 0.05V8 + 1.86$	0.79	0.61

Sl. No.	*Variables*	*Predictor Equations*	*R*	*R²*
67.	V5,V6,V7,V9	$\bar{V}_{10}^{-} = 23.5 + 0.11V5 + 0.13V6 + 0.19V7 + 0.11V9 + 1.75$	0.81	0.65
68.	V5,V6,V8,V9	$\bar{V}_{10}^{-} = 27.3 + 0.16V5 + 0.14V6 + 0.05V8 + 0.14V9 + 2.11$	0.70	0.49
69.	V5,V7,V8,V9	$\bar{V}_{10}^{-} = 27.1 + 0.12V5 + 0.20V7 + 0.05V8 + 0.10V9 + 1.90$	0.77	0.59
70.	V6,V7,V8,V9	$\bar{V}_{10}^{-} = 22.5 + 0.13V6 + 0.21V7 + 0.05V8 + 0.16\ V9 + 1.83$	0.79	0.62

Source: SPSS (Statistical Package for Social Sciences) Output of Analysis of Primary Data.

The Table 4.18.4 reveals that the best fit four variable predictor equation is the combination of Accessibility and Control Over Private Property (V_2), Accessibility and Control Over Public Property (V_3), Control Over Income and Employment (V_4) and Autonomy over Politics (V_7), since it has the highest Correlation value of 0.90 and Correlation square of 0.80 with the dependent variable Women Empowerment ($\bar{V}_{10}^{-}$). The best fit equation with the independent variables Accessibility and Control Over Private Property (V_2), Accessibility and Control Over Public Property (V_3), Control Over Income and Employment (V_4) and Autonomy over Politics (V_7) is:

$$\overline{V_{10}}^{-} = B_0 + B_2V_2 + B_3V_3 + B_4V_4 + B_7V_7 + \varepsilon$$

After the calculation of constant, the beta coefficient of variables V_2,V_3,V_4, and V_7 and standard error, the best fit from variable predictor equation is:

$$= 11.8 + 0.13V_2 + 0.16V_3 + 0.29V_4 + 0.17V_7 + 1.31$$

5. Five Variable Predictor Equations

In this variable Predictor Equation, there are Fifty Six (56) combinations of Independent variables. The Correlation (R) and Correlation Square (R^2) of each such combination are given in Table 5.18.5

Table 5.18.5: Five Variable Predictor Equations

Sl. No.	*Variables*	*Predictor Equations*	*R*	R^2
1.	V2, V3, V4,V5,V6	$\bar{V}_{10}$ = 8.9 + 0.12V2 + 0.23V3 + 0.24V4 + 0.15V5 + 0.10V6 + 1.26	0.90	0.82
2.	V2, V3, V4,V5,V7	$\bar{V}_{10}$ = 9.7 + 0.14V_2 + 0.08V_3 + 0.22V_4 + 0.12V_5 + 0.14V_7 + 1.08	0.93	0.87
3.	V2, V3, V4,V5,V8	$\bar{V}_{10}$ = 9.9 + 0.15V2 + 0.23V3 + 0.24V4 + 0.15V5 + 0.04V8 + 1.36	0.89	0.79
4.	V2, V3, V4,V5,V9	$\bar{V}_{10}$ = 11.6 + 0.15V2 + 0.21V3 + 0.24V4 + 0.12V5 + 0.07V9 + 1.33	0.89	0.80
5.	V2, V3, V4,V6,V7	$\bar{V}_{10}$ = 8.7 + 0.10V2 + 0.18V3 + 0.28V4 + 0.09V6 + 0.16V7 + 1.19	0.92	0.84
6.	V2, V3, V4,V6,V8	$\bar{V}_{10}$ = 9.8 + 0.11V2 + 0.23V3 + 0.33V4 + 0.10V6 + 0.04V8 + 1.54	0.85	0.73
7.	V2, V3, V4,V6,V9	$\bar{V}_{10}$ = 10.0 + 0.12V2 + 0.20V3 + 0.28V4 + 0.11V6 + 0.12V9 + 1.33	0.89	0.80
8.	V2, V3, V4,V7,V8	$\bar{V}_{10}$ = 10.0 + 0.13V2 + 0.17V3 + 0.29V4 + 0.17V7 + 0.04V8 + 1.27	0.90	0.82
9.	V2, V3, V4,V7,V9	$\bar{V}_{10}$ = 10.4 + 0.14V2 + 0.16V3 + 0.25V4 + 0.15V7 + 0.09V9 + 1.13	0.92	0.85
10.	V2, V3, V4,V8,V9	$\bar{V}_{10}$ = 11.3 + 0.15V2 + 0.19V3 + 0.29V4 + 0.04V8 + 0.12V9 + 1.45	0.87	0.76
11.	V2, V3, V5,V6,V7	$\bar{V}_{10}$ = 9.9 + 0.11V2 + 0.28V3 + 0.16V5 + 0.10V6 + 0.15V7 + 1.20	0.91	0.84
12.	V2, V3, V5,V6,V8	$\bar{V}_{10}$ = 9.3 + 0.11V2 + 0.33V3 + 0.21V5 + 0.12V6 + 0.06V8 + 1.46	0.87	0.76
13.	V2, V3, V5,V6,V9	$\bar{V}_{10}$ = 11.5 + 0.12V2 + 0.30V3 + 0.57V5 + 0.12V6 + 0.10V9 + 1.41	0.88	0.77
14.	V2, V3, V5,V7,V8	$\bar{V}_{10}$ = 10.6 + 0.14V2 + 0.27V3 + 0.17V5 + 0.15V7 + 0.05V8 + 1.29	0.90	0.81
15.	V2, V3, V5,V7,V9	$\bar{V}_{10}$ = 12.7 + 0.15V2 + 0.25V3 + 0.13V5 + 0.15V7 + 0.08V9 + 1.27	0.90	0.82
16.	V2, V3, V5,V8,V9	$\bar{V}_{10}$ = 12.7 + 0.16V2 + 0.30V3 + 0.16V5 + 0.06V8 + 0.09V9 + 1.52	0.86	0.74

Sl. No.	*Variables*	*Predictor Equations*	*R*	R^2
17.	V2, V3, V6,V7,V8	$\bar{V}_{10} = 11.7 + 0.10V2 + 0.29V3 + 0.11V6 + 0.19V7 + 0.06V8 + 1.55$	0.85	0.73
18.	V2, V3, V6,V7,V9	$\bar{V}_{10} = 11.3 + 0.11V2 + 0.25V3 + 0.11V6 + 0.17V7 + 0.13V9 + 1.30$	0.90	0.81
19.	V2, V3, V6,V8,V9	$\bar{V}_{10} = 11.6 + 0.11V2 + 0.31V3 + 0.13V6 + 0.06V8 + 0.16V9 + 1.62$	0.84	0.70
20.	V2, V3, V7,V8,V9	$\bar{V}_{10} = 12.6 + 0.14V2 + 0.25V3 + 0.17V7 + 0.05V8 + 0.13V9 + 1.42$	0.88	0.77
21.	V2, V4, V5,V6,V7	$\bar{V}_{10} = 12.0 + 0.11V2 + 0.31V4 + 0.11V5 + 0.08V6 + 0.16V7 + 1.25$	0.91	0.82
22.	V2, V4, V5,V6,V8	$\bar{V}_{10} = 14.1 + 0.12V2 + 0.36V4 + 0.14V5 + 0.09V6 + 0.04V8 + 1.59$	0.84	0.71
23.	V2, V4, V5,V6,V9	$\bar{V}_{10} = 14.2 + 0.13V2 + 0.33V4 + 0.10V5 + 0.09V6 + 0.10V9 + 1.49$	0.86	0.75
24.	V2, V4, V5,V7,V8	$\bar{V}_{10} = 12.7 + 0.14V2 + 0.31V4 + 0.11V5 + 0.16V7 + 0.03V8 + 1.31$	0.90	0.80
25.	V2, V4, V5,V7,V9	$\bar{V}_{10} = 13.4 + 0.14V2 + 0.29V4 + 0.07V5 + 0.15V7 + 0.08V9 + 1.25$	0.91	0.82
26.	V2, V4, V5,V8,V9	$\bar{V}_{10} = 15.5 + 0.15V2 + 0.33V4 + 0.10V5 + 0.04V8 + 0.09V9 + 1.57$	0.85	0.72
27.	V2, V4, V6,V7,V8	$\bar{V}_{10} = 11.7 + 0.10V2 + 0.36V4 + 0.08V6 + 0.18V7 + 0.03V8 + 1.38$	0.85	0.78
28.	V2, V4, V6,V7,V9	$\bar{V}_{10} = 11.3 + 0.11V2 + 0.31V4 + 0.09V6 + 0.16V7 + 0.11V9 + 1.19$	0.92	0.84
29.	V2, V4, V6,V8,V9	$\bar{V}_{10} = 13.3 + 0.12V2 + 0.37V4 + 0.10V6 + 0.04V8 + 0.13V9 + 1.56$	0.85	0.72
30.	V2, V4, V7,V8,V9	$\bar{V}_{10} = 12.4 + 0.14V2 + 0.31V4 + 0.17V7 + 0.04V8 + 0.10V9 + 1.28$	0.90	0.81
31.	V2, V5, V6,V7,V8	$\bar{V}_{10} = 19.3 + 0.11V2 + 0.17V5 + 0.09V6 + 0.20V7 + 0.05V8 + 1.74$	0.81	0.66
32.	V2, V5, V6,V7,V9	$\bar{V}_{10} = 19.1 + 0.12V2 + 0.12V5 + 0.09V6 + 0.18V7 + 0.11V9 + 1.61$	0.84	0.70

Sl. No.	*Variables*	*Predictor Equations*	*R*	R^2
33.	V2, V5, V6,V8,V9	$\bar{V}_{10}$ = 22.4 + 0.13V2 + 0.16V5 + 0.11V6 + 0.05V8 + 0.14V9 + 1.98	0.74	0.55
34.	V2, V5, V7,V8,V9	$\bar{V}_{10}$ = 19.9 + 0.15V2 + 0.12V5 + 0.19V7 + 0.04V8 + 0.11V9 + 1.68	0.82	0.68
35.	V2, V6, V7,V8,V9	$\bar{V}_{10}$ = 18.6 + 0.11V2 + 0.10V6 + 0.21V7 + 0.05V8 + 0.16V9 + 1.71	0.82	0.67
36.	V3, V4, V5,V6,V7	$\bar{V}_{10}$ = 10.5 + 0.20V3 + 0.21V4 + 0.12V5 + 0.12V6 + 0.14V7 + 1.11	0.93	0.86
37.	V3, V4, V5,V6,V8	$\bar{V}_{10}$ = 10.1 + 0.25V3 + 0.23V4 + 0.15V5 + 0.13V6 + 0.05V8 + 1.36	0.89	0.79
38.	V3, V4, V5,V6,V9	$\bar{V}_{10}$ = 12.4 + 0.23V3 + 0.22V4 + 0.11V5 + 0.14V6 + 0.08V9 + 1.34	0.89	0.79
39.	V3, V4, V5,V7,V8	$\bar{V}_{10}$ = 14.0 + 0.19V3 + 0.22V4 + 0.12V5 + 0.15V7 + 0.05V8 + 1.32	0.90	0.80
40.	V3, V4, V5,V7,V9	$\bar{V}_{10}$ = 16.2 + 0.17V3 + 0.22V4 + 0.09V5 + 0.15V7 + 0.06V9 + 1.36	0.89	0.80
41.	V3, V4, V5,V8,V9	$\bar{V}_{10}$ = 16.9 + 0.22V3 + 0.23V4 + 0.12V5 + 0.05V8 + 0.07V9 + 1.58	0.85	0.72
42.	V3, V4, V6,V7,V8	$\bar{V}_{10}$ = 9.6 + 0.19V3 + 0.27V4 + 0.12V6 + 0.17V7 + 0.05V8 + 1.25	0.91	0.82
43.	V3, V4, V6,V7,V9	$\bar{V}_{10}$ = 10.8 + 0.18V3 + 0.24V4 + 0.13V6 + 0.15V7 + 0.10V9 + 1.12	0.93	0.86
44.	V3, V4, V6,V8,V9	$\bar{V}_{10}$ = 10.8 + 0.22V3 + 0.26V4 + 0.15V6 + 0.05V8 + 0.12V9 + 1.42	0.88	0.77
45.	V3, V4, V7,V8,V9	$\bar{V}_{10}$ = 14.8 + 0.16V3 + 0.25V4 + 0.16V7 + 0.04V8 + 0.09V9 + 1.36	0.89	0.79
46.	V3, V5, V6,V7,V8	$\bar{V}_{10}$ = 10.0 + 0.29V3 + 0.16V5 + 0.14V6 + 0.15V7 + 0.06V8 + 1.24	0.91	0.82
47.	V3, V5, V6,V7,V9	$\bar{V}_{10}$ = 12.8 + 0.26V3 + 0.12V5 + 0.14V6 + 0.15V7+ 0.08V9 + 1.24	0.91	0.82
48.	V3, V5, V6,V8,V9	$\bar{V}_{10}$ = 11.8 + 0.32V3 + 0.15V5 + 0.15V6 + 0.07V8 + 0.10V9 + 1.47	0.87	0.76

Sl. No.	*Variables*	*Predictor Equations*	*R*	R^2
49.	V3, V5, V7,V8,V9	$\bar{V}_{10} = 16.8 + 0.26V3 + 0.13V5 + 0.16V7 + 0.06V8 + 0.07V9 + 1.47$	0.87	0.75
50.	V3, V6, V7,V8,V9	$\bar{V}_{10} = 11.2 + 0.27V3 + 0.15V6 + 0.17V7 + 0.06V8 + 0.13V9 + 1.34$	0.89	0.80
51.	V4, V5, V6,V7,V8	$\bar{V}_{10} = 14.0 + 0.31V4 + 0.10V5 + 0.11V6 + 0.17V7 + 0.04V8 + 1.37$	0.89	0.79
52.	V4, V5, V6,V7,V9	$\bar{V}_{10} = 15.0 + 0.29V4 + 0.07V5 + 0.12V6 + 0.16V7 + 0.08V9 + 1.30$	0.90	0.81
53.	V4, V5, V6,V8,V9	$\bar{V}_{10} = 16.8 + 0.33V4 + 0.09V5 + 0.13V6 + 0.04V8 + 0.10V9 + 1.62$	0.84	0.70
54.	V4, V5, V7,V8,V9	$\bar{V}_{10} = 18.5 + 0.29V4 + 0.07V5 + 0.17V7 + 0.04V8 + 0.07V9 + 1.48$	0.87	0.75
55.	V4, V6, V7,V8,V9	$\bar{V}_{10} = 13.2 + 0.31V4 + 0.12V6 + 0.17V7 + 0.04V8 + 0.11V9 + 1.30$	0.90	0.81
56.	V5, V6, V7,V8,V9	$\bar{V}_{10} = 20.5 + 0.11V5 + 0.13V6 + 0.19V7 + 0.05V8 + 0.11V9 + 1.70$	0.82	0.67

Source: SPSS (Statistical Package for Social Sciences) Output of Analysis of Primary Data.

The Table 5.18.5 reveals that the best fit five variable predictor equation is the combination with Accessibility and Control Over Private Property (V_2), Accessibility Control Over Public Property (V_3), Control Over Income and Employment(V_4), Control on the Decision on Own Body (V_5) and Autonomy over Politics (V_7) since it has the highest Correlation value of 0.93 and Correlation square of 0.87 with the dependent variable Women Empowerment ($\bar{V}_{10}$).The best fit equation with the independent variables Accessibility and Control Over Private Property (V_2), Accessibility Control Over Public Property (V_3), Control Over Income and Employment(V_4), Control on the Decision on Own Body (V_5) and Autonomy over Politics (V_7) is:

$$\overline{V_{10}} = B_0 + B_2V_2 + B_3V_3 + B_4V_4 + B_5V_5 + B_7V_7 + \varepsilon$$

After the calculation of constant, the beta coefficient of variables V_2 V_3 V_4, V_5 and V_7

And the standard error, the best fit from variable predictor equation is:

$$= 9.7 + 0.14V_2 + 0.08V_3 + 0.22V_4 + 0.12V_5 + 0.14V_7 + 1.08$$

6. Six Variable Predictor Equations

In six variable Predictor Equations, there are twenty eight (28) combinations of independent variables. The Correlation (R) and Correlation Square (R^2) of each such combination are given in Table 5.18.6

Table 5.18.6: Six Variable Predictor Equations

Sl. No.	*Variables*	*Predictor Equations*	*R*	*R^2*
1.	V2,V3,V4,V5,V6,V7	$\bar{V}_{10} = 6.5 + 0.11V_2 + 0.20V_3 + 0.21V_4 + 0.12V_5 + 0.9V_6 + 0.14V_7 + 0.90$	0.95	0.91
2.	V2,V3,V4,V5,V6,V8	$\bar{V}_{10}$ = 6.9 + 0.11V2 + 0.25V3 + 0.23V4 + 0.15V5 + 0.10V6 + 0.05V8 + 1.18	0.92	0.84
3.	V2,V3,V4,V5,V6,V9	$\bar{V}_{10}$ = 7.9 + 0.11V2 + 0.22V3 + 0.22V4 + 0.12V5 + 0.11V6 + 0.08V9 + 1.14	0.92	0.85
4.	V2,V3,V4,V5,V7,V8	$\bar{V}_{10}$ = 7.4 + 0.14V2 + 0.19V3 + 0.21V4 + 0.12V5 + 0.14V7 + 0.04V8 + 1.01	0.94	0.88
5.	V2,V3,V4,V5,V7,V9	$\bar{V}_{10}$ = 9.2 + 0.14V2 + 0.17V3 + 0.21V4 + 0.09V5 + 0.14V7 + 0.06V9 + 1.00	0.94	0.89
6.	V2,V3,V4,V5,V8,V9	$\bar{V}_{10}$ = 9.2 + 0.15V2 + 0.21V3 + 0.23V4 + 0.12V5 + 0.05V8 + 0.07V9 + 1.27	0.90	0.82
7.	V2,V3,V4,V6,V7,V8	$\bar{V}_{10}$ = 6.4 + 0.11V2 + 0.29V3 + 0.17V4 + 0.11V6 + 0.15V7 + 0.06V8 + 1.09	0.93	0.87
8.	V2,V3,V4,V6,V7,V9	$\bar{V}_{10}$ = 8.8 + 0.11V2 + 0.26V3 + 0.13V4 + 0.11V6 + 0.14V7 + 0.08V9 + 1.06	0.93	0.87
9.	V2,V3,V4,V6,V8,V9	$\bar{V}_{10}$ = 7.6 + 0.12V2 + 0.31V3 + 0.16V4 + 0.12V6 + 0.06V8 + 0.10V9 + 1.30	0.90	0.81

Sl. No.	*Variables*	*Predictor Equations*	*R*	R^2
10.	V2,V3,V4,V7,V8,V9	$\widehat{V_{10}} = 8.1 + 0.14V2 + 0.16V3 + 0.24V4 + 0.15V7 + 0.04V8 + 0.10V9 + 1.10$	0.93	0.87
11.	V2,V3,V5,V6,V7,V8	$\widehat{V_{10}} = 6.4 + 0.11V2 + 0.29V3 + 0.17V5 + 0.11V6 + 0.15V7 + 0.06V8 + 1.10$	0.93	0.87
12.	V2,V3,V5,V6,V7,V9	$\widehat{V_{10}} = 8.7 + 0.11V2 + 0.26V3 + 0.13V5 + 0.11V6 + 0.14V7 + 0.08V9 + 1.10$	0.93	0.87
13.	V2,V3,V5,V6,V8,V9	$\widehat{V_{10}} = 7.6 + 0.12V2 + 0.31V3 + 0.16V5 + 0.12V6 + 0.06V8 + 0.10V9 + 1.30$	0.90	0.81
14.	V2,V3,V5,V7,V8,V9	$\widehat{V_{10}} = 9.7 + 0.14V2 + 0.25V3 + 0.13V5 + 0.15V7 + 0.05V8 + 0.08V9 + 1.18$	0.92	0.84
15.	V2,V3,V6,V7,V8,V9	$\widehat{V_{10}} = 7.7 + 0.10V2 + 0.26V3 + 0.12V6 + 0.17V7 + 0.06V8 + 0.13V9 + 1.19$	0.92	0.84
16.	V2,V4,V5,V6,V7,V8	$\widehat{V_{10}} = 10.1 + 0.11V2 + 0.31V4 + 0.11V5 + 0.08V6 + 0.16V7 + 0.04V8 + 1.20$	0.91	0.84
17.	V2,V4,V5,V6,V7,V9	$\widehat{V_{10}} = 10.8 + 0.11V2 + 0.28V4 + 0.07V5 + 0.08V6 + 0.15V7 + 0.08V9 + 1.11$	0.93	0.86
18.	V2,V4,V5,V6,V8,V9	$\widehat{V_{10}} = 12.2 + 0.12V2 + 0.33V4 + 0.10V5 + 0.10V6 + 0.04V8 + 0.10V9 + 1.45$	0.87	0.76
19.	V2,V4,V5,V7,V8,V9	$\widehat{V_{10}} = 11.7 + 0.14V2 + 0.28V4 + 0.08V5 + 0.16V7 + 0.04V8 + 0.08V9 + 1.21$	0.91	0.84
20.	V2,V4,V6,V7,V8,V9	$\widehat{V_{10}} = 9.3 + 0.11V2 + 0.31V4 + 0.09V6 + 0.16V7 + 0.04V8 + 0.11V9 + 1.13$	0.92	0.85
21.	V2,V5,V6,V7,V8,V9	$\widehat{V_{10}} = 16.4 + 0.11V2 + 0.12V5 + 0.10V6 + 0.18V7 + 0.05V8 + 0.12V9 + 1.55$	0.85	0.73
22.	V3,V4,V5,V6,V7,V8	$\widehat{V_{10}} = 7.4 + 0.22V3 + 0.20V4 + 0.12V5 + 0.13V6 + 0.14V7 + 0.05V8 + 1.01$	0.94	0.89

Sl. No.	*Variables*	*Predictor Equations*	*R*	*R^2*
23.	V3,V4,V5,V6,V7,V9	$\bar{V}_{10}$ = 9.8 + 0.19V3 + 0.20V4 + 0.09V5 + 0.13V6 + 0.14V7 + 0.07V9 + 1.00	0.94	0.89
24.	V3,V4,V5,V6,V8,V9	$\bar{V}_{10}$ = 9.0 + 0.24V3 + 0.21V4 + 0.12V5 + 0.14V6 + 0.06V8 + 0.08V9 + 1.25	0.91	0.82
25.	V3,V4,V5,V7,V8,V9	$\bar{V}_{10}$ =13.7 + 0.18V3 + 0.21V4 + 0.09V5 + 0.15V7 + 0.05V8 + 0.06V9 + 1.26	0.91	0.82
26.	V3,V4,V6,V7,V8,V9	$\bar{V}_{10}$ = 7.7 + 0.19V3 + 0.22V4 + 0.13V6 + 0.15V7 + 0.05V8 + 0.10V9 + 1.02	0.94	0.88
27.	V3,V5,V6,V7,V8,V9	$\bar{V}_{10}$ = 8.8 + 0.27V3 + 0.12V5 + 0.14V6 + 0.15V7 + 0.06V8 + 0.08V9 + 1.11	0.93	0.86
28.	V4,V5,V6,V7,V8,V9	$\bar{V}_{10}$ =12.7 + 0.28V4 + 0.07V5 + 0.12V6 + 0.26V7 + 0.04V8 + 0.08V9 + 1.24	0.91	0.83

Source: SPSS (Statistical Package for Social Sciences) Output of Analysis of Primary Data.

The Table 5.18.6 reveals that the best fit four variable predictor equation is the combination with Accessibility and Control Over Private Property (V_2), Accessibility Control Over Public Property (V_3), Control Over Income and Employment(V_4), Control on the Decision on Own Body (V_5), Autonomy on Mobility (V_6), and Autonomy Over Politics (V_7). Since it has the highest correlation value of 0.95 and correlation square of 0.91 with the dependent variable, Women Empowerment ($\bar{V}_{10}$) is: $= \beta_0 + \beta_2 V_{2+} \beta_3 V_3 + \beta_4 V_4 + \beta_5 V_5 + \beta_6 V_6 \beta_7 V_7 + \varepsilon$

After the calculation of constant, the beta coefficient of variables (V_2), (V_3) (V_4) (V_5) (V_6), and (V_7) and the standard error, the best fit from variable predictor equation is:

$$= 6.5 + 0.11V_2 + 0.20V_3 + 0.21V_4 + 0.12V_5 + 0.9V_6 + 0.14V_7 + 0.90$$

6. Seven Variable Predictor Equations

In seven variable Predictor Equations, there are eight (8) combinations of independent variables. The Correlation (R) and Correlation Square (R^2) of each such combination are given in Table 5.18.7

Table 5.18.7: Seven Variable Predictor Equations

Sl. No.	*Variables*	*Predictor Equations*	*R*	R^2
1.	V2,V3,V4,V5,V6, V7,V8	$\widehat{V_{10}}$ = 3.8 + 0.11V2 + 0.21V3 + 0.20V4 + 0.12V5 + 0.10V6 + 0.14V7 + 0.05V8 + 0.79	0.96	0.93
2.	V2,V3,V4,V5,V6,V7, V9	$\widehat{V_{10}}$ = 5.8 + 0.11V2 + 0.19V3 + 0.20V4 + 0.09V5 + 0.10V6 + 0.13V7 + 0.07V9 + 0.76	0.97	0.93
3.	V2,V3,V4,V5,V6,V8, V9	$\widehat{V_{10}}$ = 4.9 + 0.12V2 + 0.23V3 + 0.21V4 + 0.12V5 + 0.11V6 + 0.05V8 + 0.08V9 + 1.04	0.94	0.88
4.	V2,V3,V4,V5,V7,V8, V9	$\widehat{V_{10}}$ = 6.8 + 0.14V2 + 0.18V3 + 0.20V4 + 0.10V5 + 0.14V7 + 0.05V8 + 0.07V9 + 0.91	0.95	0.91
5.	V2,V3,V4,V6,V7,V8, V9	$\widehat{V_{10}}$ = 4.1 + 0.10V2 + 0.18V3 + 0.23V4 + 0.11V6 + 0.15V7 + 0.05V8 + 0.10V9 + 0.82	0.96	0.93
6.	V2,V3,V5,V6,V7,V8, V9	$\widehat{V_{10}}$ = 5.1 + 0.11V2 + 0.27V3 + 0.13V5 + 0.12V6 + 0.14V7 + 0.06V8 + 0.09V9 + 0.91	0.95	0.91
7.	V2,V4,V5,V6,V7,V8, V9	$\widehat{V_{10}}$ = 8.7 + 0.11V2 + 0.28V4 + 0.07V5 + 0.09V6 + 0.15V7 + 0.04V8 + 0.09V9 + 1.05	0.94	0.87
8.	V3,V4,V5,V6,V7,V8, V9	$\widehat{V_{10}}$ = 6.6 + 0.21V3 + 0.18V4 + 0.09V5 + 0.13V6 + 0.14V7 + 0.05V8 + 0.07V9 + 0.88	0.96	0.91

Source: SPSS (Statistical Package for Social Sciences) Output of Analysis of Primary Data.

The Table 5.18.7 reveals that the best fit seven variable predictor equation is the combination with Accessibility and Control Over Private Property (V_2), Accessibility Control Over Public Property (V_3), Control Over Income and Employment(V_4), Control on the Decision on Own Body (V_5), Autonomy on Mobility (V_6), Autonomy Over Politics (V_7) and Legal Status and Accessibility to Legislature (V_9) since it has the highest Correlation value of 0.97 and Correlation square of 0.93 with the dependent variable Women Empowerment ($\bar{V_{10}}$). The best fit equation with the independent variables, Accessibility and Control Over Private Property (V_2), Accessibility Control Over Public Property (V_3), Control over Income and Employment(V_4), Control on the Decision on Own Body (V_5), Autonomy on Mobility (V_6,), Autonomy Over Politics (V_7) and Legal Status and Accessibility to Legislature (V_9) is:

$$\overline{V_{10}}^{-} = B_0 + B_2V_2 + B_3V_3 + B_4V_4 + B_5V_5 + B_7V_7 + B_9V_9 + \varepsilon$$

After the calculation of constant, the beta coefficient of (V_2), (V_3), (V_4), (V_5), (V_6), (V_7) and (V_9) And the standard error, the best fit from variable predictor equation is:

$$= 5.8 + 0.11V_2 + 0.19V_3 + 0.20V_4 + 0.09V_5 + 0.10V_6 + 0.13V_7 + 0.07V_9 + 0.76$$

8. Eight Variable Predictor Equations

Table 5.18.8 Eight Variable Predictor Equations

Sl. No.	*Variables*	*Predictor Equations*	*R*	*R^2*
1.	V2,V3, V4,V5,V6,V7, V8, V9	$\bar{V_{10}}$ = 2.9+ 0.11V2+ 0.20V3 + 0.18V4 + 0.09V5+0.11V6 + 0.13V7 + 0.05V8 + 0.08V9 + 0.61	0.98	0.96

Source: SPSS (Statistical Package for Social Sciences) Output of Analysis of Primary Data.

In Table 5.18.8, regression equation is formed with the Independent Variables Accessibility and Control Over Private Property (V_2), Accessibility Control Over Public Property (V_3), Control Over Income and Employment (V_4), Control on the Decision on Own Body (V_5), Autonomy on Mobility (V_6), Autonomy Over Politics (V_7), Professional

Autonomy in Knowledge and Information (V_8) and Legal Status and Accessibility to Legislature (V_9) The multiple correlation (R) with a correlation square (R^2) between all independent variable and dependent variable is 0.98 and 0.96. The best fit equation for the five independent variables (V_2),(V_3),(V_4),(V_5),(V_6), (V_7), (V_8)and (V_9)is:

$$\overline{V_{10}}^{-} = B_0 + B_2V_2 + B_3V_3 + B_4V_4 + B_5V_5 + B_7V_7 + B_8V_8 + B_9V_9 + \varepsilon$$

After the calculation of the constant, beta coefficient of the (V_2),(V_3),(V_4),(V_5),(V_6), (V_7), (V_8)and (V_9) and the standard error, the best fit five variable predictor equation is:

$$\bar{V}_{10} = 2.9 + 0.11V_2 + 0.20V_3 + 0.18V_4 + 0.09V_5 + 0.11V_6 + 0.13V7 + 0.05V_8 + 0.08V_9 + 0.61$$

The selected Eight Predictor Equation is shown in Table 5.18.9

Table 5.18.9: Multiple Regression Model of Women Empowerment

Sl. No.	*Variables*	*Predictor Equations*	*R*	*R^2*
1.	V4	$\bar{V}_{10}$ = 28.2 + 0.45V4 + 2.11	0.70	0.49
2.	V4, V7	$\bar{V}_{10}$ = 22.0 + 0.37V4 + 0.19V7 + 1.70	0.82	0.70
3.	V2, V4, V7	$\bar{V}_{10}$ = 15.7 + 0.13V2 + 0.37V4 + 0.18V7 + 1.50	0.86	0.74
4.	V2,V3,V4,V7	$\bar{V}_{10}$ = 11.8 + 0.13V2 + 0.16V3 + 0.29V4 + 0.17V7 + 1.31	0.90	0.80
5.	V2,V3,V4,V5,V7	$\bar{V}_{10}$ = 9.7 + 0.14V2 + 0.08V3 + 0.22V4 + 0.12V5 + 0.14V7 + 1.08	0.93	0.87
6.	V2,V3,V4,V5,V6,V7	$\bar{V}_{10}$ = 6.5 + 0.11V2 + 0.20V3 + 0.21V4 + 0.12V5 + 0.9V6 + 0.14V7 + 0.90	0.95	0.91
7.	V2,V3,V4,V5,V6,V7,V9	$\bar{V}_{10}$ = 5.8 + 0.11V2 + 0.19V3 + 0.20V4 + 0.09V5 + 0.10V6 + 0.13V7 + 0.07V9 + 0.76	0.97	0.93
8.	V2,V3,V4,V5,V6,V7,V8,V9	$\bar{V}_{10}$ = 2.9+0.11V2 + 0.20V3+0.18V4 +0.09V5 +0.11V6+ 0.13V7+ 0.05V8 + 0.08V9 + 0.61	0.98	0.96

Source: SPSS (Statistical Package for Social Sciences) Output of Analysis of Primary Data.

To sum up, Accessibility and Control Over Private Property (V_2), Accessibility Control Over Public Property (V_3), Control Over Income and Employment(V_4), Control on the Decision on Own Body (V_5), Autonomy on Mobility (V_6), Autonomy Over Politics (V_7), Professional Autonomy in Knowledge and Information (V_8) and Legal Status and Accessibility to Legislature (V_9) are the main variable contributing to Women Empowerment in Kerala which is seen from the selected activities undertaken by women in Thiruvnanthapuram District. The mean score, standard deviation and co-efficient of variation is ascertained based on their opinion at different levels to know the significance of the variables. It is made clear that all these variables are significant. The existence of these variables is analysed and compared with the help of individual mean score of opinion level with that of combined mean of all the sub variables that falls under eight heads. It is seen significant in the sense that the mean score exceeds the combined mean.

The regression analysis is made to know the relationship of the independent variables such as Accessibility and Control Over Private Property, Accessibility Control Over Public Property, Control Over Income and Employment, Control on the Decision on Own Body, Autonomy on Mobility, Autonomy Over Politics, Professional Autonomy in Knowledge and Information and Legal Status and Accessibility to Legislature with the dependent variable Women Empowerment. It is analysed through One variable, Two variable, Three variable, Four variable, Five variable, Six variable, Seven variable and Eight variable predictor equations (Regression Model). It is seen proved from the regression model that the major factors such as Control over Income and Employment, Autonomy over Politics, Accessibility and Control over Public Property and Accessibility and Control over Private Properties are very significant in assessing the Women Empowerment and their status and development compared to others.

The testing of the Hypothesis are made in Chapter-6.

6

Empowerment Disparities a Cross Section Analysis

This chapter contain the testing of hypotheses relating to empowerment disparities across different groups. The total sample of 400 respondents was drawn from 2 groups viz., Urban and Rural areas of 264 urban respondents consisting of 50 Government Organisations, 80 Non-government Organisations and 134 Un organised sectors and 136 rural respondents consisting of 20 Government Organisations, 50 Non-government Organisations and 66 Unorganised sectors. The composition of respondents in each group is shown in Table 6.1.

Table 6.1: Composition of Respondents

Sl. No.	*Location*	*Number of Respondents*			
		Government Organisation	*Non-government Organisation*	*Unorganised Sector*	*Total*
1.	Urban	50	80	134	**264**
2.	Rural	20	50	66	**136**
	Total	**70**	**130**	**200**	**400**

Source: SPSS output on analysis of Primary Data.

One of the major areas of the study was to undertake certain statistical test on seven (7) postulations put forth by the researcher on the relationships of component variables of women empowerment among different groups. These hypotheses were subjected to appropriate statistical tests and inferences have been made accordingly. The tested hypotheses are the following:

H_1: There is no significant difference in women empowerment as to income, employment and entitlement among women in different locations viz., urban and rural areas.

H_2: There is no significant difference in women empowerment as to income, employment and entitlement among women in different organisational setup viz., Government, Non-government and Unorganised sectors.

H_3: There is no significant difference in women empowerment as to income, employment and entitlement among women in different job status viz., Gazetted and Non-gazetted officials.

H_4: There is no significant difference in women empowerment as to income, employment and entitlement among women in different levels of educational attainment viz., Below Primary, Primary – SSLC, SSLC – Degree and Above Degree.

H_5: There is no significant difference in women empowerment as to income, employment and entitlement among women in different religions viz., Hindu, Muslim, Christian and Others.

H_6: There is no significant difference in women empowerment as to income, employment and entitlement among women in different occupational groups viz., Farm Activities, Hospitality, Micro Enterprises, Solid Waste Management, Health sector and Education.

H_7: There is no significant difference in women empowerment as to income, employment and entitlement among women in different age groups viz., Below 20 years, Between 20 – 35 years, Between 35 – 50 years and Above 50 years.

For testing the significance of difference between the women empowerment among rural and urban areas and among Gazetted and Non-gazetted officers, i.e., hypothesis at serial numbers 1 and 3, independent samples test is conducted. Similarly, for testing the significance of difference in women empowerment among the women respondents of Government, Non-government and Unorganised sectors; different age groups; different educated levels; different religious groups and different occupational groups, i.e., for hypothesis at serial numbers 2, 4, 5, 6 and 7, Analysis of Variance (ANOVA) one way classification test is undertaken. The results of analysis are explained in the following paragraphs.

Testing the Significance of Differences

H_1: There is no significant difference in women empowerment as to income, employment and entitlement among women in different locations viz., urban and rural areas.

In order to test the tenability of this hypothesis, independent samples test is undertaken. In order to see the mean empowerment of women in rural and urban areas, the group statistics is computed using the computer software package, Statistical Package for Social Sciences (SPSS). The details of group statistics is shown in Table 6.2

Table 6.2: Group Statistics

	Location	N	Mean	Std. Deviation	Std. Error Mean
Empowerment	1	264	51.47	2.230	.137
	2	136	48.85	3.370	.289

Source: SPSS output on analysis of Primary Data

The location is coded as 1 for urban area and 2 for rural area. There are 264 respondents from urban and 136 respondents from rural areas with 51.47 and 48.85 as corresponding mean values of empowerment with respective standard deviation of 2.230 and 3.370. There is a difference of mean values of empowerment among the urban and rural areas as seen in Table 5.2, but whether the difference is significant or not is to be determined by test of hypothesis using independent samples test the result of which is shown in Table 6.3.

The result is presented in two parts: (i) the *Levene's Test for Equality of Variance* and *t–test for Equality of Means*. The table contains two sets of analysis, the first one assuming equal variances in the two groups and the second one assuming unequal variances. The Levene's test indicates which statistics to consider analysing the equality of the means. It tests the null hypothesis that the two locations have equal variances. A small value of significance associated with Levene's test indicates that the two regions, Urban and Rural have unequal variances and the null hypothesis is false. In Table 6.3, a very small value of this test statistic indicates that the two regions do not have equal variance. Therefore, the statistic associated with *equal variance not assumed* should be used for Equality of Means.

Table 6.3: Independent Samples Test

		Levene's Test for Equality of Variances		t-test for Equality of Means						
									95% Confidence Interval of the Difference	
		F	Sig.	t	df	Sig. (2-tailed)	Mean Difference	Std. Error Difference	Lower	Upper
Empowermer	Equal variance assumed	49.916	.000	9.266	398	.000	2.613	.282	2.059	3.167
	Equal variance not assumed			8.168	197.609	.000	2.613	.320	1.982	3.244

Source: SPSS output on analysis of Primary Data.

The *t*–test result (with equal variances not assumed) shows *t*–statistic of 8.168 with 197.609 degrees of freedom. The corresponding two-tailed *p*–value is 0.00, which is less than 0.05 and 0.01. Therefore, the null hypothesis is rejected at 5 per cent and one per cent significance level, which means that the average empowerment of women in these two regions, Urban and Rural areas are significantly different from each other, that is the empowerment is not the same in Urban and Rural areas.

H_2: There is no significant difference in women empowerment as to income, employment and entitlement among women in different organisational setup viz., Government, Non-government and Unorganised sectors.

In order to test the tenability of this hypothesis, Analysis of Variance (ANOVA) one way classification is undertaken. In order to see the mean empowerment of women in Government Organisations, Non-government Organisations and Unorganised sector, and their combinations, the Post Hoc Test has also been performed. The details of group statistics is shown in Table 6.3.

The result of the analysis for testing the omnibus hypothesis is given in the Table 6.4.

Table 6.4: ANOVA

Empowerment

	Sum of Squares	df	Mean Square	F	Sig.
Between Groups	1990.691	2	995.345	270.114	.000
Within Groups	1462.907	397	3.685		
Total	3453.598	399			

Source: SPSS output on analysis of Primary Data.

The result of the analysis in Table 6.4 is shown in three rows. The first row labeled *Between Groups* gives the variability due to the form of organisation (between-groups variability), viz., Government Organisation, Non-government Organisation and Unorganised sector, the second row labeled *Within Groups* gives variability due to random error, and the third row labeled *Total* gives total variability. In this case, the F-value is 270.114 and the corresponding *p*-value is < 0.000. Therefore, the null hypothesis can be safely rejected and can conclude that, the average women empowerment is not the same in all the three forms of organisation, say, Government organisation, Non-government organisation and in the Unorganised sector.

Thus, the result of the test is reported as "There is a significant difference in the women empowerment in the Government sector, Non-government sector and the Unorganised sector,

$$F_{(2,\ 397)} = 270.114,\ p < 0.001".$$

The F-statistic in ANOVA only indicates that the dependent variables vary for different levels of factor(s). In cases of more than two levels, as in this hypothesis testing, F-statistic does not indicate the exact way in which the dependent variable differs by the levels of factor(s). So as to gain a deeper understanding of the subject, the researcher has relied on unplanned comparisons, i.e., exploring the difference in means of women empowerment between all possible pairs of groups using Post Hoc Tests.

The hypothesis is subjected to Post Hoc Test selecting *Tukey* (same as *Tukey HSD test*) as this is the most commonly reported statistic in economic research. The Government Organisation is coded as '1'; the Non-government Organisation is coded as '2'; and the Unorganised sector is coded as '3'. The test result is shown in Table 6.5.

Table 6.5 presents the Post Hoc Test result of the comparison between all the possible pairs and hence in three groups, a total of six pairs is shown in which three will be mirror images (1 – 2 and 2 – 1; 1 – 3 and 3 – 1; and 2 – 3 and 3 – 2). The results are shown in three rows. The *p*-value for Government Organisation – Non-government Organisation and Non-government Organisation – Government Organisation comparison is shown as 0.000. This means that the average empowerment of women in Government Organisation and Non-government Organisation is significantly different. Same is the case with all other combinations, i.e., Government Organisation – Unorganised sector and Unorganised sector – Government Organisation; and Non-government Organisation – Unorganised sector.

The same result is also shown in another form in Table 6.6 as its homogeneous subsets.

In Table 6.6, the groups are arranged in the increasing order by the mean value. The unorganised sector having the least mean value of women empowerment is listed first followed by Non-government Organisation and Government Organisation. As there is no homogeneity among these three groups, they are shown separately in the right-hand side.

Table 6.5: Multiple Companies

Dependent Variable: Empowerment

Tukey HSD

(I) Organisation	(J) Organisation	Mean Difference (I-J)	Std. Error	Sig.	95% Confidence Interval	
					Lower Bound	Upper Bound
1	2	3.419*	.284	.000	2.75	4.09
	3	6.020*	.265	.000	5.40	6.64
2	1	-3.419*	.284	.000	-4.09	-2.75
	3	2.601*	.217	.000	2.09	3.11
3	1	-6.020*	.265	.000	-6.64	-5.40
	2	-2.601*	.217	.000	-3.11	-2.09

*. The mean difference is significant at the .05 level.

Source: SPSS output on analysis of Primary Data.

Table 6.6: Homogeneous Subsets

Empowerment

Tukey HSD[a,b]

Organisation	N	Subset for alpha = .05		
		1	2	3
3	200	48.67		
2	129		51.27	
1	71			54.69
Sig.		1.000	1.000	1.000

Means for groups in homogeneous subsets are displayed.

a. Uses Harmonic Mean Sample Size = 111.788.

b. The group sizes are unequal. The harmonic mean of the group sizes is used. Type I error levels are not guaranteed.

Source: SPSS output on analysis of Primary Data

H_3: There is no significant difference in women empowerment as to income, employment and entitlement among women in different job status viz., Gazetted and Non-gazetted officials.

In order to test the tenability of this hypothesis, independent samples test is undertaken. In order to see the mean empowerment of women in gazetted and non-gazetted cadre, the group statistics is computed using the computer software package, Statistical Package for Social Sciences (SPSS). The details of group statistics is shown in Table 6.7.

Table 6.7: Group Statistics

	Status	N	Mean	Std. Deviation	Std. Error Mean
Empowerment	1	33	55.91	1.042	.181
	2	367	50.10	2.559	.134

Source: SPSS output on analysis of Primary Data

The location is coded as 1 for gazetted cadre and 2 for non-gazetted cadre. There are 33 respondents of gazetted cadre and 136 respondents of non-gazetted cadre with 55.91 and 50.10 as corresponding mean values of empowerment with respective standard deviation of 1.042 and 2.559. There is a difference of mean values of empowerment among the urban and rural areas as seen in Table 5.7, but whether the difference is significant or not is to be determined by test of hypothesis using independent samples test, the result of which is shown in Table 6.8.

Table 6.8: Independent Sample Test

		Levene's Test for Equality of Variances		t-test for Equality of Means						
									95% Confidence Interval of the Difference	
		F	Sig.	t	df	Sig. (2-tailed)	Mean Difference	Std. Error Difference	Lower	Upper
Empowerme	Equal variance assumed	23.106	.000	12.937	398	.000	5.811	.449	4.928	6.694
	Equal variance not assumed			25.801	74.230	.000	5.811	.225	5.362	6.260

Source: SPSS output on analysis of Primary Data

The result is presented in two parts, (i) the *Levene's Test for Equality of Variance* and *t-test for Equality of Means*. The table contains two sets of analysis, the first one assuming equal variances in the two groups and the second one assuming unequal variances. The Levene's test indicates which statistics to consider analysing the equality of the means. It tests the null hypothesis that the two locations have equal variances. A small value of significance associated with Levene's test indicates that the two groups of officials, Gazetted and Non-gazetted have unequal variances and the null hypothesis is false. In Table 6.8, a very small value of this test statistic indicates that the two regions do not have equal variance. Therefore, the statistic associated with *equal variance not assumed* should be used for Equality of Means.

The t – test result (with equal variances not assumed) shows t-statistic of 25.801 with 74.230 degrees of freedom. The corresponding two-tailed p – value is 0.00, which is less than 0.05 and 0.01. Therefore, the null hypothesis is rejected at 5 per cent and one per cent significance level, which means that the average empowerment of women in these two groups, gazetted and non-gazetted cadres are significantly different from each other, that is, the empowerment is not the same for gazetted and non-gazetted cadre.

H_4: There is no significant difference in women empowerment as to income, employment and entitlement among women in different levels of educational attainment viz., Below Primary, Primary – SSLC, SSLC – Degree and Above Degree.

In order to test the tenability of this hypothesis, Analysis of Variance (ANOVA) one way classification is undertaken. In order to see the mean empowerment of women at various educational level viz., Below Primary, Primary - SSLC, SSLC - Degree and Above Degree, and their combinations, the Post Hoc Test has also been performed. The details of group statistics is shown in Table 6.9.

The result of the analysis for testing the omnibus hypothesis is given in the Table 6.9.

The result of the analysis in Table 6.9 is shown in three rows. The first row labeled *Between Groups* gives the variability due to the level of educational attainment (between-groups variability), viz., Below Primary, Primary - SSLC, SSLC - Degree and Above Degree, the second row labeled *Within Groups* gives variability due to random error,

Table 6.9: ANOVA

Empowerment

	Sum of Squares	df	Mean Square	F	Sig.
Between Groups	1165.590	3	388.530	67.245	.000
Within Groups	2288.007	396	5.778		
Total	3453.598	399			

Source: SPSS output on analysis of Primary Data.

and the third row labeled *Total* gives total variability. In this case, the F-value is 67.245 and the corresponding *p*-value is < 0.000. Therefore, the null hypothesis can be safely rejected and can conclude that, the average women empowerment is not the same in all the four categories of educational attainment, say, Below Primary, Primary - SSLC, SSLC - Degree and Above Degree.

Thus the result of the test is reported as "There is a significant difference in the women empowerment in different groups of educational attainment viz., Below Primary, Primary - SSLC, SSLC - Degree and Above Degree, $F_{(3,396)} = 67.245$, $p < 0.001$".

The F-statistic in ANOVA only indicates that the dependent variables vary for different levels of factor(s). In cases of more than two levels as in this hypothesis testing, F-statistic does not indicate the exact way in which the dependent variable differs by the levels of factor(s). So as to gain a deeper understanding of the subject, the researcher has relied on unplanned comparisons, i.e., exploring the difference in means of women empowerment between all possible pairs of groups using Post Hoc Tests.

The hypothesis is subjected to Post Hoc Test selecting *Tukey* (same as *Tukey HSD test*) as this is the most commonly reported statistic in economic research. The Below Primary level is coded as '1'; Primary - SSLC is coded as '2'; SSLC – Degree is coded as '3'; and the Above Degree is coded as '4'. The test result is shown in Table 6.10.

Table 6.10 presents the Post Hoc Test result of the comparison between all the possible pairs and hence in four groups, a total of twelve pairs is shown in which six will be mirror images (1 – 2 and 2 – 1; 1 – 3 and 3 – 1; 1 – 4 and 4 – 1; 2 – 3 and 3 – 2; 2 – 3; and 3 – 2; 2 – 4 and 4 – 2; and 3 – 4 and 4 – 3). The results are shown in four rows. The *p*-value for all combinations i.e., Below Primary – Between Primary and SSLC and Between Primary and SSLC – Below Primary; Below Primary – Between SSLC and Degree and Between SSLC and Degree – Below Primary; Below Primary – Above Degree and Above Degree – Below Primary; Between Primary and SSLC – Between SSLC and Degree and Between SSLC and Degree – Between Primary and SSLC; Between Primary and SSLC – Above Degree and Above Degree – Between Primary and SSLC; and Between SSLC and Degree – Above Degree and Above Degree – Between SSLC and Degree are shown as 0.000. This means that the average empowerment of

Table 6.10: Multipe Comparisons

Dependent Variable: Empowerment

Tukey HSD

(I) Education	(J) Education	Mean Difference (I-J)	Std. Error	Sig.	95% Confidence Interval	
					Lower Bound	Upper Bound
1	2	-1.859*	.659	.026	-3.56	-.16
	3	-4.312*	.619	.000	-5.91	-2.72
	4	-5.947*	.609	.000	-7.52	-4.38
2	1	1.859*	.659	.026	.16	3.56
	3	-2.452*	.371	.000	-3.41	-1.50
	4	-4.087*	.354	.000	-5.00	-3.17
3	1	4.312*	.619	.000	2.72	5.91
	2	2.452*	.371	.000	1.50	3.41
	4	-1.635*	.271	.000	-2.34	-.93
4	1	5.947*	.609	.000	4.38	7.52
	2	4.087*	.354	.000	3.17	5.00
	3	1.635*	.271	.000	.93	2.34

*. The mean difference is significant at the .05 level.

Source: SPSS output on analysis of Primary Data

women in all the combinations of different groups of education level is significantly different as their mean difference is significantly different at 5 per cent level.

The same result is also shown in another form in Table 5.11 as its homogeneous subsets.

Table 6.11 : Homogeneous Subsets

Empowerment

Tukey HSD[a,b]

Education	N	Subset for alpha = .05			
		1	2	3	4
1	17	46.06			
2	61		47.92		
3	135			50.37	
4	187				52.01
Sig.		1.000	1.000	1.000	1.000

Means for groups in homogeneous subsets are displayed.

a. Uses Harmonic Mean Sample Size = 45.469.

b. The group sizes are unequal. The harmonic mean of the group sizes is used. Type I error levels are not guaranteed.

Source: SPSS output on analysis of Primary Data.

In Table 6.11, the groups are arranged in the increasing order by the mean value. The Below Primary class is having the least mean value of women empowerment is listed first followed by Between Primary and SSLC, Between SSLC and Degree and Above Degree. As there is no homogeneity in empowerment among these four groups, they are shown separately in the right-hand side.

H_5: There is no significant difference in women empowerment as to income, employment and entitlement among women in different religions viz., Hindu, Muslim, Christian and Others.

In order to test the tenability of this hypothesis, Analysis of Variance (ANOVA) one way classification is undertaken. In order to see the mean empowerment of women among various religious groups viz., Hindu, Muslim, Christian and other religions, and their combinations, the Post Hoc Test has also been performed. The details of group statistics is shown in Table 6.13.

The result of the analysis for testing the omnibus hypothesis is given in the Table 6.12.

Table 6.12: ANOVA

Empowerment

	Sum of Squares	df	Mean Square	F	Sig.
Between Groups	11.315	3	3.772	.434	.729
Within Groups	3442.283	396	8.693		
Total	3453.598	399			

Source: SPSS output on analysis of Primary Data

The result of the analysis in Table 6.12 is shown in three rows. The first row labeled *Between Groups* gives the variability due to the level of educational attainment (between-groups variability), viz., Hindu, Muslim, Christian and other religions, the second row labeled *Within Groups* gives variability due to random error, and the third row labeled *Total* gives total variability. In this case, the F-value is 0.434 and the corresponding *p*-value is < 0.729. Therefore, the null hypothesis can be safely accepted and can conclude that, the average women empowerment is the same in all the four categories of religious groups, say, Hindu, Muslim, Christian and Other religions.

Thus, the result of the test is reported as "There is no significant difference in the women empowerment in different groups of religion viz., Hindu, Muslim, Christian and Other communities, $F_{(3, 396)} = 0.434$, $p > 0.05$".

The F-statistic in ANOVA only indicates that the dependent variables vary for different levels of factor(s). In cases of more than two levels, as in this hypothesis testing, F-statistic does not indicate the exact way in which the dependent variable differs by the levels of factor(s). So as to gain a deeper understanding of the subject, the researcher has relied on unplanned comparisons, i.e., exploring the difference in means of women empowerment between all possible pairs of groups using Post Hoc Tests.

The hypothesis is subjected to Post Hoc Test selecting *Tukey* (same as *Tukey HSD test*) as this is the most commonly reported statistic in economic research. The Hindu religion is coded as '1'; Muslim religion is coded as '2'; Christian religion is coded as '3'; and the other religions are coded as '4'. The test result is shown in Table 6.13.

Table 6.13: Multiple Comparisons

Dependent Variable: Empowerment
Tukey HSD

(I) Religion	(J) Religion	Mean Difference (I-J)	Std. Error	Sig.	95% Confidence Interval	
					Lower Bound	Upper Bound
1	2	.078	.382	.997	-.91	1.06
	3	.093	.370	.994	-.86	1.05
	4	-.549	.558	.759	-1.99	.89
2	1	-.078	.382	.997	-1.06	.91
	3	.015	.432	1.000	-1.10	1.13
	4	-.627	.601	.724	-2.18	.92
3	1	-.093	.370	.994	-1.05	.86
	2	-.015	.432	1.000	-1.13	1.10
	4	-.642	.593	.701	-2.17	.89
4	1	.549	.558	.759	-.89	1.99
	2	.627	.601	.724	-.92	2.18
	3	.642	.593	.701	-.89	2.17

Source: SPSS output on analysis of Primary Data.

Table 6.13 presents the Post Hoc Test result of the comparison between all the possible pairs and hence in four groups, a total of twelve pairs is shown in which six will be mirror images (1 – 2 and 2 – 1; 1 – 3 and 3 – 1; 1 – 4 and 4 – 1; 2 – 3 and 3 – 2; 2 – 3; and 3 – 2; 2 – 4 and 4 – 2; and 3 – 4 and 4 – 3). The results are shown in four rows. The *p*-value for all combinations i.e., Hindu – Muslim and Muslim – Hindu; Hindu – Christian and Christian – Hindu; Hindu – Others and Others – Hindu; Muslim – Christian and Christian - Muslim; Muslim – Others and Others – Muslim and Christian – Others and Others – Christian are shown as > 0.05. This means that the average empowerment of women in all the combinations of different religious groups is not significantly different as their mean difference is not significantly different at 5 per cent level.

The same result is also shown in another form in Table 6.14 as its homogeneous subsets.

Table 6.14: Homogeneous Subsets

Empowerment

Tukey HSD[a,b]

Religion	N	Subset for alpha = .05
		1
3	98	50.48
2	89	50.49
1	180	50.57
4	33	51.12
Sig.		.573

Means for groups in homogeneous subsets are displayed.

a. Uses Harmonic Mean Sample Size = 69.810.

b. The group sizes are unequal. The harmonic mean of the group sizes is used. Type I error levels are not guaranteed.

Source: SPSS output on analysis of Primary Data

In Table 6.14, the groups are arranged in the increasing order by the mean value. The Christian community having the least mean value of women empowerment is listed first followed by Muslims, Hindus and Other religions. As there is homogeneity in empowerment among all these four groups, they are shown in a group in the right-hand side.

H_6: There is no significant difference in women empowerment as to income, employment and entitlement among women in different occupational groups viz., Farm activities, Hospitality, Micro Enterprises, Solid waste management, Health sector and Education.

In order to test the tenability of this hypothesis, Analysis of Variance (ANOVA) one way classification is undertaken. In order to see the mean empowerment of women among various occupational / activity groups viz., Farm activities, Hospitality management, Micro Enterprises, Solid waste management, Health sector and Education sectors, and their combinations, the Post Hoc Test has also been performed. The details of group statistics is shown in Table 6.16.

The result of the analysis for testing the omnibus hypothesis is given in the Table 6.15.

Table 6.15: ANOVA

Empowerment

	Sum of Squares	df	Mean Square	F	Sig.
Between Groups	2724.232	5	544.846	294.324	.000
Within Groups	729.365	394	1.851		
Total	3453.598	399			

Source: SPSS output on analysis of Primary Data.

The result of the analysis in Table 5.15 is shown in three rows. The first row labeled *Between Groups* gives the variability due to the categories of occupational groups (between-groups variability), viz., Farm activities, Hospitality management, Micro Enterprises, Solid waste management, Health sector and Education sectors; the second row labeled *Within Groups* gives variability due to random error, and the third row labeled *Total* gives total variability. In this case, the F-value is 294.324 and the corresponding p-value is < 0.000. Therefore, the null hypothesis can be safely rejected and can conclude that, the average women empowerment is not the same in all the four categories of occupational groups, say, Farm activities, Hospitality management, Micro Enterprises, Solid waste management, Health sector and Education sector.

Thus the result of the test is reported as "There is significant difference in the women empowerment in different occupational groups, viz., Farm activities, Hospitality management, Micro Enterprises, Solid waste management, Health sector and Education sectors,

$$F_{(5,\ 394)} = 294.324,\ p < 0.001\text{''}.$$

The F-statistic in ANOVA only indicates that the dependent variables vary for different levels of factor(s). In cases of more than two levels as in this hypothesis testing, F-statistic does not indicate the exact way in which the dependent variable differs by the levels of factor(s). So as to gain a deeper understanding of the subject, the researcher has relied on unplanned comparisons, i.e., exploring the difference in means of women empowerment between all possible pairs of groups using Post Hoc Tests.

Table 6.16: Post Hoc Tests

Multiple Comparisons

Dependent Variable: Empowerment
Tukey HSD

(I) Sector	(J) Sector	Mean Difference (I-J)	Std. Error	Sig.	95% Confidence Interval	
					Lower Bound	Upper Bound
1	2	-5.054*	.213	.000	-5.66	-4.44
	3	-4.192*	.225	.000	-4.84	-3.55
	4	-2.298*	.247	.000	-3.01	-1.59
	5	-7.292*	.259	.000	-8.03	-6.55
	6	-7.138*	.217	.000	-7.76	-6.52
2	1	5.054*	.213	.000	4.44	5.66
	3	.861*	.223	.002	.22	1.50
	4	2.755*	.245	.000	2.05	3.46
	5	-2.238*	.257	.000	-2.97	-1.50
	6	-2.084*	.214	.000	-2.70	-1.47
3	1	4.192*	.225	.000	3.55	4.84
	2	-.861*	.223	.002	-1.50	-.22
	4	1.894*	.256	.000	1.16	2.63
	5	-3.100*	.268	.000	-3.87	-2.33
	6	-2.946*	.227	.000	-3.59	-2.30
4	1	2.298*	.247	.000	1.59	3.01
	2	-2.755*	.245	.000	-3.46	-2.05
	3	-1.894*	.256	.000	-2.63	-1.16
	5	-4.993*	.286	.000	-5.81	-4.17
	6	-4.839*	.248	.000	-5.55	-4.13
5	1	7.292*	.259	.000	6.55	8.03
	2	2.238*	.257	.000	1.50	2.97
	3	3.100*	.268	.000	2.33	3.87
	4	4.993*	.286	.000	4.17	5.81
	6	.154	.260	.992	-.59	.90
6	1	7.138*	.217	.000	6.52	7.76
	2	2.084*	.214	.000	1.47	2.70
	3	2.946*	.227	.000	2.30	3.59
	4	4.839*	.248	.000	4.13	5.55
	5	-.154	.260	.992	-.90	.59

*. The mean difference is significant at the .05 level.

Source: SPSS output on analysis of Primary Data.

The hypothesis is subjected to Post Hoc Test selecting *Tukey* (same as *Tukey HSD test*) as this is the most commonly reported statistic in economic research. The Farm activity is coded as '1'; Hospitality is coded as '2'; Micro Enterprises is coded as '3'; Solid waste management is coded as '4'; Health sector is coded as '5'and Education sector is coded as '6'. The test result is shown in table 6.16.

Table 6.16 presents the Post Hoc Test result of the comparison between all the possible pairs and hence in six groups, a total of fifteen pairs is shown in which six will be mirror images (1 – 2 and 2 – 1; 1 – 3 and 3 – 1; 1 – 4 and 4 – 1; 1 – 5 and 5 – 1; 1 – 6 and 6 – 1; 2 – 3 and 3 – 2; 2 – 4 and 4 – 2; 2 – 5 and 5 – 2; 2 – 6 and 6 – 2; 3 – 4 and 4 – 3; 3 – 5 and 5 – 3; 3 – 6 and 6 – 3; 4 – 5 and 5 – 4; 4 – 6 and 6 – 4; and 5 – 6 and 6 – 5). The results are shown in six rows. The *p*-value for all combinations except Health sector – Education sector and Education sector – Health sector i.e., Farm activities – Hospitality management and Hospitality management – Farm activities; Farm activities – Micro Enterprises and Micro Enterprises – Farm activities; Farm activities – Solid waste management and Solid waste management – Farm activities; Farm activities – Health sector and Health sector – Farm activities; Farm activities – Education sector and Education sector – Farm activities; Hospitality management – Micro Enterprises and Micro Enterprises – Hospitality management; Hospitality management – Solid waste management and Solid waste management – Hospitality management; Hospitality management – Health sector and Health sector – Hospitality management; Hospitality management – Education sector and Education sector – Hospitality management; Micro Enterprises – Solid waste management and Solid waste management – Micro Enterprises; Micro Enterprises – Health sector and Health sector – Micro Enterprises; Micro Enterprises – Education sector and Education sector – Micro Enterprises; Solid waste management – Health sector and Health sector – Solid waste management; and Solid waste management – Education sector and Education sector – Solid waste management are shown as < 0.05. This means that the average empowerment of women in all the combinations of different occupational groups is significantly different as their mean difference is significantly different at 5 per cent level. For Health sector – Education sector and Education sector – Health sector, the *p*-value is > 0.05. This means that the average empowerment of women in this combination of occupational groups is not significantly different as their mean difference is not significantly different at 5 per cent level.

The same result is also shown in another form in Table 6.17 as its homogeneous subsets.

Table 6.17 Homogeneous Subsets

Empowerment

Tukey HSD

Sector	N	Subset for alpha = .05				
		1	2	3	4	5
1	80	46.38				
4	49		48.67			
3	67			50.57		
2	84				51.43	
6	78					53.51
5	42					53.67
Sig.		1.000	1.000	1.000	1.000	.989

Means for groups in homogeneous subsets are displayed.

a. Uses Harmonic Mean Sample Size = 62.261.

b. The group sizes are unequal. The harmonic mean of the group sizes is used Type I error levels are not guaranteed.

Source: SPSS output on analysis of Primary Data.

In Table 6.17, the groups are arranged in the increasing order by the mean value. The respondents of farm activity is having the least mean value of women empowerment and is listed first followed by Solid waste management, Micro Enterprises, Hospitality management, Education sector and Health sector. As there is homogeneity in empowerment among respondents engaged in Education and Health sectors, they are grouped in 5th group on the right hand side. In all other cases, there is no homogeneity in empowerment among respondents (i.e., those engaged in farm activity, solid waste management, micro enterprises and hospitality management), they are shown in separate groups from 1 to 4 groups in the right-hand side.

H_7: There is no significant difference in women empowerment as to income, employment and entitlement among women in different age groups viz., Below 20 years, Between 20 – 35 years, Between 35 – 50 years and Above 50 years.

In order to test the tenability of this hypothesis, Analysis of Variance (ANOVA) one way classification is undertaken. In order to see the mean empowerment of women among various age-groups viz., Below 20 years, Between 20 – 35 years, Between 35 – 50 years and Above 50 years, and their combinations, the Post Hoc Test has also been performed. The details of group statistics is shown in Table 6.19.

The result of the analysis for testing the omnibus hypothesis is given in the Table 6.18.

Table 6.18: ANOVA

Empowerment

	Sum of Squares	df	Mean Square	F	Sig.
Between Groups	316.642	3	105.547	13.324	.000
Within Groups	3136.956	396	7.922		
Total	3453.598	399			

Source: SPSS output on analysis of Primary Data.

The result of the analysis in Table 6.18 is shown in three rows. The first row labeled *Between Groups* gives the variability due to the level of age groups (between-groups variability), viz., Below 20 years, Between 20 – 35 years, Between 35 – 50 years and Above 50 years, the second row labeled *Within Groups* gives variability due to random error, and the third row labeled *Total* gives total variability. In this case, the F-value is 13.324 and the corresponding p-value is < 0.000. Therefore, the null hypothesis can be safely rejected and can conclude that, the average women empowerment is not the same in all the four categories of age groups, say, Below 20 years, Between 20 – 35 years, Between 35 – 50 years and Above 50 years.

Thus the result of the test is reported as "There is significant difference in the women empowerment in different occupational groups, viz., Below 20 years, Between 20 – 35 years, Between 35 – 50 years and Above 50 years, $F_{(3,\ 396)} = 13.324$, $p < 0.001$".

The F-statistic in ANOVA only indicates that the dependent variables vary for different levels of factor(s). In cases of more than two levels as in this hypothesis testing, F-statistic does not indicate the exact way in which the dependent variable differs by the levels of factor(s). So as to gain a deeper understanding of the subject, the researcher has relied on unplanned comparisons, i.e., exploring the difference in means of women empowerment between all possible pairs of groups using Post Hoc Tests.

The hypothesis is subjected to Post Hoc Test selecting *Tukey* (same as *Tukey HSD test*) as this is the most commonly reported statistic in economic research. The respondents below 20 years are coded as '1'; Between 20 years and 35 years are coded as '2'; Between 35 years and 50 years are coded as '3'; and those above 50 years are coded as '4'. The test result is shown in Table 6.19.

Table 6.19: Post Hoc Tests

Multiple Comparisons

Dependent Variable: Empowerment
Tukey HSD

(I) Age	(J) Age	Mean Difference (I-J)	Std. Error	Sig.	95% Confidence Interval	
					Lower Bound	Upper Bound
1	2	-3.088*	.524	.000	-4.44	-1.74
	3	-2.485*	.523	.000	-3.84	-1.13
	4	-1.639*	.575	.024	-3.12	-.16
2	1	3.088*	.524	.000	1.74	4.44
	3	.603	.329	.260	-.25	1.45
	4	1.449*	.406	.002	.40	2.50
3	1	2.485*	.523	.000	1.13	3.84
	2	-.603	.329	.260	-1.45	.25
	4	.846	.405	.158	-.20	1.89
4	1	1.639*	.575	.024	.16	3.12
	2	-1.449*	.406	.002	-2.50	-.40
	3	-.846	.405	.158	-1.89	.20

*. The mean difference is significant at the .05 level.

Table 6.19 presents the Post Hoc Test result of the comparison between all the possible pairs and hence in four groups, a total of twelve pairs is shown in which six will be mirror images (1 – 2 and 2 – 1; 1 – 3 and 3 – 1; 1 – 4 and 4 – 1; 2 – 3 and 3 – 2; 2 – 4 and 4 – 2; and 3 – 4 and 4 – 3). The results are shown in four rows. The *p*-value for all combinations, i.e., below 20 years – between 20 years and 35 years and between 20 years and 35 years – below 20 years; below 20 years – between 35 years and 50 years and between 35 years – below 20 years; below 20 years – above 50 years and above 50 years – below 20 years; and between 20 years and 35 years – above 50 years and above 50 years – between 20 years and 35 years are shown as < 0.05. This means that the average empowerment of women in all the combinations of different religious groups is significantly different as their mean difference is significantly different at 5 per cent level.

The *p*-value for all combinations, i.e., between 20 years and 35 years – between 35 years and between 35 years – between 20 years and 35 years; and between 35 years – above 50 years and above 50 years – between 35 years are shown as > 0.05. This means that the average empowerment of women in all the combinations of different religious groups is not significantly different as their mean difference is not significantly different at 5 per cent level.

The same result is also shown in another form in Table 6.20 as its homogeneous subsets.

Empowerment

Tukey HSD

Age	N	Subset for alpha = .05		
		1	2	3
1	36	48.25		
4	72		49.89	
3	147		50.73	50.73
2	145			51.34
Sig.		1.000	.272	.571

Means for groups in homogeneous subsets are displ

a. Uses Harmonic Mean Sample Size = 72.247.

b. The group sizes are unequal. The harmonic mea of the group sizes is used. Type I error levels ar not guaranteed.

Source: SPSS output on analysis of Primary Data.

Table 6.20 : Homogeneous Subsets

In Table 6.20, the groups are arranged in the increasing order by the mean value. The respondents of below 20 years of age group are having the least mean value of women empowerment and are listed first followed by those above 50 years of age group, between the age of 35 and 50 group and those between the age of 20 and 35 group. As there is homogeneity in empowerment among respondents in the age group of above 50 years and those between 35 years and 50 years, they are grouped in to the 2nd group. Similarly as there is homogeneity in empowerment among respondents in the age group of between the age of 35 and 50 group and those in the age group of between 20 years and 35 years, they are grouped in 3rd group on the right hand side.

Tenability of Hypotheses

In all, the tenability of all the seven hypotheses which were subjected to the statistical test is shown in Table 6.21.

Table 6.21: The Acceptance or Rejection of Hypotheses

Sl. No.	*Hypotheses*	*Acceptance/ Rejection*
1.	H_{01}: There is no significant difference in women empowerment as to income, employment and entitlement among women in different locations viz., urban and rural areas.	Rejected
2.	H_{02}: There is no significant difference in women empowerment as to income, employment and entitlement among women in different organisational setup viz., Government, Non-government and Unorganised sectors.	Rejected
3.	H_{03}: There is no significant difference in women empowerment as to income, employment and entitlement among women in different job status viz., Gazetted and Non-gazetted officials.	Rejected
4.	H_{04}: There is no significant difference in women empowerment as to income, employment and entitlement among women in different levels of educational attainment viz., Below Primary, Primary – SSLC, SSLC – Degree and Above Degree.	Rejected
5.	H_{05}: There is no significant difference in women empowerment as to income, employment and entitlement among women in different religions viz., Hindu, Muslim, Christian and Others.	Accepted

Sl. No.	*Hypotheses*	*Acceptance/ Rejection*
6.	H_{06}: There is no significant difference in women empowerment as to income, employment and entitlement among women in different occupational groups viz., Farm activities, Hospitality, Micro Enterprises, Solid waste management, Health sector and Education.	Rejected
7.	H_{07}: There is no significant difference in women empowerment as to income, employment and entitlement among women in different age groups viz., Below 20 years, Between 20 – 35 years, Between 35 – 50 years and Above 50 years.	Rejected

7

Summary of Findings

This Chapter contains a summary of findings, conclusions and suggestions relating to socio-economic background of the respondents, results on variable-wise analysis and predictor equation model.

(a) The analysis on the socio-economic background (V_1) reveals the following:

Age: Age is another important variable which changes the attitude of women and also determines the status. A majority of the respondents in the sample are in the age group of 20 to 50 years.

Educational qualification: As far qualification of the respondents is concerned, most of them have an education level above Degree.

Nature of sector : A large majority of the respondents fall under unorganised sector, i.e., 200 respondents (50 per cent); 128 respondents (32 per cent) are working under Non-governmental organisations and 72 respondents (18 per cent) are working in Government organisations.

Job status : There are 368 respondents (92 per cent) working in the Non-gazetted cadre and only 32 respondents (8 per cent) are working in Gazetted posts.

Location : Women empowerment to a great extent is location-specific. Hence, it is an important variable. It is found that 264 respondents (66 per cent) are residing in urban areas, and only 136 respondents (34 per cent) are residing in the rural areas. A large majority of the respondents in the sample are residing in urban areas.

Religion: There are 180 respondents (45 per cent) and 100 respondents (25 per cent) belonging to religious group of Hindus and Christians respectively; 88 respondents (22 per cent) are from Muslim religion. It is clear that there is adequate representation of respondents from Hindu and Christian religions compared to Muslim religion community.

Nature of activity: The important activities performed by the women in Kerala are Farm activities like lease land farming, organic cultivation and as agricultural labourer in the unorganised sector; Hospitality industry like conducting canteen, catering services and so on; Micro enterprises; Solid waste management; Health sector; and Education sector. It is clear that a large majority of them are engaged in Hospitality, Farm and Education sectors.

Marital status: Another variable taken for analysing the personal profile of women respondents is marital status. It is clear from the analysis that the majority of the sample respondents are married and only a few are single.

(b) The Women Empowerment Index : Selected activities in rural and urban areas based on educational and other variables show that women empowerment is high in those cases where the women had higher education and were living in urban areas, compared to those in rural areas. The empowerment of women among Gazetted officers of the Government organisation with higher educational status is higher than that of women with lower education. In respect of activities selected, like farm activities, hospitality activities, micro enterprises activities, solid waste management, health sector activities and activities in the education sector, the women empowerment is high only in those cases where they are placed in the higher educational status groups.

(c) Variablewise analysis: On Employment, Income, Entitlement and Empowerment of women in Kerala, this analysis revealed the following :

The selected eight variables and their sub-variables which determine women empowerment are : Accessibility to and control over Private Properties (V_2), Accessibility to and control over Public Properties (V_3), Accessibility to and control over Income and Employment (V_4), Control over Decision on own body (V_5), Independence on mobility (V_6), Accessibility to and control over Politics (V_7), Accessibility to and control over Knowledge, Information and Proficiency (V_8) and Legal Status and Accessibility to Legislature (V_9).

1. Accessibility and Control Over Private Properties

The matriarchal system that prevailed among some of the dominant communities in the past, the progressive social movements, government policies, and a historically conducive climate are a few factors identified as contributors to the success of women in Kerala. The traditional matriarchal system gave women the freedom to access several services including education. Their empowerment started when they got the right to access property, both private and public. The identified eleven sub-variables give the following results of the analysis. They are :

(i) Savings

Savings is an important variable which leads to surplus amount as income to women which can be utilised for their own purposes. This leads to empowerment and accessibility and control over private property according to 220 respondents who recorded their level of opinion at 20 to 40 per cent. As many as 84 respondents (21 per cent) recorded their level at 50 per cent and the rest recorded a level up to 80 per cent. The mean score of the opinions is 31 per cent, which is less than combined mean (52 per cent). This shows that there is no impact of savings to control over private properties.

(ii) Family Income

Another sub-variable identified for accessibility to and control over private properties is family income. One of the important factors which contributes to the earning of private property is the income from the family. The opinion level of respondents shows that family income is a determining factor in acquiring private property as is seen from the means score of 57 per cent, which exceeds the combined mean of 52 per cent. As many as 290 respondents (73 per cent) recorded a level of 60 per cent.

(iii) Food

Food is an important dire necessity for people of every walk of life including women. The mean score of the level of opinion is 52 per cent and it is equal to the combined mean which indicates that this is an important variable which contributes to the accessibility to and control over private property. Further, 115 respondents (29 per cent) and 157 respondents (40 per cent) recorded their opinion at 50 and 60 per cent respectively. 88 respondents recorded their opinion at 80 to 100 per cent range.

(iv) Clothing

In those families where the husband earns income and the decision to purchase is vested in him and in another case where wife also earns income, leads to acquisition by herself or taking a joint decision. Here, 112 respondents (28 per cent) and 119 respondents (30 per cent) recorded a level of 50 and 60 per cent respectively; 94 respondents (24 per cent) recorded a higher level at 80 per cent and above. The mean score of opinion is 57 per cent which is higher than the combined mean of 52 per cent which clearly indicates that this variable has a direct impact on accessibility to and control over private property by women.

(v) Shelter

Another very important dire necessities of life is shelter. It is arranged for either by husband or wife or both, depending on their earnings. Hence, 182 respondents (46 per cent) recorded a level between 40 and 50 per cent and 112 respondents (28 per cent) recorded their level of opinion at 60 per cent. The mean score in this case is 47 per cent which is less than the combined mean of 52 per cent; this shows that this variable is not so significant in determining accessibility and control over private properties.

(vi) Accessibility to Housing Loans

The opinion of women on accessibility to housing loan revealed that there is less scope as is seen from the mean score (47 per cent) which is less than the combined mean of 52 per cent. In this case, 107 respondents (27 per cent) recorded a level of 40 per cent and 131 respondents (33 per cent) recorded a level of 50 per cent; 126 respondents (32 per cent) recorded a level of 60 per cent.

(vii) Accessibility to Vehicle Loans

This facility helped women in acquiring private property. The opinions of respondents on accessibility to vehicle loans revealed that the mean score is 46 per cent, which is less than the combined mean of 52 per cent and is not significant. Here, 273 respondents (68 per cent) recorded a level between 40 and 50 per cent; 61 respondents (15 per cent) recorded a level of 60 per cent.

(viii) Accessibility to Consumption Loans

Opinions of respondents on accessibility to consumption loans revealed that the mean level of opinion is 57 per cent which is higher than the combined mean of 52 per cent. This makes it clear that there is ample chance for accessibility to consumption loans. Here, 139 respondent (35 per cent) recorded a level of 50 per cent and 168 respondents (42 per cent) recorded a level of 60 per cent; 48 respondents (13 per cent) recorded a level of 80 per cent and above.

(ix) Status and Property Laws

Opinions on the status and property laws make it clear that it is not significant as is clear from the mean score (49 per cent) which is less than the combined mean of 52 per cent. On this factor, 122 respondents out of 400 (31 per cent) recorded their level of opinion at 40 per cent and 94 respondents (24 per cent) recorded a level of 50 per cent; 107 respondents (27 per cent) recorded a level at 60 per cent.

(x) Impact of Globalisation on Expenditure Pattern

The pattern of consumption increases due to globalisation in general, and in the case of women, in particular. On this variable, 170 respondents (43 per cent) recorded their opinion level between 40 per cent and 50 per cent; 133 respondents (33 per cent) recorded a level of 60 per cent and 22 respondents (6 per cent) recorded a level of 80 per cent. The mean percentage level of opinion (52 per cent) is equal to the combined mean, which clearly indicates that there is impact on change in the expenditure pattern due to globalisation.

(xi) Role in Decision-making

The opinions on acquiring private property prove that all these contribute to women empowerment, as is noticed from the mean level of opinion of 69 per cent, which is higher than the combined mean. Here, 75 respondents (19 per cent) and 117 respondents (29 per cent) recorded a level of 50 per cent and 60 per cent respectively; 184 respondents (46 per cent) recorded a level of 80 per cent and 22 respondents (6 per cent) recorded a level of cent per cent.

2. Main Variable—Accessibility to and Control over Public Properties

Historically, Kerala has been quite different from the rest of the country in terms of the indicators of women's development. This, in turn, enhances the power of taking decisions and making use of the common facilities available as public properties. The following conclusions are derived:

(i) Labour Issues in Bringing Water

Opinions on labour issues in bringing water were collected and it is seen that there is no problem in getting water because the mean score (47 per cent) is less than the combined mean of 51 per cent. On this factor, 83 respondents (21 per cent) and 118 respondents (30 per cent) recorded their level of opinion at 40 per cent and 50 per cent respectively; 107 respondents (27 per cent) recorded a level of 60 per cent and 26 respondents (6 per cent) recorded a level of 80 per cent and above.

(ii) Labour Issues in Bringing Fuel

The mean recorded level of opinions in this case is 55 per cent, which is higher than the combined mean, which shows that this is a major issue which prevents access to public property by women. On this issue, 34 respondents (9 per cent) recorded a level of 20 per cent and less; 78 respondents (20 per cent) and 104 respondents (26 per cent) recorded their opinion level at 40 per cent and 50 per cent respectively; 99 respondents (25 per cent) recorded a level of 60 per cent, and 85 respondents (21 per cent) recorded a high level of 80 per cent to 100 per cent.

(iii) Problems related to Availability of Water

The opinions on problems related to availability of water are not significant issues as is clear from the mean score of 41 per cent which is less than the combined mean (51). There are 114 respondents (29 per cent) and 87 respondents (22 per cent) who recorded a level of opinion between 40 and 50 per cent; 50 respondents (13 per cent) recorded a level of 60 per cent.

(iv) Problems Related to Availability of Fuel

The views of respondents regarding this aspect show that there exists problems in connection with the availability of fuel as is noticed from mean score which is equal to the combined mean. Here, 106 respondents (27 per cent) recorded a level of 50 per cent and 105 respondents (27 per cent) recorded a level of 60 per cent.

(v) Problems Related to Availability of Sanitation

The mean level of opinions recorded by respondents (36 per cent) shows that there exists no such problem, because the mean score is less than the combined mean (51 per cent). A large section of the respondents (44 per cent) recorded a level of 20 per cent and less.

(vi) Problems Related to Kind of Health Issues

The mean level of opinions recorded by respondents in this case is 52 per cent which exceeds the combined mean (51 per cent). This means that this is an important variable of access to and control over public property.

Here, 108 respondents (27 per cent) recorded a level at 50 per cent and 103 respondents (26 per cent) recorded a level of 60 per cent respectively.

(vii) Availability of Security

As far as availability of security measures is concerned, there is sufficient security provided by the government to women, as is made clear from the mean level of opinion of 61 per cent which is higher than the combined mean of 51 per cent. On this factor, 110 respondents (28 per cent) and 122 respondents (31 per cent) recorded a level of 60 per cent and 80 per cent.

(viii) Expenditure on Security

As is clear from the mean recorded level, expense on security is not a prominent issue. The mean score is less than the combined mean in this case. Here, 138 respondents (34 per cent) and 99 respondents (25 per cent) recorded their opinion level at 20 per cent and less and 40 per cent respectively.

(ix) Food Security

Opinion level on food is significant for a large majority, as is clear from the mean score of 54 per cent which is higher than the combined mean (51 per cent). Here, 101 respondents (25 per cent) and 96 respondents (24 per cent) recorded 50 per cent and 60 per cent respectively.

(x) Calorie Expense

The mean recorded level of opinion clearly indicate that the expense is not much. The mean recorded level of opinion is 49 per cent which is lower than the combined mean (51 per cent). In this case, 95 respondents (24 per cent) and 131 respondents (33 per cent) recorded a level of 40 per cent and 50 per cent respectively; 111 respondents (28 per cent) recorded a level of 60 per cent.

(xi) Nutritional Status

As far as nutritional status is concerned, there is a better status as is clear from the mean score of 56 per cent which is higher than the combined mean (51 per cent). Here, 101 respondents (25 per cent) and 108 respondents (27 per cent) recorded a level of 50 per cent and 60 per cent respectively.

(xii) Non-acquisition of Primary Education

In the case of non-acquisition of primary education, the respondents argued that there is no such issue and all of them had acquired primary education, as is clear from the mean score of 29 per cent. Here, 47 respondents (12 per cent) recorded their opinion level at 20 per cent and less; 180 respondents (45 per cent) and 118 respondents (30 per cent) recorded a level of 20 per cent and 40 per cent respectively.

(xiii) Child Welfare Services

The mean recorded level of opinion is 60 per cent which is higher than the combined mean (51 per cent), which makes it clear that the child welfare services are significant in respect of accessibility to and control over public property by women. Here, 122 respondents (31 per cent) and 105 respondents (26 per cent) recorded a level of 60 per cent and 80 per cent respectively.

(xiv) Accessibility to Housing

The mean recorded level of opinions is 54 per cent, which is higher than the combined mean (51 per cent). This makes it clear that accessibility to housing is a prominent factor of accessibility and control over public property by women. In this case, 112 respondents (28 per cent) and 109 respondents (27 per cent) recorded a level of 50 per cent and 60 per cent respectively.

(xv) Accessibility to Banking

The mean recorded level of opinions is 61 per cent which shows that accessibility to banking is very important for the accessibility to and control over public property by women. Here, 124 respondents (31 per cent) recorded a level of 60 per cent and 103 respondents (26 per cent) recorded a level of 80 per cent.

(xvi) Facilities for Other Basic Needs

In this regard, the mean score is 65 per cent which is higher than the combined mean (51 per cent). This makes it clear that the facilities for other basic needs is a prominent sub-variable in the accessibility to and control over public property by women. Here, 118 respondents (30 per cent) and 128 respondents (32 per cent) recorded a level of 60 per cent and 80 per cent respectively.

(xvii) Accessibility to Loans

The mean recorded level of opinion of 52 per cent makes it clear that accessibility to loans is a prominent sub-variable in the accessibility to and control over public property by women. Here, 109 respondents (27 per cent) recorded a level of 50 per cent and 107 respondents (27 per cent) recorded a level at 60 per cent.

(xviii) Accessibility to Electricity

The mean recorded level of opinions is 60 per cent, which means that the accessibility to electricity is also a prominent sub-variable in the accessibility to and control over public property by women. Here, 128 respondents (32 per cent) recorded a level at 60 per cent and 109 respondents (27 per cent) recorded a level of 80 per cent.

(xix) Accessibility to Technical Education

The mean recorded level of opinions is 49 per cent, which means that accessibility to technical education is not a significant sub-variable in the accessibility to and control over public property by women.

3. Main Variable Bigger Control Over Income and Employment

One of the important factors that contributes to women empowerment is control over income and employment. In the unorganised sector, the conditions of work are insecure and wages are low with hardly any non-wage benefits. The conclusions drawn from the analysis on control over income and employment are:

(i) Work done which carries Wages

The women in Kerala are engaging themselves in tasks for getting wages. It is seen from the mean score which represents that most of the work done by women is unpaid or which carry no wages. Here, 258 respondents (65 per cent) marked their level of opinion between 40 and 50 per cent. The mean recorded level of opinion is 46 per cent, which is less than the combined mean (50 per cent).

(ii) Work done which carries no Wages

As far as women are concerned, they undertake numerous tasks at home for managing the family, but earn nothing as housewives. The mean recorded level of opinions is 54 per cent, which is higher than the combined mean (50 per cent). This means that this is a prominent variable contributing much to the main variable. Here, 217 respondents (54 per cent) recorded their level of opinion between 50 and 60 per cent.

(iii) Self-reliance in the Decision-making Process

Women in Kerala are self-reliant in decision-making in every walk of life. In Kerala, they take decisions regarding the purchase of articles, properties, vehicles, deposits of savings, investment, politics, starting of business, employment and management of situations. The mean score in this case is equal to the combined mean (50 per cent), which means this is a prominent variable contributing much to the main variable.

(iv) Time Spent on Different Jobs and Rest

Women in Kerala are dedicated to their family work for efficient management of the house. Working women face a lot more than the housewives according to a large majority of the respondents in the sample. The mean recorded level of opinion is 51 per cent which exceeds the combined mean (50 per cent). This means that it is a prominent variable contributing much to the main variable. Here, 211 respondents (53 per cent) marked their level of opinion between 50 and 60 per cent.

(v) Utilisation of Wages Earned

The amount of earnings from employment is spent either by her own decision or by a joint decision with her husband and other family members. In this respect, 230 respondents (58 per cent) recorded their level of opinion between 20 per cent or less and 40 per cent. The mean recorded level of opinion is 40 per cent which is less than the combined mean (50 per cent). This means that it is not a main contributory factor to the main variable.

(vi) Utilisation of Wages Earned or Handed Over

The opinions on the amount of earnings of women from employment is handed over to the husband or father or other elder members of the family, and not spent directly, revealed that the entire earnings are handed over, as is clear from the mean score which is 55 per cent. Regarding this, 103 respondents (26 per cent) and 169 respondents (42 per cent) recorded marked their level of opinion at 50 per cent and 60 per cent respectively.

(vii) The Degree of Decision-making Power on Family Expenditure

The degree of decision-making power on family expenditure is also enquired into and the collected opinions revealed that the degree of decision-making power is low as is clear from the mean score which is 47 per cent. Here, 124 respondents (31 per cent) recorded their level of opinion at 20 per cent and less.

(viii) Share of Women's Income in Family Expenditure

In the case of the single earner, who is a woman, she spends more as family expenditure. The mean recorded level of opinions of 43 per cent makes it clear that the share of women's income in family expenditure is low. Here, 212 respondents (54 per cent) recorded their level of opinion at 40 per cent and less.

(ix) Expenditure on Personal Needs

Those who are earning income by themselves can spend accordingly for meeting their personal needs. The level of opinions (mean score 60 per cent) on it shows that the expenditure on personal needs is much more than that on any other needs. Here, 185 respondents (47 per cent) marked a level between 80 per cent and 100 per cent.

(x) Accessibility to Income-Generating Jobs

In Kerala, there is ample scope for earning income through employment, whether public or private, or by starting businesses. The opinions of the respondents revealed, from the mean score (61 per cent), that there is accessibility to income-generating jobs. Here, 189 respondents (48 per cent) recorded a level between 80 and 100 per cent.

+In a majority of cases, the stream of study for women is selected by their parents and in certain cases only, the women choose a course. Now, a large majority of the girls have their own preference in studies so that they select a branch of study independently. The mean score of 70 per cent revealed that they have a certain level of independence in the selection of the stream of study. Here, 284 respondents (54 per cent) marked a level at 80 per cent and above.

(xii) Level of Independence for Selection of Jobs

As far as independence for selection of jobs is concerned, the preference is much less because getting a job is not easy in Kerala. The opinions of the respondents on it also revealed the same result (mean score is 49 per cent). Here, 205 respondents (51 per cent) marked their level of opinion between 40 per cent and 50 per cent and 136 respondents (34 per cent) recorded their level of opinion at 60 per cent.

(xiii) Wage Difference

There exists wage difference among men and women in Kerala. Depending upon the nature and type of work, the wages differ accordingly. The mean recorded level of opinions is 67 per cent, which is a clear indication of that. Here, 269 respondents (68 per cent) recorded a level between 60 and 80 per cent.

(xiv) Relationship of Women's Job with Education

The opinion of the respondents revealed that there exists no relation between women's job and education (the mean score is 41 per cent). Here, 242 respondents (61 per cent) recorded a level up to 50 per cent.

(xv) Relationship of Women's Job with Land Holding

Women have the entitlement right to acquire and control properties. The opinion level of respondents on the relationship of job with land holdings revealed that there exists no such relationship, as the mean score is only 38 per cent.

(xvi) Relationship of Women's Job with Men's Job Status

The status of women's job compared with that of men's job was also looked into and the opinions of respondents were gathered, which shows that no relation exists between the two as the mean score is 29 per cent. Here, 125 respondents (31 per cent) marked their level of opinion at 40 per cent.

(xvii) Access to and Control Over Trade and Commerce

As far as trade and commerce are concerned, the role played by women is also enquired into; the level of opinions revealed that there is no such control over trade and commerce by women (the mean score is 43 per cent).

(xviii) Intervention in New Products Market

The role of women in the intervention in new products markets was also looked into by examining the kind of intervention, such as, what to sell and what to buy. This revealed that there is only lesser intervention as far as new products market is concerned (the mean score 39 per cent).

(xix) Participation or Role of Women in Trade Unions

Almost all people in Kerala are politically conscious, in general, and women, in particular. They belong to any one political party and are active in politics on account of decentralised planning. There is high level of participation in trade unions by women, as is clear from the mean score of 61 per cent.

5. Main Variable—Control on the Decision on Own Body

The variables include freedom to take decision on their marriage, giving birth to child, sexual intercourse with partner, and also avoidance of tortures in workplace, torture of spouse, rape, and mental and physical hazards. The main conclusions drawn are:

(i) Freedom for Taking Decision on Marriage

In Kerala, marriages are usually arranged by parents or elders; sometimes with the consent of the women or without their consent. In certain circumstances, women themselves select their partners. It is the opinion of most respondents that they have their own freedom in taking decisions on marriage, as is clear from the mean score of 71 per cent. Here, 105 respondents (26 per cent) recorded their level of opinion at 60 per cent. 122 respondents (31 per cent) marked a level at 80 per cent and 77 of them (19 per cent) marked at 100 per cent.

(ii) Control over the Decisions on Child Birth

There is a need for consensus between husband and wife or life partners in respect of giving birth to child. The opinions of respondents revealed that there is sufficient freedom for control over decisions on child birth (mean score 70 per cent). Here, 250 respondents (67 per cent) recorded their level of opinion between 60 and 80 per cent.

(iii) Freedom on Decision on Sexual Intercourse with the Partner

Leading a better life and also for bettering the women status and development which requires sufficient freedom for decision on sexual intercourse with the partner. In this case, 230 respondents (58 per cent) recorded their level of opinion up to 40 per cent.The mean recorded level of opinion is 40 per cent, which shows there is less freedom in decision on sexual intercourse with the partner.

(iv) Physical and Mental Torture Like Rape

The mean recorded level of opinions is 37 per cent, which shows that the respondents are not agreed upon with physical and mental torture like rape. In this case, 274 respondents (68 per cent) recorded their level of opinion up to 40 per cent only.

(v) Physical and Mental Torture Like Caste or Religion-based Atrocities

In this case, 261 respondents (66 per cent) recorded their level of opinion up to 40 per cent. The mean recorded level of opinions is 38 per cent, which shows that there are no such caste and religion-based atrocities in Kerala.

(vi) Physical and Mental Torture like Sexual Harassment at Work Place

In this case, 119 respondents (30 per cent) marked their level of opinion at 50 per cent and 163 respondents 41 per cent) recorded their level of opinion at 60 per cent, whereas 53 respondents (13 per cent) marked a level of 80 per cent. The mean score in this case is as high as 55, which shows that there exists physical and mental torture like sexual harassment at the workplace.

(vii) Physical and Mental Torture by Spouse

In this case, 104 respondents (27 per cent) recorded their level of opinion at 20 per cent and less, and 104 respondents (26 per cent) marked their level of opinion between 40 per cent and 50 per cent.The mean recorded level of opinion is 45 per cent, which shows that there is no such torture by spouses.

(vii) Physical and Mental Torture by Close Relatives

There is no physical and mental torture from the close relatives as is noticed from the mean score of 39 per cent. A large majority recorded a level up to 40 per cent only. In this case, 236 respondents (60 per cent) recorded their level of opinion up to 40 per cent.

(viii) Societal Attitude on Women Status

Women occupy a prominent role in the society of Kerala. Now, they are having almost equal position as that of men by possessing almost all the rights for improving their status. But the opinions of the respondents revealed that the societal attitude is not up to the mark, as is clear from the mean score of 43 per cent. A large majority recorded a level up to 40 per cent and less.

(ix) Societal Attitude on Women Sexuality

Kerala women are still influenced largely by the religious and social images imposed upon them for centuries. The stereotype ideals of women have reduced them to a level of physical, mental, and spiritual subjugation. The mean recorded level of opinion is 50 per cent which indicates that this is a significant variable contributing much to the main variable.

6. Main Variable – Autonomy on Mobility

One of the important factors responsible for human development and the development of women status is free mobility. The trend in migration from Kerala to other countries of the world is increasing. The main variable 'autonomy in mobility' is analysed with eleven (11) sub-variables and the conclusions drawn from them are:

(i) Freedom for Mobility as Single

Now, in the globalised era there is free mobility of labourers from elsewhere in the world for employment, whether men or women. The mean recorded level of opinion is 50 per cent which indicates that there is freedom of mobility as single. In this regard, 107 respondents (27 per cent) and 81 respondents (20 per cent) marked their level of opinion at 40 per cent and 50 per cent respectively. 92 respondents (23 per cent) recorded their level of opinion at 60 per cent.

(ii) Freedom of Mobility with Female Companion

Women's mobility is more so when there is a companion than when single. The mean score (66 per cent) is higher than the combined mean of 50 per cent, which indicates that freedom of mobility is more when there is a woman companion. On this variable, 272 respondents (68 per cent) recorded their level of opinion at 60 per cent to 80 per cent.

(iii) Freedom of Mobility with Male Companion

The mobility of women when there is a male companion was also examined and it is seen that there is more mobility, as is clear from the mean recorded level of opinion of 66 per cent. Here, 266 respondents (67 per cent) recorded their level of opinion at 60 to 80 per cent level.

(iv) Freedom of Mobility in Day Time

The mobility of women is more during the day time than at night, as is clear from the mean score, which is 60 per cent. As many as 133 respondents (33 per cent) recorded their level of opinion at 60 per cent; 103 respondents (31 per cent) marked a level of 80 per cent.

(v) Freedom of Mobility at Night

As far as women in Kerala are concerned, there is less mobility at night, as is clear from the mean score of 43 per cent. In this case, 220 respondents (56 per cent) recorded their level of opinion at 40 per cent and less.

(vi) Lack of Freedom of Mobility due to Caste/Religion

There is less mobility for women in Kerala basically because they belong to a particular caste or religion, especially in the case of women wearing *Purdah*. The mean recorded level of opinion is 46 per cent. In this case, 256 respondents (64 per cent) recorded their level of opinion at 50 per cent and less.

(vii) Lack of Freedom of Mobility due to Special Conditions

Another important factor responsible for preventing or slowing down the process of mobility are certain special conditions. For example, there is less mobility for widows). The mean recorded level of opinion is 55 per cent, which indicates that there is adequate mobility even when special conditions are prevailing.

(viii) Lack of Freedom of Mobility due to Special Personal Issues

Another important problem which hinders the mobility of women in general is the personal issues confronted during periods and other issues such as pregnancy. There are 150 respondents (37 per cent) who recorded their level of opinion at 20 per cent and less; 68 respondents (17 per cent) and 95 respondents (24 per cent) marked their level of opinion at 40 per cent and 50 per cent respectively. The mean score is higher than the combined mean of 50 per cent which indicates that there is freedom of mobility even when there exist special personal issues.

(ix) Lack of Freedom of Mobility due to Local Customs

There are certain local customs and traditions which prevent the freedom of mobility of women in Kerala, especially in the case of tribes, as the mean recorded level of opinion is 37 per cent, which indicates that there is no such prevention as far the respondents are concerned.

(x) Lack of Freedom of Mobility due to Women Status

Those who are at the helm of affairs move faster than those at the lower strata. In this case, 190 respondents (47 per cent) recorded their level of opinion at 20 per cent and less; 94 respondents (24 per cent) and 75 respondents (19 per cent) marked their level of opinion at 40 per cent and 50 per cent respectively. The mean recorded level of opinion is 30 per cent which indicates that this not a significant variable which contributes to the main variable.

(xi) Lack of Freedom of Mobility due to Places of Worship

Another factor which is responsible for women's mobility is the place of worship. Sometimes, people reside in a place surrounding a place of worship. In that case, they won't go anywhere other than this place of worship. In this respect, 266 respondents (67 per cent) recorded their level of opinion at 20 per cent and less. The mean recorded level of opinion is 22 per cent, which means that there is no such prevention as far the respondents are concerned.

7. Main Variable – Autonomy in Politics

In Kerala, women's participation in politics is low and no difference is noticed from the rest of the country. On the contrary, going by the numbers in which they turn out for electioneering and to cast vote in various elections, women's participation can quite justifiably be described as active and the proportion of votes cast by women has improved. This variable was analysed and conclusions drawn are as under:

(i) Participation in the Capacity as Voter in General Elections

The mean score is very high compared to the combined mean of 55 per cent, which means that the respondents are of the opinion that they are actively participating in general elections as voters and nothing more than that.

(ii) Participation in the Capacity as Candidate in General Elections

There is political empowerment extended to women by 50 per cent reservation in seats of the grassroots institutions. The mean score is very high compared to the combined mean of 55 per cent, which means that the respondents are of the opinion that they are contesting as a candidates in general elections.

(iii) Freedom to Cast Vote as per Own Decision

In respect of casting of votes, women have the freedom of exercising their own decision. It means that they are not accepting the recommendation for casting vote in favour of a political party. The mean score is higher than the combined mean of 55 per cent which means that the respondents are of the opinion that women have exercised their votes by their own decisions and not under any influence or pressure.

(iv) Membership in Political Parties

Women are not active in politics and hence they do not take membership in political parties. In the case of employees, they are active in trade unions which are affiliated to certain political parties. On this factor, 110 respondents (28 per cent) marked their level of opinion at 20 per cent and less, and 113 respondents (28 per cent) marked their level of opinion at 40 per cent. The mean recorded level of opinion is 42 per cent, which means that the respondents are of the opinion that women have no membership in party politics.

(v) Membership in Community Organisations

Kudumbasree has introduced several innovative programmes for the financial, economic and social uplift of poor women, by organising them into community-based structures like Neighbourhood groups. In this case, 112 respondents (28 per cent) recorded their level of opinion at 20 per cent and less; 92 respondents (23 per cent) recorded their level of opinion at 40 per cent; and 63 respondents (16 per cent) marked their level of opinion at 50 per cent. The mean recorded level of opinion noticed is 47 per cent, which means that the respondents are of the opinion that all of them are not involved in community-based organisations.

(vi) Approach of Political Parties towards Women

The mean recorded level of opinion noticed is 41 per cent which means that the respondents are of the opinion that the treatment of political parties towards women is not appreciable.

(vii) Reservation of Seats for Women in Election to Parliament

For giving political empowerment to women in general, and those of Kerala in particular, there is reservation of seats for election to the parliament. The mean score on this sub-variable is higher than the combined mean of 55 per cent, which indicates that the respondents are very much satisfied with the pattern of reservation in parliament election.

(viii) Reservation of Seats for Women in Election to Legislative Assembly

In this case, the mean score is higher than the combined mean of 55 per cent which indicates that the respondents are very much satisfied with the pattern of reservation of seats in elections to the legislative assembly.

(ix) Reservation of Seats for Women in Elections to the Local Government Bodies

Only 1/3rd of the seats were reserved for women in local government bodies at the initial phase of the introduction of the People's Plan Campaign during the IXth Plan, and now 50 per cent of the seats are reserved. The mean recorded level of opinions is 56 per cent, which indicates that the respondents are very much satisfied with the pattern of reservation extended to women in local bodies in Kerala.

(x) The Method of Participation of Women

There are various methods by which women participate in different activities for their development as well as the development of the economy as a whole). The mean recorded level of opinions is 58 per cent, which indicates that the respondents are very much satisfied with the method of participation for the attainment of political autonomy.

(xi) Nominations of Women to Corporations/Boards

Like reservation of seats for women in legislature, parliament and local bodies, there are nominations to statutory Corporations and Boards. In this case, 121 respondents (28 per cent) marked their level of opinion at 20 per cent and less, whereas 100 respondents (25 per cent) marked their level of opinion at 40 per cent; 87 respondents (22 per cent) at 50 per cent, and 66 respondents (17 per cent) at 60 per cent. The mean recorded level of opinions is 44 per cent which indicates that the respondents were not satisfied with the method of participation for the attainment of political autonomy.

(xii) Nominations of Women as Chiefs of Political Parties

Sometimes, women are nominated as chiefs of political parties. In this case, 166 respondents (42 per cent) marked their level of opinion at 20 per cent and less, whereas 120 respondents (30 per cent) marked their level of opinion at 40 per cent, and 52 respondents (13 per cent) marked their level of opinion at 50 per cent. This indicates that the respondents are not satisfied with nomination as chiefs of political parties for attainment of political autonomy.

8. Main Variable – Professional Autonomy in Knowledge and Information

Women's autonomy is likely to have a significant impact on society by altering women's relative control over household resources, and by influencing their attitudes and abilities. This variable is analysed with the help of ten (10) sub-variables and the conclusion drawn from them are:

(i) Women's Participation in Gram Sabha

The participation of women in Gram Sabhas is more than that of men which is a notable feature in Kerala in the initial phase of the people's campaign for the Ninth Plan, but during the second phase onwards, there are dropouts on account of the lose of faith in it. Women mainly constitute the beneficiary groups and are normally concentrated in the subject groups like women welfare, sanitation or drinking water. The mean recorded level of opinions is 48 per cent, which indicates that the participation is not up to the mark.

(ii) Women's Participation in Community Organisations

Community organisations are very common among Kerala women who are the members of the organisations. The mean score in this case is 41 per cent, which indicates that the participation in community organisations is not remarkably good. A large majority of the respondents marked their level at 40 per cent and less. In this case, 222 respondents (53 per cent) marked their level of opinion at 40 per cent and less.

(iii) Ability to Bring up Own Interests

In this case, 217 respondents (52 per cent) marked their level of opinion at 40 per cent and less; 97 respondents (25 per cent) marked their level of opinion between 60 per cent and 80 per cent. The mean score in this case is 47 per cent which indicates that this variable is not a significant contributory factor to the main variable.

(iv) Ability to Bring up Consensus-building

The mean recorded level of opinion in this case is 63 per cent, which exceeds the combined mean of 51 per cent. This indicates that professional autonomy in knowledge and information is needed for creating ability to bring up consensus building. Here, 128 respondents (32 per cent) marked their level of opinion at 60 per cent and 121 respondents (30 per cent) at 80 per cent.

(v) Ability of Bargaining

Information and knowledge can increase the bargaining capacity of women. The professional autonomy in knowledge and information improves the bargaining capacity of women, which in turn, leads to better status and development. The mean recorded level of opinion in this case is 52 per cent. The mean score exceeds the combined mean of 51 per cent which indicates that professional autonomy in knowledge and information creates the ability of bargaining. Here, 74 respondents (19 per cent) marked their level of opinion at 50 per cent and 142 respondents (36 per cent) at 60 per cent; 84 respondents (21 per cent) marked a level of 80 per cent and none of them recorded a level of cent per cent.

(vi) Power of Women's Associations

On account of the power and strength of the women's associations, their ability to control and prevent violence and crimes against women is possible on the one hand and gain on status, development and empowerment on the other. Here, 110 respondents (28 per cent) marked a level at 60 per cent and 122 respondents at 80 per cent. The mean recorded level of opinion in this case is 61 per cent which exceeds the combined mean of 51 per cent. This indicates that professional autonomy in knowledge and information is obtained through women's associations.

(vii) Women's Participation in Big Organisations

The mean score is less than the combined mean of 51 per cent which indicates that women's participation in big organisations is not satisfactory. In this respect, 165 respondents (42 per cent) marked their level of opinion at 20 per cent and less. 88 respondents (22 per cent) marked their level of opinion at 40 per cent and 75 respondents (19 per cent) at 50 per cent.

(viii) Women's Participation in Big Networks

Women's participation in big networks was also enquired into and opinions of respondents were obtained. The mean recorded level of opinion in this case is 58 per cent and it exceeds the combined mean of 51 per cent. This clearly indicates that women's participation in big networks is satisfactory. In this case, 101 respondents (25 per cent) recorded a level of 50 per cent and 126 respondents (32 per cent) at 60 per cent.

(ix) Women's Membership in Women's Associations

For increasing the bargaining power through collective action, women's associations were organised. The mean recorded level of opinions in this case is 49 per cent and it is less than the combined mean of 51 per cent. This is a clear indication that women's membership in associations is not satisfactory. A large majority marked a level of 40 per cent and less, while 240 respondents (60 per cent) marked their level of opinion up to 40 per cent.

(x) Women's Membership in Information Centres like Libraries

The opinion of women on the extent of information and knowledge was gathered from them through visiting these information centres which makes it clear that their membership in information centres is satisfactory. The mean score in this case is 51 per cent. Here, 109 respondents (27 per cent) recorded a level of 50 per cent, 106 respondents (27 per cent) at 60 per cent, and 57 respondents (14 per cent) at 80 per cent.

9. Main Variable - Legal Status and Accessibility to Legislature

The matrilineal social structures and lack of organised social opposition to women's education, and social and economic advancement, contributed to women's progress. The eight sub-variables were analysed with the following inferences:

(i) The Attitude of Legislative Forums Towards Women

The opinion on the attitude of legislative forums towards women shows a favourable trend. The mean recorded level of opinion in this case is 61 per cent. Here, 112 respondents (28 per cent) recorded a level of 50 per cent and 82 respondents (21 per cent) at 60 per cent, whereas 89 respondents (22 per cent) marked their opinion level at 80 per cent.

(ii) Women's Awareness of Laws Concerned with Women and their Rights

The women's legal awareness for safeguarding their rights was looked into and opinions have been collected. The mean recorded level of opinion in this case is 51 per cent, which is higher than the combined mean of 46 per cent. This shows that the women in Kerala are legally aware about protecting their rights. On this sub-variable, 117 respondents (29 per cent) recorded a level at 50 per cent, and 106 respondents (27 per cent) at 60 per cent.

(iii) Women's Awareness of their Rights

The mean marked level of opinion on women's awareness of their rights is 51 per cent and is higher than the combined mean of 51 per cent. This shows that women in Kerala are aware of their rights.

(iv) Decision on Violation of Women's Rights

Violation of women's rights was also looked into. The mean level of opinion on it is 31 per cent. The mean score is higher than the combined mean of 46 per cent, which shows that there is no question of violation of women's rights. A large majority of the respondents in the sample recorded their opinion level at 40 per cent and less; 186 respondents (47 per cent) at 20 per cent and less, and 109 respondents (27 per cent) at 40 per cent.

(v) Decision on Violation of Atrocities against Women

In this case, a large majority of the respondents marked their opinion level at 40 per cent and less, 137 respondents (35 per cent) marked their level of opinion at 20 per cent and less. 108 respondents (27 per cent) at 40 per cent and 101 respondents (25 per cent) at 50 per cent. The mean recorded level of opinions in this case is 37 per cent. The mean score is lower than the combined mean of 46 per cent which shows that this variable is not contributing much to the main variable.

(vi) Accessibility and Experience with the Police Set-Up

The police force in the State gives protection to women. The mean recorded level of opinion in this case is 40 per cent, which is lower than the combined mean of 46 per cent. This shows that this variable is not contributing much to the main variable. In this case also, a large majority of the respondents marked their opinion level at 40 per cent and less and 129 respondents (32 per cent) at 20 per cent and less. Only 106 respondents (27 per cent) marked their level of opinion at 40 per cent.

(vii) Accessibility and Experience with Court of Law

The accessibility and experience with the court of law was enquired into. The mean level of opinions (43 per cent) reveals that this variable is not contributing much to the main variable. In this case, 111 respondents (28 per cent) marked their level of opinion at 20 per cent and less and 82 respondents (21 per cent) at 40 per cent.

(viii) Accessibility and Experience with Women's Commission

The Women's Commission of Kerala was constituted to uplift their status and to empower women. The mean recorded level of opinions in this case is 51 per cent. The mean score is higher than the combined mean of 46 per cent, which shows that women's accessibility to and experience with the Women's Commission in Kerala is high. Here, 76 respondents (19 per cent) marked their level of opinion at 40 per cent and 94 respondents (24 per cent) at 50 per cent. Only 106 respondents (27 per cent) marked a level of 60 per cent.

(c) Predictor Equation of the Women Empowerment

A predictor equation model for the Income, Employment, Entitlement and Empowerment of Women in Kerala by considering eight Independent variables and one Dependent variable for knowing the extent of influence of the Independent variables on the Dependent variable in relation to the Women Empowerment were examined (Regression Analysis).

The item-wise analysis of the eight (8) independent variables of women empowerment gives a detailed itemwise picture of the opinions of the respondents. The Multiple Regression Analysis with different combinations of Independent variables with the Dependent variables is used to frame a Predictive Model for Women Empowerment in Kerala.

The different combinations of Independent variables consisting of one (1) Independent Variable, two (2) Independent Variables, three (3) Independent Variables, four (4) Independent Variables, five (5) Independent Variables, six (6) Independent Variables, seven (7) Independent Variables and eight (8) Independent Variables equations are framed.

1. One Variable Predictor Equation

In one variable predictor equation, there are eight (8) combinations of equations for each set. The Independent Variable is Control over Income and Employment (V_4), since it has the highest correlation of 0.70 and correlation square of 0.49 with the independent variable women empowerment (V_{10}).$\bar{V}_{10} = 28.2 + 0.45V_4 + 2.11$

2. Two Variable Predictor Equations

In the two variable predictor equation, there are twenty eight (28) combinations of Independent Variables with Dependent Variables. Control over Income and Employment (V_4), and Autonomy over Politics (V_7); it has the highest correlation (0.82) and correlation square (0.70) with the dependent variable, Women empowerment (V_{10}).

$= 22.0 + 0.37V4 + 0.19V7 + 1.70$

3. Three Variable Predictor Equations

In three variable predictor equations, there are fifty six (56) combinations of Independent Variables. The best fit three variable predictor equation is the combination with the Accessibility and Control Over Private Property (V_2), operational problem(V_2), Control Over Income and Employment (V_4) and Autonomy over Politics (V_7). It has the highest correlation value of 0.86 and correlation square of 0.74 with the dependent variable women empowerment ($\bar{V}_{10}$). The best fit equation is with the Independent Variable Accessibility and Control Over Private Property (V_2), Control Over Income and Employment (V_4) and Autonomy over Politics (V_7). $= 15.7 + 0.13V_2 + 0.37V_4 + 0.18V_7 + 1.50$

4. Four Variable Predictor Equations

In this variable predictor equation, there are seventy (70) combinations of Independent Variables.

The best fit four variable predictor equation is the combination of Accessibility and Control Over Private Property (V_2), Accessibility and Control Over Public Property (V_3), Control Over Income and Employment (V_4) and Autonomy over Politics (V_7), since it has the highest correlation value of 0.90 and correlation square of 0.80 with the dependent variable Women Empowerment ($\bar{V}_{10}$). The best fit equation with the Independent Variables Accessibility and Control Over Private Property (V_2), Accessibility and Control Over Public Property (V_3), Control Over Income and Employment (V_4) and Autonomy over Politics (V_7):

$= \beta_0 + \beta_2 V_2 + \beta_3 V_3 + \beta_4 V_4 + \beta_7 X_7 + \varepsilon$

After the calculation of constant, the beta coefficient of variables V_2, V_3, V_4, and V_7 and standard error, the best fit from variable predictor equation is:

$= 11.8 + 0.13V_2 + 0.16V_3 + 0.29V_4 + 0.17V_7 + 1.31$

5. Five Variable Predicted Equations

In this variable predictor equation, there are fifty six (56) combinations of Independent Variables. The best fit equation with the independent variables Accessibility and Control Over Private Property (V_2), Accessibility Control Over Public Property (V_3), Control Over Income and Employment (V_4), Control on the Decision on Own Body (V_5) and Autonomy over Politics (V_7) is:

$$= 9.7 + 0.14V_2 + 0.08V_3 + 0.22V_4 + 0.12V_5 + 0.14V_7 + 1.08$$

6. Six Variable Predictor Equations

In this variable predictor equation, there are twenty eight (28) combinations of Independent Variables. Accessibility and Control Over Accessibility and Control Over Private Property (V_2), Accessibility Control Over Public Property (V_3), Control Over Income and Employment (V_4), Control on the Decision on Own Body (V_5), Autonomy on Mobility (V_6), Autonomy Over Politics (V_7) and Legal Status and Accessibility to Legislature (V_9), since it has the highest correlation value of 0.97 and correlation square of 0.93 with the dependent variable Women Empowerment ().The best fit equation with the independent variables, Accessibility and Control Over Private Property (V_2), Accessibility Control Over Public Property (V_3), Control Over Income and Employment (V_4), Control on the Decision on Own Body (V_5), Autonomy on Mobility (V_6), Autonomy Over Politics (V_7) and Legal Status and Accessibility to Legislature (V_9) is:

$$= 5.8 + 0.11V_2 + 0.19V_3 + 0.20V_4 + 0.09V_5 + 0.10V_6 + 0.13V_7 + 0.07V_9 + 0.76$$

7. Seven Variable Predictor Equations

In seven variable predictor equations, there are eight (8) combinations of Independent Variables. The best fit seven variable predictor equation is the combination with Accessibility and Control Over Private Property (V_2), Accessibility Control Over Public Property (V_3), Control Over Income and Employment(V_4), Control on the Decision on Own Body (V_5), Autonomy on Mobility (V_6), Autonomy Over Politics (V_7) and Legal Status and Accessibility to Legislature (V_9), since it has the highest Correlation value of 0.97 and Correlation square of 0.93 with the dependent variable Women Empowerment ().The best fit equation with the independent variables, Accessibility and Control Over Private Property (V_2), Accessibility Control Over Public Property (V_3), Control Over Income and Employment (V_4), Control on the Decision on Own Body (V_5), Autonomy on Mobility (V_6), Autonomy Over Politics (V_7) and Legal Status and Accessibility to Legislature (V_9) is:

$$= \beta_0 + \beta_2 V_2 + \beta_3 V_3 + \beta_4 V_4 + \beta_5 V_5 + \beta_6 V_6 + \beta_7 X_7 + \beta_9 V_9 \ \varepsilon$$

After the calculation of Constant, the Beta Coefficient of (V_2), (V_3),

(V_4), (V_5), (V_6), (V_7) and (V_9) and the standard error, the best fit from variable predictor equation is:

= 5.8 + 0.11V2 + 0.19V3 + 0.20V4 + 0.09V5 + 0.10V6 + 0.13V7 + 0.07V9 + 0.76.

8. Eight Variable Predictor Equations

In respect of Accessibility and Control Over Private Property (V_2), Accessibility Control Over Public Property (V_3), Control Over Income and Employment (V_4), Control on the Decision on Own Body (V_5), Autonomy on Mobility (V_6), Autonomy Over Politics (V_7), Professional Autonomy in Knowledge and Information (V_8) and Legal Status and Accessibility to Legislature (V_9). The multiple correlation (R) with a correlation square (R^2) between all the independent variables and the dependent variable is 0.98 and 0.96. The best fit equation for the five independent variables (V_2), (V_3), (V_4), (V_5), (V_6), (V_7), (V_8) and (V_9) is: $= 2.9 + 0.11V_2 + 0.20V_3 + 0.18V_4 + 0.09V_5 + 0.11V_6 + 0.13V_7 + 0.05V_8 + 0.08V_9 + 0.$

The selected Eight Predictor Equations are:

Multiple Regression Model of Women Empowerment

Sl. No.	*Variables*	*Predictor Equations*	*R*	*R^2*
1.	V4	$\bar{V}_{10}$ = 28.2 + 0.45V4 + 2.11	0.70	0.49
2.	V4, V7	$\bar{V}_{10}$ = 22.0 + 0.37V4 + 0.19V7 + 1.70	0.82	0.70
3.	V2, V4, V7	$\bar{V}_{10}$ = 15.7 + 0.13V2 + 0.37V4 + 0.18V7 + 1.50	0.86	0.74
4.	V2,V3,V4,V7	$\bar{V}_{10}$ = 11.8 + 0.13V2 + 0.16V3 + 0.29V4 + 0.17V7 + 1.31	0.90	0.80
5.	V2,V3,V4,V5,V7	$\bar{V}_{10}$ = 9.7 + 0.14V2 + 0.08V3 + 0.22V4 + 0.12V5 + 0.14V7 + 1.08	0.93	0.87
6.	V2,V3,V4,V5,V6,V7	$\bar{V}_{10}$ = 6.5 + 0.11V2 + 0.20V3 + 0.21V4 + 0.12V5 + 0.9V6 + 0.14V7 + 0.90	0.95	0.91
7.	V2,V3,V4,V5,V6,V7,V9	$\bar{V}_{10}$ = 5.8 + 0.11V2 + 0.19V3 + 0.20V4 + 0.09V5 + 0.10V6 + 0.13V7 + 0.07V9 + 0.76	0.97	0.93
8.	V2,V3,V4,V5,V6,V7,V8, V9	$\bar{V}_{10}$ = 2.9 + 0.11V2 + 0.20V3 + 0.18V4 + 0.09V5 + 0.11V6 + 0.13V7 + 0.05V8 + 0.08V9 + 0.61	0.98	0.96

Source: SPSS (Statistical Package for Social Sciences) Output of Analysis of Primary Data.

To sum up, Accessibility and Control Over Private Property (V_2), Accessibility Control Over Public Property (V_3), Control Over Income and Employment(V_4), Control on the Decision on Own Body (V_5), Autonomy on Mobility (V_6), Autonomy Over Politics (V_7), Professional Autonomy in Knowledge and Information (V_8) and Legal Status and Accessibility to Legislature (V_9) are the main variables contributing to women empowerment in Kerala. The mean score, standard deviation and co-efficient of variation are ascertained, based on opinions at different levels to know the significance of the variables. It is made clear that all these variables are significant. The existence of these variables is analysed and compared with the help of the individual mean score of opinions with the combined mean of all the sub-variables under eight heads. It is seen significant in the sense that the mean score exceeds the combined mean.

The regression analysis is made to know the relationship of the independent variables such as Accessibility and Control Over Private Property, Accessibility Control Over Public Property, Control Over Income and Employment, Control on the Decision on Own Body, Autonomy on Mobility, Autonomy Over Politics, Professional Autonomy in Knowledge and Information and Legal Status and Accessibility to Legislature with the dependent variable women empowerment.

(d) Summary of Empowerment Disparities Across Different Groups

This summary reveals the following :

1. There is no significant difference in women empowerment as to employment, income and entitlement among women in different locations, viz., urban and rural areas. Therefore, the null hypothesis is rejected at 5 per cent and one per cent significance level, which means that the average empowerment of women in these two regions, urban and rural areas is significantly different from each other, that is, the empowerment is not the same in urban and rural areas.

2. There is no significant difference in women empowerment as to employment, income and entitlement among women in different organisational set-ups, viz., Government, Non-government and Unorganised sectors. The average women empowerment is not the same in all the three forms of organisation, say, Government organisation, Non-government organisation and the Unorganised sector. Thus, the result of the test is reported as "There is a significant difference in the women empowerment in the Government sector, Non-government sector and the Unorganised

sector. This means that the average empowerment of women in Government Organisation and Non-government Organisation is significantly different. The same is the case with all other combinations, i.e., Government Organisation – Unorganised sector, Unorganised sector – Government Organisation, and Non-government Organisation – Unorganised sector.

3. There is no significant difference in women empowerment as to employment, income and entitlement among women in different job status,viz., Gazetted and Non-gazetted officials. Therefore, the null hypothesis is rejected at 5 per cent and one per cent significance level, which means that the average empowerment of women in these two groups, Gazetted and Non-gazetted cadres, is significantly different from each other, that is, the empowerment is not the same for Gazetted and Non-gazetted cadre.

4. There is no significant difference in women empowerment as to employment, income and entitlement among women in different levels of educational attainment viz., Below Primary, Primary – SSLC, SSLC – Degree and Above Degree. Therefore, the null hypothesis can be safely rejected and it can be concluded that the average women empowerment is not the same in all the four categories of educational attainment, say, Below Primary, Primary - SSLC, SSLC - Degree and Above Degree. This means that the average empowerment of women in all the combinations of different groups of education level is significantly different as their mean difference is significantly different at 5 per cent level.

5. There is no significant difference in women empowerment as to employment, income and entitlement among women in different religions, viz., Hindu, Muslim, Christian and Others. In this case, the average women empowerment is the same in all the four categories of religious groups. This means that the average empowerment of women in all the combinations of different religious groups is not significantly different as their mean difference is not significantly different at 5 per cent level.

6. There is no significant difference in women empowerment as to income, employment and entitlement among women in different occupational groups viz., Farm activities, Hospitality, Micro Enterprises, Solid waste management, Health sector and Education. The null hypothesis can be safely rejected and it can be concluded that the average women empowerment is not the same in all the four categories of occupational groups, say, Farm activities,

Hospitality management, Micro Enterprises, Solid waste management, Health sector and Education sectors. This means that the average empowerment of women in all the combinations of different occupational groups is significantly different as the mean difference is significantly different at 5 per cent level. For Health sector – Education sector and Education sector – Health sector, the p-value is > 0.05. This means that the average empowerment of women in this combination of occupational groups is not significantly different, as the mean difference is not significantly different at 5 per cent level.

7. There is no significant difference in women empowerment as to income, employment and entitlement among women in different age groups, viz., Below 20 years, Between 20 – 35 years, Between 35 – 50 years and Above 50 years. The average women empowerment is not the same in all the four categories of age groups. This means that the average empowerment of women in all the combinations of different religious groups is significantly different as the mean difference is significantly different at 5 per cent level. This means that the average empowerment of women in all the combinations of different religious groups is not significantly different as their mean difference is not significantly different at 5 per cent level.

8

Conclusions and Suggestions

The following are the suggestions based on the findings of the study:

(a) There is a need for full empowerment training to all women, irrespective of their religion, age, job or occupational status.

(b) For improving the political empowerment of women, sufficient training should be given for governance practice and project preparations in local governments.

(c) Sufficient support must be given by the government in the form of guidance and support - oral and financial - to women enterprises, to develop in them entrepreneurial talents.

(d) Adequate measures should be initiated to avoid disparity in the empowerment level of women in urban and rural areas and also in the organised (Government and Non-governmental organisations) and unorganised sectors.

(e) Women entrepreneurs should be trained in undertaking technologically high industries for earning profit than in starting traditional activities in the farming sector, like rearing of goats and cows.

(f) Adequate steps should be taken by local governments to ensure the participation of all members in the Neighbourhood group, Area Development Society (ADS) and Community Development Society (CDS) for improving their empowerment status.

(g) The local governments should ensure legal literacy to make women aware of their legal rights.

(h) The higher the education level, the better is the level of empowerment; so sufficient measurers should be initiated for extending higher education to women as far as possible.

(i) Sufficient training should be extended in all categories of activities such as farm activities, hospitality, micro enterprise, solid waste management, health sector and education sectors, and it should be ensured that all of them reach the same level of empowerment.

(j) A separate women code should be formulated by the government through which the women of various religions, can enjoy legal entitlements.

(k) The local government may be empowered to initiate locally specific means to study the women status and formulate gender budgeting so as to improve the empowerment of women.

(l) While different development departments draft their Five Year and Annual Plans, at least a 10 per cent provision should be earmarked for women development schemes.

Appendix

(I) Personal Details

1	Name	: ------------------------------------
2	Locality	: 1. Rural ☐ 2. Urban ☐
3	Sector	: 1. GO ☐ 2. NGO ☐ 3. UNO ☐
4	Age	:
5	Religion	:
6	Academic Qualifications	: 1. Below Primary ☐ 2. Primary – SSLC ☐ 3. SSLC – Degree ☐ 4. Above Degree ☐
7	Marital Status	1. Married ☐ 2. Unmarried ☐
8	Status	1. Gazetted ☐ 2. Non-gazetted ☐
9	Activity Sector	1. Farm operation ☐ 2. Hospitality Management ☐ 3. Micro Enterprises ☐ 4. Solid waste Management ☐ 5. Health Sector ☐ 6. Education Sector ☐

Kindly put a tick (√) mark for your level of satisfaction on 1,2,3,4,5,6, or 7 based on the following scale

100%	80%	60%	50%	40%	20%	0%
1	2	3	4	5	6	7

(II) Accessibility and control over Private Properties [V_1]

		1	2	3	4	5	6	7
1	Savings							
2	Family income							
3	Food							
4	Accessibility to housing loans							
5	Status and property laws							
6	Impact of Globalisation in Expenditure pattern							
7	Role in decision making							

(III) Accessibility and control over public properties [V_2]

		1	2	3	4	5	6	7
1	Labour issues in bringing water/fuel							
2	Problems related to availability of water/fuel							

3. Availability and expenditure on security

1	2	3	4	5	6	7

4. Food security

1	2	3	4	5	6	7

5. Calorie expense and nutritional status

1	2	3	4	5	6	7

6. Non-acquisition of primary education

1	2	3	4	5	6	7

7. Child welfare services

1	2	3	4	5	6	7

8. Accessibility to housing

1	2	3	4	5	6	7

9. Accessibility to banking

1	2	3	4	5	6	7

10. Facilities to basic needs

1	2	3	4	5	6	7

11. Accessibility to loans

1	2	3	4	5	6	7

12. Accessibility to electricity

1	2	3	4	5	6	7

13. Accessibility to technical education

1	2	3	4	5	6	7

(IV) Control over Income and Employment [V_3]

1. Work done which carry wages

1	2	3	4	5	6	7

2. Work done which carry no wages

1	2	3	4	5	6	7

3. Self-reliance in the decision-making process

1	2	3	4	5	6	7

4. Time spent on different job and rest

1	2	3	4	5	6	7

5. Utilisation of wages earned (spent/handed over)

1	2	3	4	5	6	7

6. The degree of decision-making power in family expenditure

1	2	3	4	5	6	7

7. Share of woman's income in family expenditure

1	2	3	4	5	6	7

8. Expenditure on personal needs

1	2	3	4	5	6	7

9. Accessibility to income generating jobs

1	2	3	4	5	6	7

10. Level of independence for selection of jobs

1	2	3	4	5	6	7

11. Wage difference

1	2	3	4	5	6	7

12. Relationship of woman's job with education, land holding and men's job status

1	2	3	4	5	6	7

13. Access and control over trade and commerce (who sells, at what cost, at what location, etc.)

1	2	3	4	5	6	7

14. Intervention in new products' market (what to sell, what to buy)

1	2	3	4	5	6	7

15. Participation (role) of women in trade unions

1	2	3	4	5	6	7

(V) Control on the decision on own body [V_4]

1. Freedom for taking decision on marriage

1	2	3	4	5	6	7

2. Control over the decisions on child birth

1	2	3	4	5	6	7

3. Freedom on decision on sexual intercourse with the partner

1	2	3	4	5	6	7

4. Physical and mental torture like rape

1	2	3	4	5	6	7

5. Physical and mental torture like caste-religion based atrocities

1	2	3	4	5	6	7

6. Physical and mental torture like

1	2	3	4	5	6	7

sexual harassment at work place

1	2	3	4	5	6	7

7. Physical and mental torture by spouse

8. Societal attitude on women sexuality

1	2	3	4	5	6	7

(VI) Autonomy on Mobility [V_5]

1. Freedom for mobility in single

1	2	3	4	5	6	7

2. Freedom for mobility only along with someone

1	2	3	4	5	6	7

3. Freedom for mobility in night

1	2	3	4	5	6	7

4. Lack of freedom for mobility due to caste-religion issues being women*

1	2	3	4	5	6	7

5. Lack of freedom for mobility due to special conditions such as being widow*

1	2	3	4	5	6	7

6. Lack of freedom for mobility due to special conditions such as menses periods*

1	2	3	4	5	6	7

7. Relationship with Caste and Religion

1	2	3	4	5	6	7

(VII) Autonomy over Politics (V_6)

1. Participation in the capacity as voter and candidate in general elections

1	2	3	4	5	6	7

2. Freedom to caste vote as per own decision

1	2	3	4	5	6	7

3. Membership in Political parties and community organisations

1	2	3	4	5	6	7

4. The method of participation of women

1	2	3	4	5	6	7

(VIII) Professional Autonomy in Knowledge and Information [V_7]

1. Women's participation in Gram sabha / Community organisations

1	2	3	4	5	6	7

2. Ability to bring up own interests and power of bargaining and consensus building

1	2	3	4	5	6	7

3. Power of women's associations

1	2	3	4	5	6	7

4. Women's participation in biggest organisation, networks etc.

1	2	3	4	5	6	7

(IX) Legal Status and accessibility to legislature [V_8]

1	2	3	4	5	6	7

1. The attitude of legislative forums towards women

1	2	3	4	5	6	7

2. Women's awareness on laws and their rights

1	2	3	4	5	6	7

3. The decisions on the violation of women's rights and atrocities against women

1	2	3	4	5	6	7

4. Accessibility and experience with the police set up

1	2	3	4	5	6	7

5. Accessibility and experience with the court of law

1	2	3	4	5	6	7

Bibliography

1. Lucy, T.V.: Empowerment for women for sustainable Development, Social Action, Vol. 45, No. 2, 1995, pp. 224-230.
2. Mahaljan, A: Women's Tow Roles- A study of role conflict in India, Journal of Social Work, 1996, Vol. 25, No. 4, pp. 377-80.
3. Gopalan Sarala : Empowerment of women, a case study of Andhra Pradesh, Southern Economist, Vol. XXX, No. 15, 1997, pp. 18-23.
4. Gopalan Suseela: Empowerment of Women Through Education and Employment, Kerala Calling, Vol. 19, No. 5, 1999, pp. 5-6.
5. Kulathoor Nair and Premakumaran, S.V.: Empowering Women, to be or not to be, Calling, Vol. 19, No. 5, 1999, pp. 7-9.
6. Subha, K. and Bhargava, B.S: Panchayati Raj System and Political Empowerment of Women, All India Institute of Local Self Government, Vol. XXI, No. 12, January-June-2001, Mumbai, pp. 11-15.
7. Shalu Nigam : Empower Women Enrich Family, Social Welfare, Vol. 48, No. 5, 2001, pp. 35-38.
8. Murugaiah, K: Women's Work and Empowerment, Interventions to Enhance Women's Income, Social Welfare, Vol. 49, No. 7, pp. 3-8, 2002.
9. Anand Jaya: Self Help Groups in Empowering Women, A Case Study of Selected SHGs and NHGs,. Kerala Research Programme on Local Level Development, Discussion Paper, No. 38, Centre for Development Studies, Thiruvananthapuram, 2002, pp. 1-70.
10. Das, Shrimati: Gender Justice and Empowerment, Social Welfare, Vol. 49, No. 9, pp. 14-19, 2002.
11. Paricha, A.K.: Strategies of empowerment of women in Panchayati Raj Institutions, Local Government, Quarterly, Vol. XXII, No. 1.2, February to March, 2002, pp. 6-7.
12. Srivstava Ramesh: Policies for Socio-Economic Development of Women, Social Welfare, Vol. 49, No. 7, 2002, pp. 24-27.
13. Vasudev Rao: Empowerment Concepts and Charity, Social Welfare, Vol. 49, No. 9 2002, pp. 9-13.
14. Nanavathy Reema: Empowering Women by the Women, for the Women, the SEWA Experience, Women's Link, Vol. 9, No. 3, 2003, pp. 16-19.
15. Nandal Santhosh: Women's empowerment perspectives- A critical analysis, Women's Link, Vol. 9, No. 3, 2003, pp. 28-31.
16. Tucker Veena: Theoretical perspectives of Women's Empowerment and the Role of NGOs, Women's Link, Vol. 9, No. 3, 2003, pp. 2-8.
17. Kamalam, M.: Women Empowerment Role of Women's Commission, Kerala Calling, Vol. 24, No. 5, March 2004, pp. 5-17.
18. Mridual Eapen: Empowering Kerala Women, Kerala Calling, March 2004, Vol. 24, No. 5, pp. 9-13.

19. Bala Madhur and Monga, O.P.: Impact of Women's Employment on Decision Making in Families, Social Welfare, Vol. 5, No. 51, 2004, pp. 14-16.
20. Kishor Sunita and Gupta Kamala: Women's Empowerment in India and its States Evidence from the National Family Health Survey, Economic and Political Weekly, Vol. XXXIX, No. 7, 2004, pp. 694-703.
21. Mohammad Noor and Shahid Mohammad: Rethinking Women's Participation, Empowerment and Gender Equality: A Micro Analysis, Women's Link, Vol. 10, No. 3, 2004, pp. 7-12.
22. S. Ramanathan, Malathi: Women and empowerment- Shri Mahila Giriha Udyog, Hijjat Papad, Economic and Political Weekly, Vol. XXXIX, No. 17, 2004, pp. 1689-96.
23. Ram Kumar Usha: Education and Empowerment of Women Experience in India, Indian Journal of Adult Education, Vol. 65, No. 1-2, 2004, pp. 22-31.
24. Renganathan, R.: Women's Empowerment Through Development Programmes, Kisan World, Vol. 31, No. 6, June, 2004, pp. 13-14.
25. Rosa, K.D.: Empowerment of Women Through Employment, Ph.D thesis submitted to the University of Calicut, 2004.
26. Singh Surat: Empowerment of Women Representatives in Panchayati Raj—A profile from Haryana, Kurukshetra, Vol. 52, No. 10, 2004, p. 18.
27. Sood Archana: Sustainable Rural Development–Focus on Women, Kurushetra, Vol. 52, No. 6, 2004, p. 30.
28. Narayan and Deepa: Empowerment and Poverty Reduction—A Source Book, Washington: World Bank, 2005.
29. The Hindu, September 18, 2005, p. 15.
30. Bishoji, Deepak: Information Technology–New Mantra for Women's Empowerment, Social Welfare, Vol. 52, No. 5, 2005, pp. 10-13.
31. Kelkar Govind : Development Effectiveness Through Gender Mainstreaming, Gender Equality and Poverty Reduction in South Asia, Economic and Political Weekly, Vol. XL, No. 44 and 45, 2005, pp. 4690-98.
32. Lalithabai, K.N.: Women Empowerment and Panchayati Raj, Journal of Local Governance, April-June 2005, Quarterly Publication, KILA, pp. 38-46.
33. Lakshmidevi, K.R. and Pillai, P.P.: Micro Credit Programmes, Poverty Alleviation and Empowerment of Women-some Empirical Evidence from Kerala, Institute Francais, Pondichery, 2005, pp. 322-324.
34. Naila, Kabeer: Is Micro Finance a Magic Bullet for Women's Empowerment? Analysis of Findings from South Asia, Economic and Political Weekly, Vol. XL, No. 44 and 45, 2005, pp. 4709-18.
35. Omvedi Gail: Women in governance in Asia, EPW, Vol. XL, No. 44 and 45, 2005, pp. 4747-4750.
36. Pattnaik Sathyanarayana and Trupty Mayee Pradhan: Empowering Women by Ending Gender Violence, Social Welfare, Vol. 52, No. 52, 2005, pp. 21-24.
37. Paul Cithara: Kudumbasree Mission Failed to Achieve Purpose, The New Indian Express, Kochi, September 2, 2005, p. 5.
38. Thambi Binitha and Devika : Changing Order of Empowerment and Kudumbasree Activities, Shastra Gathi, Vol. 41, No. 7, 2006, pp. 17-21.
39. The Hindu, Oct. 11, 2006, p. 15.
40. The Hindu, November 19, 2006, p6.
41. The Hindu, February 6, 2006.
42. The Hindu, March 22, 2006.

43. The Hindu, February 26, 2006.
44. Jyothi S. Nair: Ph.D thesis submitted to the University of Kerala (Dept. of Sociology) in 2007.
45. Ruby, J.A.: Micro Finance and Women Empowerment- A Study of Kudumbasree Project in Kerala, Ph.D thesis submitted to the M.G. University (Dept. of Economics) July, 2008.
46. Lathika K.K.: A Study of Women Empowerment in Kerala with Special Reference to Kudumbasree Projects, Ph.D thesis submitted to M.G. University (Dept. of Economics) March, 2008.
47. Bushra Beegom: Women Executives in Kerala, Ph.D thesis submitted to University of Kerala, (Dept. of Sociology), 2008.
48. Lathika, K.K.: Ph.D Thesis submitted to the M.G. University, March, 2008.
49. Ruby, J.A.: Ph.D. Thesis submitted to M.G. University (Dept. of Economics) July, 2008.
50. Beena George: Ph.D thesis submitted to M.G. University (Dept. of Economics), October, 2008.
51. Promila Yadava: Literacy and Women's Empowerment, Yojana, Vol. 83, March 2009, pp. 47-50.
52. Emmanuel K. A. Kanipilly: Ph.D thesis submitted to M.G. University (Dept. of Zoology), January, 2009.
53. Manju Singh: Empowerment of Women: Gaps in Technology Diffusion, Social Change, Vol. 40, No. 4, December, 2010, pp. 564-576.
54. Santhosh Nandal, Kavita, Suman Rani and Gautam, N.C.: Women's Empowerment and National Development Policies: A Critical Analysis, Social Action, Vol. 60, No. 3, July-September, 2010, pp. 302-313.
55. Dijo Augustine and Minu M Kumar: Women Empowerment Through the SHG Approach – The Kudumbashree Model, The Indian Journal of Social Work, Vol. 71, No. 4, October 2010, pp. 601-610.
56. Atonu Chatterjee: Women in Panchayats: A Review, Yojana, Vol. 55, Feb., 2011, Government of India, pp. 24-25.
57. Patil, B.G. and Nandana, G.B.: Women empowerment–A Spiritual Approach SELP Journal of Social Science, Vol. 5, January-March, 2011, pp. 14-15.
58. Paramasivan, C.: Economic Empowerment of Women Through SHG in YARCARD, SELP Journal of Social Science, Vol. 5, January-March, 2011.
59. Rajamani, B.: Self Help Groups and Women Empowerment, SELP Journal of Social Science, Vol. 5, January-March, 2011, pp. 86-89.
60. Naipendra Kishore Mishra, Tulika Tripathi: Conceptualising women's Agency, Autonomy and Empowerment, Economic and Political Weekly, Vol. XLVI, No. 11, March 12, 2011, pp. 58-65.
61. Staffan Lindbery, Venkitesh, B. Athrey, R., Vidhyasagar, Goran Djurfeldt, Rajagopalan: A Silent Revolution? Women's Empowerment in Rural Tamil Nadu, EPW, Vol. XLVI, No. 13, March 16, 2011, pp. 111-120.
62. Sreekumar, S.S. Education and Empowerment of Women: The Case of Andaman and Nicobar Islands, Social Science in Perspective Achudamenon Study Centre, Thiruvananthapuram, Vol. 3, No. 1, January-March 2011, pp. 39-60.
63. Nripendra Kishore Mishra, Tulika Tripathi: Conceptualising Women's Agency, Autonomy and Empowerment, EPW, Vol. XLVI, No. 11, March 12, 2011, pp. 58-65.
64. Naomi Neft and Ann. D. Levine: Where Women stand, An international Report on the status of women in 140 countries -1997-98, Random House,

New York, 1998, pp. 1-2.
65. *Ibid.,* p. 8.
66. *Ibid.,* pp. 9-10.
67. *Ibid.,* p. 12.
68. Naomi Neft and Ann.D. Levine: Women's Right, Random House, New York, 1998, p. 13.
69. Naomi Neft and Ann.D. Levine: Women's Right, Random House, New York, 1998, pp.13-14.
70. YWCA of India : The educated women in Indian Society Today, Tata Mac Graw Hill Publishing Company, Bombay-1971, p. 240.
71. *Ibid.,* p. 249.
72. *Ibid.,* p. 248.
73. Ralph E. Smith: Projecting the size of the Female Labour Force: What makes a difference in Book of Llyod, Andrew and Gilroy, Women in the Labour Market Columbia University Press, New York.
74. *Ibid.,* p. 65.
75. *Ibid.,* p. 59.
76. Sharan R.R: Status of Women : A historical perspective, Uppal Publishing House, New Delhi, 1992.
77. Kane.P.V: History of Dharmashastra, Vol. II, Part I, Hindu Social Organisation, Bombay, 1961.
78. Srinivas, M.N.: Social Change in India, Orient Publications, Bombay, 1972.
79. Altekar A.S.: The Position of Women in Hindu Civilisation, The Cultural Publication House, Calcutta, 1938.
80. Tripathi S.N.: Unorganised Women Labour in India, Discovery Publishing House, New Delhi,1994.
81. Sharma R.R.: Status of Indian Women - A Historical Perspective, Uppal Publishing House, New Delhi, 1992.
82. Article 14th,15th and 16th of the Constitution of India.
83. Fried: Women and Men, Academic Press, New York, 1983, p 20.
84. Joyce M. Nielson: Sex in Society: Perspective on Stratification (Belmont. C.A., Wordsworth) 1978.
85. Michelle Z. Rosaldo: Women, Culture and Society: A Theoretical Overview, Schocken Books, New York, 1982.
86. Tawney R.H. : Religion and the Rise of Capitalisation, Preface, (Quoted by Neogi H.C.); Origin of Feudalism in Ancient India – Land system and Feudalism in Ancient India, ed., D.C. Sir Car, p. 96.
87. Quoted in A.R. Desai – Rural sociology in India, p. 33.
88. Karve.I.- Kinship Organisation in India, p. 10.
89. Karve – Kinship Organisation in India, p. 48.
90. Srimad Devi Bhagavatham, Part III B. VII.Chapter XXV, p. 679.
91. Likhita Smriti: p. 153 cited by Vinayaka Ganesha Apte.
92. Dhanapala – Tilakamanjari, pp. 17-18 Upaniti, p. 698.
93. Iravati Karve – Kinship Organisation in India, p. 72.
94. Ashraf K.M. : Life and Conditions of People of Hindustan, p. 135.
95. The Arthasashtra 2, 23.
96. Baudhayana – II 2, 3. p. 135 ed. by A. Chinnaswami Shastri.
97. Agni Purana, 253, pp. 63-64.
98. Jaimini, Vol. 1-14 p. 983.

99. Vashishta S., Chapter 17, M.N. Dutt – The Dharmashastra, p. 804.
100. Manu Smriti, Chapter – IX, p. 185.
101. Yogendra Singh : 1988, Modernising Indian Tradition, Rawat Publications, Jaipur, p.101.
102. Yogendra Singh : 1988, Modernising Indian Tradition, Rawat Publications, Jaipur, p. 102.
103. Mishra. B.B : 1960, Supra, pp. 302-305.
104. Yogendra Singh : 1988, Modernising Indian Tradition, Rawat Publications, Jaipur, p. 105.
105. Yogendra Singh : 1988, Modernising Indian Tradition, Rawat Publications, Jaipur, p. 102.
106. Ralph E. Smith: Projecting the size of the Female Labour Force: What makes a difference, Book of Lloyds, Andrew and Gilroy, Women in the Labour Market, Columbia University Press, New York.
107. *Ibid.,* p. 65.
108. *Ibid.,* p. 59.
109. Amartya Sen : Development as Freedom, Oxford University Press, 1999.
110. Meera Bai. M: Women's Development in Kerala Some Current Issues, Women and Economic Reforms Kerala Experience, Serial Publications, 2006, New Delhi, p. 1.
111. Safa, H.T. : Gender equality and women's wage labour: In Valentine M (ed), A Theoretical and Empirical analysis in Patriarchy and Development, 1986.
112. Jagajeevan, N and Ramakanthan, N. (2000) *Gram sabhas-A democratic structure for development planning.* Paper presented in International Conference on Democratic Decentralisation. State Planning Board.
113. Bava Khan, Pareethu P.M, Oomman, John, Kumari, Leela. (2001) *Report of study of Women Component Plan in Kerala,* State Institute of Rural Development, Kottarakkara.
114. Ramanathan, Mala. Vijayan, Aleyamma. Varatharajan, D. and Sukanya, R. (2002). *A Study Report on Political Decentralisation and Primary Health Care System,* Achutha Menon Centre for Health Science Studies.
115. Sukumar, Mini. (2003) *Experience of Kerala in local governance,*Paper presented in the open forum on 24th October 2003 at Chinese Academy of Social Sciences Hall, Beijing, organised by ARENA as part of ARENA Regional School in Local Governance.
116. Muraleedharan, Sarada (2005) *Decentralisation and gender – the Kerala experience of the WCP,* Paper presented in a workshop on 'Gender Based Planning in Local Governance: Issues and Concerns, on 8th February, 2005 Organised by Sakhi Women's Resource Centre, Trivandrum.
117. Ramanathan, Mala. Vijayan, Aleyamma. Varatharajan, D and Sukanya, R (2002). *A Study Report on Political Decentralisation and Primary Health Care System.* Achutha Menon Centre for Health Science Studies.
118. Muraleedharan, Sarada. (2005) *Decentralisation and gender – the Kerala experience of the WCP,* Paper presented in a workshop on 'Gender Based Planning in Local Governance: Issues and Concerns', on 8th February, 2005 Organised by Sakhi Women's Resource Centre, Trivandrum.
119. Muraleedharan, Sarada. (2005) *Decentralisation and gender – the Kerala experience of the WCP,* Paper presented in a workshop on 'Gender Based Planning In Local Governance: Issues and Concern's, on 8th February, 2005 Organised by Sakhi Women's Resource Centre, Trivandrum.

120. Sukumar, Mini. (2003) *Experience of Kerala in local governance,* Paper presented in the open forum on 24th October 2003 at Chinese Academy of Social Sciences Hall, Beijing, organised by ARENA as part of ARENA Regional School in Local Governance.
121. Bava Khan, Pareethu P.M., Oomman, John, Kumari, Leela. (2001) *Report of study of Women Component.*
122. Issac, Thomas. Seema, T.N. and Guptha, Smitha. (2003) *Women elected representatives in Kerala (1995-2000), From symbolism to empowerment.* Paper presented in a seminar on a Decade of women's empowerment through local government in India.
123. Radha, S. and Choudhary, Roy Bulu. (2002) *Women in local bodies,* KRPLLD, Centre for Development Studies, Trivandrum *Plan in Kerala,* State Institute of Rural Development, Kottarakkara.
124. Muraleedharan, K. (2000) *Women's Participation in Development - the Kerala experience.* Paper presented in International Conference on Democratic Decentralisation.
125. Sanitha, Baby. (2003) *Women's empowerment in Ninth Plan- Case Study of Ezhupunna panchayath.* M.A. Dissertation, Mahatma Gandhi University.
126. UNRISD: Working towards a more gender equitable Macro economic agenda, 1997, Report of UNRISD/CPD workshop 1996.
127. Lalitha Bai: Women's Empowerment, Kerala Institute of Local Administration, 2003.
128. Economic Review, 2009, State Planning Board, Thiruvananthapuram, p. 440.
129. Devi Lakshmy: Determinants of Labour Force Participation among Women in Kerala – Some Evidence from a Micro level study, The Asian Economic Review, 38, April, 1996.
130. Economic Review, 2008, State Planning Board, Thiruvanantha-puram, p. 432.
131. Economic Review 2009, State Planning Board, Thiruvananthapuram, p. 432.
132. Economic Review 2009, State Planning Board, Thiruvananthapuram, p. 444.
133. Economic Review 2009, State Planning Board, Thiruvananthapuram, p. 322.
134. Human Development Report of UNDP, 2005.
135. Dreze, Jean and Sen A.K.: India: Economic Development and social opportunity, Delhi: Oxford University Press, 1995.
136. Eapen and Kadoth, Praveen: Demystifying the High Status of Women in Kerala: An Attempt to Understand the Contradiction in Social Development, Report submitted to New Delhi Institute of Social Studies Trust, 2001.
137. Gender, Special Issue, Economic and Political Weekly, Vol. 31, No. 43, 1996.
138. The expression used by the Sate Government of Kerala to promote tourism in the State..
139. Government of India, Census of India, 2001, URL, www. Censusindia.net.
140. Dreze, Jean and Sen A.K.: India: Economic Development and Social Opportunity, Delhi: Oxford University Press, 1995.
141. Government of India : Women and Men in India 2002, New Delhi, CSO, 2002, p. 20.
142. Chakraborty, Lekh. S.: Public expenditure and Human Development: An Empirical Investigation, 2003 (Http://www.wider.unu.edu/conference-2002-/conference%202003-2 papers/papers pdf/Chakraborty%20120403.pdf).
143. Daya Baga Chapter XI, Section I, 15 and 47 c.f. D.N. Mitter: Position of Women.

Index